RETRIEVAL & RENEWAL
Ressourcement
IN CATHOLIC THOUGHT

The middle years of this century marked a particularly intense time of crisis and change in European society. During this period (1930-1950), a broad intellectual and spiritual movement arose within the European Catholic community, largely in response to the secularism that lay at the core of the crisis. The movement drew inspiration from earlier theologians and philosophers such as Möhler, Newman, Gardeil, Rousselot, and Blondel, as well as from men of letters like Charles Péguy and Paul Claudel.

The group of academic theologians included in the movement extended into Belgium and Germany, in the work of men like Emile Mersch, Dom Odo Casel, Romano Guardini, and Karl Adam. But above all the theological activity during this period centered in France. Led principally by the Jesuits at Fourviére and the Dominicans at Le Saulchoir, the French revival included many of the greatest names in twentieth-century Catholic thought: Henri de Lubac, Jean Daniélou, Yves Congar, Marie-Dominique Chenu, Louis Bouyer, and, in association, Hans Urs von Balthasar.

It is not true — as subsequent folklore has it — that those theologians represented any sort of self-conscious "school": indeed, the differences among them, for example, between Fourviére and Saulchoir, were important. At the same time, most of them were united in the double conviction that theology had to speak to the present situation, and that the condition for doing so faithfully lay in a recovery of the Church's past. In other words, they saw clearly that the first step in what later came to be known as *aggiornamento* had to be *ressourcement* — a rediscovery of the riches of the whole of the Church's two-thousand-year tradition. According to de Lubac, for example, all of his own works as well as the entire *Sources chrétiennes* collection are based on the presupposition that "the renewal of Christian vitality is linked at least partially to a renewed exploration of the periods and of the works where the Christian tradition is expressed with particular intensity."

In sum, for the *ressourcement* theologians theology involved a "return to the sources" of Christian faith, for the purpose of drawing out the meaning and significance of these sources for the critical questions of our time. What these theologians sought was a spiritual and intellectual communion with Christianity in its most vital moments as transmitted to us in its classic texts, a communion that would nourish, invigorate, and rejuvenate twentieth-century Catholicism.

The *ressourcement* movement bore great fruit in the documents of the Second Vatican Council and has deeply influenced the work of Pope John Paul II and Cardinal Joseph Ratzinger, Prefect of the Sacred Congregation of the Doctrine of the Faith.

The present series is rooted in this twentieth-century renewal of theology, above all as the renewal is carried in the spirit of de Lubac and von Balthasar. In keeping with that spirit, the series understands *ressourcement* as revitalization: a return to the sources, for the purpose of developing a theology that will truly meet the challenges of our time. Some of the features of the series, then, will be:

- a return to classical (patristic-mediaeval) sources;
- a renewed interpretation of St. Thomas;
- a dialogue with the major movements and thinkers of the twentieth century, with particular attention to problems associated with the Enlightenment, modernity, liberalism.

The series will publish out-of-print or as yet untranslated studies by earlier authors associated with the *ressourcement* movement. The series also plans to publish works by contemporary authors sharing in the aim and spirit of this earlier movement. This will include interpretations of de Lubac and von Balthasar and, more generally, any works in theology, philosophy, history, literature, and the arts which give renewed expression to an authentic Catholic sensibility.

The editor of the Ressourcement series, David L. Schindler, is Gagnon Professor of Fundamental Theology at the John Paul II Institute in Washington, D.C., and editor of the North American edition of *Communio: International Catholic Review,* a federation of journals in thirteen countries founded in Europe in 1972 by Hans Urs von Balthasar, Jean Daniélou, Henri de Lubac, Joseph Ratzinger, and others.

Ressourcement
Retrieval and Renewal in Catholic Thought

available

Mysterium Paschale
by Hans Urs von Balthasar

The Letter on Apologetics *and* History and Dogma
by Maurice Blondel

Prayer: The Mission of the Church
Jean Daniélou

Letters from Lake Como:
Explorations in Technology and the Human Race
by Romano Guardini

The Portal of the Mystery of Hope
Charles Péguy

In the Beginning:
A Catholic Understanding of the Story of Creation and the Fall
by Cardinal Joseph Ratzinger

Hans Urs von Balthasar: A Theological Style
by Angelo Scola

The Discovery of God
Henri de Lubac

The Discovery of God

Henri de Lubac

Translated by
Alexander Dru

Footnotes translated by
Mark Sebanc
and
Cassian Fulsom, O.S.B.

WILLIAM B. EERDMANS PUBLISHING COMPANY
GRAND RAPIDS, MICHIGAN

Originally published as
Sur les chemins de Dieu
© 1956 Aubier, Paris

Original abridged English translation © 1960
Darton Longman & Todd, Ltd, and P. J. Kenedy and Sons

This edition © 1996 Wm. B. Eerdmans Publishing Co.
255 Jefferson Ave. S.E., Grand Rapids, Michigan 49503
All rights reserved

Printed in the United States of America

01 00 99 98 97 96   7 6 5 4 3 2 1

Library of Congress Cataloging-in-Publication Data

Lubac, Henri de, 1896-
[Sur les chemins de Dieu. English]
The discovery of God / Henri de Lubac;
translated by Alexander Dru. — [New ed.]
p.   cm.   — (Ressourcement)
Originally published: Darton Longman & Todd, Ltd.,
and P. J. Kenedy and Sons, c1960.
Includes bibliographical references.
ISBN 0-8028-4089-2 (pbk.: alk. paper)
1. God — Knowableness. I. Title.
II. Series: Ressourcement (Grand Rapids, Mich.)
BT102.L813   1996
231'.042 — dc20   96-43367
                                                CIP

Contents

Preface	ix
Our Knowledge of God	3
Abyssus abyssum invocat	5
1. The Origin of the Idea of God	15
2. The Affirmation of God	35
3. The Proof of God	57
4. The Knowledge of God	87
5. The Ineffable God	117
6. The Search for God	145
7. God in Our Time	177
Postscript	205

Preface

The Discovery of God is the first unabridged English translation of Henri de Lubac's *Sur les chemins de Dieu* (1956), which is itself a revised and greatly expanded edition of *De la connaissance de Dieu* (1945, with a slightly different version in 1948). De Lubac republished the book in its present form — with its addition of extensive notes — mainly to show that its teaching was firmly rooted in the tradition. Although the book provoked much controversy at the time of its original (1945) publication, de Lubac insisted that its intention was simply to draw on the double treasure of the *philosophia perennis* and Christian experience, in order "to lend a helping hand to a few people in their search for God." The passages that were often criticized, he insisted, were scarcely more than translations or paraphrases of very traditional texts.

The Discovery of God expresses the original point of departure for de Lubac's thought, which had already been sketched out earlier, especially in *Catholicisme* (1938) and *Surnaturel* (1946). This point of departure is certainly "Augustinian," if one views Augustine as the "pinnacle of the patristic age" and the most important inspiration of the Middle Ages and even of the modern period (cf. the claim of E. Przywara). But de Lubac is keenly aware of the limits of any one historical system or "school" of thought. Indeed, it could as well be said that the book develops almost as a gloss on the dictum of St. Thomas that, in every act of thought and will, God is also thought and willed implicitly (*De Veritate*, XXII, a.2, ad 1).

Bringing together the Augustinian and Thomistic traditions, then, the author shows how the dynamism of the "restless heart," of that "habitual" longing for the absolute that breathes in the soul, while not involving any vision of absolute being, precedes every act of thinking and willing. Recognizing the necessity of rational concepts and of modes of proof and "systems" in our knowledge of God, de Lubac argues that these nonetheless serve as reflexive clarifications of a notion that has always already been present *implicitly*, by virtue of God's initiative.

One will find in *The Discovery of God* not only the main themes of de Lubac's theology but also many of the key issues in twentieth-century and indeed classical Christian theology and philosophy: the relation between nature and grace; the place of "natural theology" in our understanding of the God of biblical revelation; the "power of affirmation that surpasses both our power to conceive and our power to argue"; the proper place of "negative theology" (*"via negationis"*) in our approach to God. And evoked in all of these issues is the thought-form of "paradox" which de Lubac saw as fundamental for any authentic Christian theology. Opposing expressions, when conceived properly in terms of paradox, are understood neither to contradict one another nor to fuse into each other dialectically. Instead, together they point beyond themselves to the phenomenon that lies both "beneath" and "above" them. Paradox thus interpreted does not sin against logic but is its most profound expression.

The Discovery of God is a timely book, in the light of our age's theoretical and — more often in Anglo-America — practical atheism. The study brings into relief the startling fact that no instance of human consciousness or human action is *without implication* of God, hence is ever simply *neutral* with respect to God. The importance of such a fact can scarcely be exaggerated for a liberal culture whose claim is that it can, in its public institutions and way of life, safely bracket just such an implication regarding the existence and meaning of God.

In bringing into relief the implied "presence" of God in every act of human consciousness, *The Discovery of God* invites attention also to the important fact that our affirmations always exceed the explicit contents of our understanding. Whatever terms one employs to explain this, it is crucial to see that the feature of *implicitness*, by virtue of its being basic in every act of knowledge, is therefore ineliminable: it must be integrated into any notion of "rationality" or indeed "objectivity," adequately conceived. Again, it seems hard to exaggerate the importance of this achievement, in a culture whose presuppositions regarding "objectivity" have been so decisively shaped by Descartes.[1]

---

1. In this connection, we might highlight how de Lubac's book provides support — and ontological broadening and deepening — for such significant "postcritical" cognitional theory as that of Michael Polanyi (cf., for example, his *Personal Knowledge* and

PREFACE

Those interested in the history surrounding de Lubac's writing of *The Discovery of God* may usefully consult his memoir on the circumstances that occasioned his books: *At the Service of the Church* (Ignatius Press, 1993), pp. 41ff. and 81ff.

DAVID L. SCHINDLER
1 June 1996
Washington, D.C.

The Tacit Dimension) regarding the "from-to" structure of knowing and the existential commitment tacitly involved in all thinking.

As for me, I feel that by far my most pressing duty to God is to speak of him in all that I think and all that I say.

> St. Hilary, *De Trinitate*, 1, 37

I have never written anything on the real purpose of my endeavor.

> Plato, *Letter 7*

What men lack most is knowledge of God.

> Fénelon, *Sentiments et avis chrétiens*, 1

Forte substomacharis, si adhuc pergimus quaerere: quid est Deus? tum quia toties jam quaesitum est, tum quia diffidis inventum iri. Dico tibi, pater Eugeni, solus est Deus, qui frustra numquam quaeri potest nec cum inveniri non potest.

> St. Bernard, *De consideratione*, 5, 11, 24

Our Knowledge of God

As chapel ended, one of the boys turned into the recreation ground and began ridiculing the sermon he had just been subjected to. Like many another, it had been a poor one. In his attempt to say something about God, the preacher had fed his youthful congregation on a flow of abstract formulae and pious platitudes which produced the most absurd effect on those whose minds were not entirely dulled. The master in charge, who was a man of God, called over the young scoffer, but instead of scolding him simply asked him: "Hasn't it ever occurred to you that it is the most difficult subject to speak about that you can think of?" The boy was no fool. He pondered the question, and that incident became his first conscious realization of the mystery, his first contact with the twofold mystery, of God and man.

Although the thoughts in this book differ considerably from many sermons, they will not necessarily seem less ridiculous. They are deliberately fragmentary, and make no claim to replace the classic treatises on the subject or even to supplement them. They are marginal notes which make no attempt to gloss over the salutary sense of embarrassment which overcomes the mind on such an occasion. No less deliberately, they refrain from crossing the threshold of the mystery where the spiritual life is nourished, the life hidden from the eyes of the world, the intimate history of the Church which is beyond the reach of the profane. Their inadequacy, their very awkwardness may, however, provoke the reader to thought. May his reflections lead him beyond the realm of words and of human thought to find God!

Abyssus abyssum invocat

Was Moses right, or Xenophanes? Did God make man in his image, or is it not rather man who has made God in his?

Appearances, certainly, are on the side of Xenophanes — yet it is Moses who is right. And at bottom Xenophanes agrees. For they are not speaking of the same God, or of the same image; which is why the argument seems unending. In fact, Xenophanes has no intention of denying the divinity; on the contrary, his purpose is to recall man to the divine when he loses himself among the gods he has fashioned.[1] In this the Christian can only approve[2] the "intellectual revolutionary," and reckon him among those who have "blazed a trail" to the truth.[3] His contempt for anthropomorphic gods conceals a very important positive

---

1. Charles Renouvier saw clearly the importance of Xenophanes' critique; but in conformity with his consistent thesis, he finds this critique unfortunate, as negating the only real God, a God (according to Renouvier) who is finite and anthropomorphic: *Histoire et solution des problèmes métaphysiques*, p. 15; *Philosophie analytique de l'histoire*, vol. 1 (1896), p. 447.

2. As does Clement of Alexandria, *Stromata*, 7, 4.

3. "The theology of Xenophanes," says Werner Jaeger, "springs from an immediate sense of awe at the sublimity of the Divine. It is a feeling of reverence that leads Xenophanes to deny all the finite shortcomings and limitations laid upon the gods by traditional religion, and makes him a unique theological figure, despite his dependence on the views of the natural philosophers. His religious motif — the demand for utter sublimity in the Godhead — is expressed with particular clarity..., etc. Werner Jaeger, *The Theology of the Early Greek Philosophers*, 3rd ed. (1952), p. 49; cf. p. 41.

lesson, and in effect his words evoke man's secret sympathy. They release an energy not at first distinctly understood, but which inevitably leads him on, far beyond the denial of his gods. But let us take another example, nearer our own time, in which his meaning is echoed:

> Monde, tout le mal vient de la forme des dieux. . . .
> Pourquoi mettre, au-dessus de l'Être, des Fantômes?[4]

> (World, all the ill comes from the form the gods take,
> Why put Phantoms above Being itself?)

Away, then, with all the projections, sublimations and creations of our passions or our dreams, of our fears or anger, of our nightmares or desires! Away with the gods who "seem to have been invented of set purpose by the enemy of mankind, in order to sanction crime and turn the divine to ridicule!"[5] Away with the gods of nothingness which leave us to ourselves and keep us in bondage! Away with all false gods! — for God is indeed the God of whom Moses speaks, a God without countenance, a God who is the negation of human gods. For the God who denies the gods of our desires is nonetheless the sole God of human desire. The God before whom everything is as though it were not is nonetheless the sole God of all that is noblest in man.

All our representations of the divine are woven of elements taken from our world, whether from the natural or the social world; there is, however, a faculty or power in man which always drives him on beyond them: the power of reason itself. That is because in his most intimate being, made in the image of God, there is always something which he is quite unable to represent to himself, though he is not without experience of it. "He bears within himself a source of wonder, a source of infinite self-transcendence."[6] And that, in the last analysis, is what allows him to know God in truth. *Abyssus abyssum invocat* (Abyss calls to abyss).

God, Moses says, made man in his image. To which Christian tradition adds that man, made in the image of the incomprehensible God, is ultimately incomprehensible to himself. "Who can enter into himself and

---

4. Victor Hugo, *La Légende des siècles*, "Le Satyre."
5. Fénelon.
6. Fénelon, *Traité de l'existence de Dieu*, pt. I, ch. 2, n. 52.

understand himself?"⁷ "Our spirit bears the imprint of inscrutable Nature through the mystery within it."⁸

Der Abgrund meines Geistes ruft immer mit Geschrei
Den Abgrund Gottes: Sag welcher tiefer sei?⁹

(The abyss of my spirit calls for ever with a cry
To the abyss of God: Tell me, which is deeper?)

And so one cannot say that this knowledge, at its root, is a human acquisition. It is an "image," an "imprint," a "seal." It is the mark of God upon us. We do not construct it; we do not borrow it from elsewhere; it is in us, for all our misery; it is our very selves — more, even, than ourselves. It comes before the operation of will and intellect, presupposed by consciousness itself, and our initiative goes for nothing. And so it is true, indeed indispensable, to say: *Auctor nobis de Deo, Deus est; non nisi se auctore cognoscitur*¹⁰ . . . *Deum scire nemo potest, nisi Deo docente*¹¹ (God himself is our authority about God; otherwise he is not known. . . . No one can have any knowledge of God unless God teaches him).

That does not mean the suppression of our natural activity of mind; it indicates the prime condition and guarantee of its validity. It does not mean substituting another principle in the place of reason; rather it means digging down to its foundation. Going back, and up, to the source.¹² It means

---

7. Among a host of others, St. Augustine, *De symbolo,* ch. 1, n. 2: "He also made man in his image and likeness in the mind: for in that is the image of God. This is the reason why the mind cannot be comprehended even by itself, because it is the image of God" (PL 40:628); *De anima et ejus origine,* bk. 4, ch. 6, n. 8 (PL 44:529). Cf. Cardinal Tolet, *In Primam Partem sancti Thomae,* q.1, a.1, q.2 (Rome, 1869), vol. 1, p. 20; or Bossuet, *Elévations sur les Mystères,* 2e Semaine, 6e élévation, on the Trinity: "God has infused in our souls, which represent it (i.e., the Trinity), something incomprehensible. . . . I am an impenetrable mystery to myself . . ." (*Oeuvres complètes,* ed. F. Lachat, vol. 7 [1862], pp. 36, 38).

8. St. Ephrem. Cf. Edmund Beck, "Die Theologie des hl. Ephraem," *Studia Anselmiana* 21, pp. 98, 52. St. Gregory of Nyssa, *On the Creation of Man,* ch. 11 (PG 44:156b).

9. Angelus Silesius, *Der Cherubinische Wandersmann,* I, 68. Cf. Tauler, *Sermon* 44.

10. St. Hilary, *De Trinitate,* bk. 5, ch. 21 (PL 10:143).

11. St. Irenaeus, *Adversus Haereses,* bk. 4, ch. 6, n. 4 (PG 7:988), etc.

12. Stanislas Lyonnet, S.J.: *Quaestiones in Epistolam ad Romanos prima series* (Rome, 1955), ch. 2, "De naturali Dei cognitione, Rom. 1:18-23," pp. 68-108. Cf. p. 78, on verse 19: "*because God has shown it to them:* this is not a mere tautology; for the emphasis is placed on the action of God: it happened thus because God himself made it known"; and on verse

saying, with St. Thomas, and according to the teaching of St. Paul, that God, the creative God, manifests himself to us through his works as in a book, and that he is, moreover, the principle of the knowledge which we have to acquire by the exercise of natural reason:

> He has put an eye into their hearts
> To show them the greatness of his works.[13]

20: "Herein is explained *how* God made it known . . . by the created world and the inner light. . . ." Cf. St. Thomas Aquinas, *In Epistol. Pauli ad Romanos,* ch. 1, lectio 6: ". . . For God makes a thing known to man in two ways: In one way, by pouring out an interior light, by which man knows; Ps. 42:3: *Send forth your light and your truth.* In another way by fashioning exterior signs of his wisdom, namely sensible creatures; Sirach 1:9: *He poured her out, that is, wisdom, upon all his works.* Therefore God made it known to them thus: either by pouring out his light interiorly, or by fashioning visible creation exteriorly, in which created things the mind of God can be read as in a book. *Ibid.:* "Then when it says: *God has shown it to them,* it emphasizes who the author is, who had shown this kind of knowledge to them. . . ." (In this commentary, wrote Martini, *Prefazione alla Epistola di S. Paolo ai Romani,* St. Thomas gathered together "the flower of the teaching of the Fathers.") Cf. *De Magistro,* a.1. St. Irenaeus, *Adversus Haereses,* bk. 4, ch. 5, n. 1: "Since it was impossible without God to come to a knowledge of God, He teaches men, through his Word, to know God"; ch. 6, n. 6: "By means of the creation itself, the Word reveals God the Creator" (PG 7:984a and 988-989). Let us take these texts in their most general meaning: whatever the path is by which our spirit raises itself to God, and whatever part in this movement the spirit's own natural activity has, it is salutary to remind ourselves that, radically, the initiative always comes from God; it is always God who "manifests himself." Cf. Austin Farrer, *Naturel et surnaturel:* "The most avidly theoretical speculation, the typical case of rational theology, should be attributed to the divine initiative, to God acting in the natural order, God who wants to manifest himself in the stars and elevate the spirit of a philosopher by means of the path of the contemplation of the stars" (trans. Jean Daniélou, in *Dieu Vivant* 21, pp. 124-125). See note 15, below, and also Chapter 4.

Cf. A. Feuillet, P.S.S., "La connaissance naturelle de Dieu par les hommes d'après Rom. I," in *Lumière et Vie* 14 (1954), p. 74: "Instead of showing, in the manner of a philosopher, men taking the initiative to raise themselves from the created world to God, it is God himself to whom the Apostle assigns the initiative in the manifestation of his attributes: "God," he says, "has revealed what can be known of him." It is a question, however, of a knowledge acquired by the light of human reason alone, reflecting on the works of creation, and not in any way, as has been believed heretofore, of revelation properly so-called, revelation given to the Jews or primitive revelation by which God would have desired to supernaturally increase the stock of the religious knowledge of humanity. In brief, Paul speaks in terms of revelation of a purely natural knowing." However, seeing in this language of the Apostle an "anomaly," the author tries to find an explanation that seems to me a bit minimalizing.

13. Sirach 17:8.

The initiative is a double one, and our most natural and most spontaneous activity is no more than a response. If the reason which enlightens us were, from the first, enlightened as to its own nature, it would be driven to make the mystic's cry its own: "Behold me, O my aim and end and meaning! I cry to thee.... Yet, no, it is thou who callest me!"[14]

Whatever the order in which things are set, God comes before everything. He goes before us on the road, and is always there before us. On whatever plane, it is he who makes himself known to us. It is he who reveals himself to us.[15]

---

14. Hallaj, *Qasida 1* (Dîwân, from the French translation of Louis Massignon [1955], p. 4).

15. Several friends have asked why I use the terms "reveal" and "revelation" since it is still at this point a matter of the natural knowledge of God, and not of that knowledge that comes from positive and supernatural revelation. I do so for the following three reasons:

(1) Because this term expresses an important traditional idea, and is itself traditional. Cf. St. Irenaeus, *Adversus Haereses*, bk. 2, ch. 4, n. 5: "When reason (= verbum) infused in the mind moves minds and reveals to them that there is one God, the Lord of all" (ed. Harvey, vol. 1, pp. 263-264). St. Maximus the Confessor, *Ambigua*: the visible world, "this unique masterpiece, in which God makes himself known by a silent revelation" (PG 91:1328a), etc. The term has been passed down as far as certain of our manuals. It was more than authorized by St. Paul (Rom. 1:19), where Gk. ἐφανέρωσε y to which the Vulgate *manifestavit* corresponds, is often translated in the older versions as *revelavit*. Again, in the Middle Ages, in William of St.-Thierry, *Letter to the Brethren of Mont-Dieu*, 114: "Since what is known of God has been manifested to man by God revealing it in nature," in Peter Lombard, *Sentences*, bk. I, dist. 3: "The Apostle, in Rom. 1:19, says that God revealed (revelavit) to them ...," or in Alexander of Hales, *In 1 Sent.*, d. 2, n. 6: "the revelation of the Trinity occurs in three ways: through doctrine, or through creation, or by the inspiration of faith." Or in St. Thomas, *In Epist. ad Romanos*, ch. 1, lectio 6: "First, it shows what they knew about God; second, it shows from whom they received knowledge of this kind, for God *revealed* (revelavit) it to them; third, it shows in what way the invisible things of God [are known]. Or *Compendium Theologiae*, bk. 3, ch. 8: "What is known of God, that is, what is knowable about God through natural reason, has been manifested to them, that is, the Gentiles; for God *revealed* (revelavit) it, namely, through the light of reason and through the created things which he fashioned...." (One can certainly discern the nuance of the [author's] restrictive intention in relation to an Augustinian-type interpretation. But the nuance allows the fundamental idea which this word expresses, along with the word used by St. Paul — and his translator, to remain intact and whole. St. Thomas is a witness of this [usage], as are all the great doctors of the Catholic tradition.) Cf. I. A. Moehler, *La Symbolique*: "We draw the knowledge of God from two sources: natural revelation and supernatural revelation."

The working of reason which carries us to him — not to him so much as to the threshold of his mystery — is never but the second wave of the rhythm which he himself has set in motion. Whatever explanation may be given of knowledge — and St. Thomas's explanation is not in every respect that of St. Augustine or St. Bonaventure, for example — traditional philosophy is unanimous on that point. In the intimacy of the spirit, God is always the "illuminating light" of our "illuminated light."[16] He is "that uncreated Light without which I should not be eye,"[17] and unless he pronounced his *fiat lux* upon me, the abyss within me would be dark indeed. He is the hearth from which the souls of men, like so many lamps, take their light.[18] He is the *ipse qui illuminat* at the heart of reason.[19]

---

(2) Because this word seems to be the best one here, or rather, the only correlative of the word "image," in itself equally biblical and traditional. Cf. among a thousand other attestations St. Bonaventure, *In 2 Sent.*, dist. 16, q.1, a.2: "To be the image of God is not accidental to man, but rather substantial"; or St. Thomas, *Prima Secundae*, prologue, etc.

(3) Finally, because it seems to be the right term in order to make it more clearly understood that the knowledge of God, even natural, in the concrete reality, especially if it is already in some sense and in some degree the knowledge of a personal God, surpasses, wherever one encounters it, the profane order and causes us to penetrate into the domain of the sacred. (This a domain, moreover, which itself surpasses, but not without considerable ambivalence, the religious affirmation of a personal God.) Cf. Lyonnet, *Quaestiones,* p. 105, "Conclusio generalis," 3: "This pertains, almost certainly, to knowledge that is not merely abstract but living, by which man orders his end for himself as he should . . ." and pp. 97-102. Let us add that it is not a question here of equivocation, given that the text is clear enough by itself, and that, in addition, a "that is to say" immediately gives the explanation.

16. St. Thomas, *Tertia,* q.5, a.4, ad 2: "The intellect or mind of man is, as it were, a light illuminated by the divine light of the Word," *De Veritate,* q.16, a.3. St. Bonaventure, *In hexameron,* collatio 13, n. 8: God "is illuminating Light" (Quaracchi, vol. 5, p. 385).

17. Gabriel Marcel, *Le Mystère de l'être* 2, Foi et réalité (1951), p. 178.

18. St. Augustine, *De civitate Dei,* bk. 11, ch. 27, a.2: "[Irrational creatures] cannot penetrate that incorporeal light which, as it were, illumines our mind and makes us able to judge correctly of all other things" (PL 41:341). *De peccatorum meritis et remissione,* bk. 1, ch. 25, n. 37: "That which is said in the Gospel: 'He was the true light, which enlightens every man coming into this world' has this meaning: that no man is enlightened, except with that light of truth which is God . . ." (PL 44:130). *De fide et symbolo,* ch. 4, n. 6: "We, however, are not light by nature, but we are illumined by that Light . . ." (PL 40:185). *De Genesi ad litteram:* "from which source souls, like lamps, are lit," etc. (PL 34:251-254, 292).

19. St. Augustine, *Soliloques,* ch. 6, n. 12 (PL 32:875). *In Joannem,* tract. 23, n. 5 (PL

Lux lucis et fons luminis
Diem dies illuminans.[20]

(Light of light, and source of illumination,
Day which enlighteneth the day.)

That is to say, there is something sacred in our humble reason.[21]

In this way the scruples of agnosticism and the self-sufficiency of the profane are set aside. But man must have the courage to use his reason; he must neither despise the power which is in him nor take pride in it. And in the supreme use of his faculty of knowing, he should be neither hesitant

---

35:1584). *De vera religione*, ch. 39, n. 72: "whence the light itself of reason is lit" (ed. J. Pegon, p. 130). As will be seen more clearly below, I do not hold completely to the Augustinian explanation which, besides, it is not possible to summarize here. But he who would retain it, would rightly call to mind the remark made by R. P. Blaise Romeyer in this regard, in *La philosophie chrétienne jusqu'à Descartes*, vol. 3 (1937), p. 61: "It is best to avoid the ridicule of accusing Augustine of ontologism." In fact, "all Christian thinkers agree in admitting that the evidence of the principles of theoretic reason and those of practical reason 'hangs upon divine illumination'" (Etienne Gilson, *L'esprit de la philosophie médiévale*, 2nd ed. [1944], pp. 309-310, note). The divergence comes only afterwards. Some, too quickly attentive to this divergence, do not grant the fundamental and common principle all the attention which it deserves. St. Thomas, *In Epist. Pauli ad Romanos*, ch. 1, lectio 6: "They grasped the truth of God. For true knowledge of God was in them in respect to some thing: for what is known of God, that is, what is knowable of God by man through reason, is manifest to them from that which is in them, from an interior light." Cf. *In Joannem*, ch. 1, lectio 2, n. 2: "The light, that is, that life which is the light of men, shines in the darkness, that is to say, in created souls and minds, by always shining forth *(irradiando)* upon them all." (The Augustinian expression can be recognized here.) *Prima Secundae*, q.109, a.1, ad 2: "The material sun sheds its light outside us; but the intelligible Sun, Who is God, shines within us. Hence the natural light itself, bestowed upon the soul, is God's enlightenment, whereby we are enlightened by Him to see what pertains to natural knowledge." *Contra Gentiles*, bk. 1 ch. 10: "For just as the light of the sun is the principle of all visible perception, so also the divine light is the principle of all intelligible knowledge, since the divine light is that in which intelligible illumination is found first and in its highest degree." The same for practical reason, principle of the natural law; *Prima Secundae*, q.91, a.2: "The natural law is nothing other than a participation of the eternal law in the rational creature."

20. Hymn, *feria secunda, ad Laudes* (St. Ambrose).

21. Clearly I am not speaking here — as a certain critic has misrepresented me, due to an obviously mistaken reading — of a revelation "which is directed to our humble reason" (as if to supply its defect). Rather, I am speaking in the first place of this humble reason itself, which thus finds itself, quite to the contrary, magnified.

nor sacrilegious. Be the windings of his thought what they may — let him at last find his way to the source and return to the spring.

Above all — though this may seem no more than a secondary thought, very often repressed — God reveals himself continuously to man by imprinting his image upon him.[22] That divine operation constitutes the very center of man. That is what makes him spirit and constitutes his reasonableness.[23] That is why, strictly speaking, no other revelation of God is absolutely necessary; that "natural revelation" suffices, quite apart from any supernatural intervention. But in order to avoid exaggeration, let us say that it suffices in principle. Sin has not entirely extinguished it. For if the human soul only knows itself in actual knowledge, reaching that knowledge through its acts,[24] it possesses nevertheless a certain "habitual knowledge" of itself, real in spite of being obscure and veiled, constant although forever fleeting — owing to the fact that it is always present to itself;[25] the presence of the soul present to

---

22. See, for example, St. Thomas: *Prima*, q.45, a.7: "The image represents the cause as regards the similitude of its form, as fire generated represents fire generating." St. Augustine, *De Trinitate*, bk. 15, ch. 7, n. 14: "We have, therefore, tried to do this in order that through this image which we are, we might see Him by whom we have been made, in some manner or other as though through a mirror" (PL 42:1067). St. Isidore of Seville, *De ordine creaturarum*, ch. 15, n. 9: "The prophet makes mention of this stamped likeness of the image of God, when he says: 'The light of your face has been stamped upon us' (Psalm 4:7)" (PL 83:952B). St. Bonaventure, *Itinerarium mentis in Deum*, bk. 2, ch. 12. St. Bernard, *Sermo 45 de diversis*, n. 1 (PL 183:667), etc. It is this which made the author of the *Sententiae divinae Paginae* say (ch. 3): "Even the knowledge of the entire Trinity is seen to be naturally inserted into human reason" (Münster [1919], p. 7), etc. But the discussion of this last sentence would lead us to problems that are outside of our purview. (On the links between creation and the Trinity in St. Thomas, consult the work of F.-P. Sladek, analyzed in the *Bulletin de théologie ancienne et médiévale*, vol. 4, p. 295.)

23. St. Augustine, *De Genesi ad litteram*, bk. 12, ch. 7, n. 18: "The rational mind itself is also called spirit, which is, as it were, the eye of the soul, to which pertains the image and knowledge of God" (PL 34:460). Garnier de Rochefort, *Sermo 3* (PL 205:584a), etc. Cf. St. John Damascene, *De fide orthodoxa*, bk. 2, ch. 12 (PG 94:920), and St. Thomas, *Prima Secundae*, prologue.

24. St. Thomas, *In Boetium de Trinitate*, q.1, a.3; *De anima*, a.3, ad 4; *Prima*, q.87, a.1: "The human intellect of itself has the power to understand, but not to be understood, except according to that which it becomes in act"; *De veritate*, q.8, a.6, etc.

25. St. Thomas, *De Veritate*, q.10, a.8: "For this, the essence alone of the soul suffices, which is present to the mind." (Blaise Romeyer drew attention to this text: "Saint Thomas et notre connaissance de l'esprit humain," *Archives de Philosophie* 2 [1928], p. 57.) *Ibid.*, ad 1: "The mind before it withdraws from phantasms, has a habitual knowledge of itself, by which it can perceive itself to be"; ad 6: "The soul knows itself in a certain way by its

itself, in which it may learn, as in a mirror, the presence of God to the soul.[26] In the same way that the reality of the divine image in the soul is at the center and principle of all rational activity, which should lead it from knowledge of the world to the affirmation of God, so, in the same way, the soul's habitual knowledge of itself can become the principle of an intimate process of reflection, enabling it to recognize its reality as "image."[27]

... Forget, then, your greatness and confess your dependence. Reflect upon the splendor you bear within you.[28] Do not neglect the light that is given to you, but do not attribute the source to yourself.[29] Try to discover your reality as a mirror and as an image. Know yourself by knowing your God. Begin, as far as it is possible for a mortal, to contemplate his Face in recollection.[30]

---

essence"; and ad 9. On the experience of "the presence of the spirit to itself," cf. Aimé Forest, *La vocation de l'esprit* (1953), ch. 5, "La présence spirituelle." For St. Augustine: P. Agaësse, Bibliothèque aug., *Oeuvres de saint Augustine, la Trinité* 2 (1955), pp. 591-593, 603-607.

26. Again according to St. Thomas, the same kind of presence of God in the soul: thus *De Veritate*, q.10, a.2, ad 5: "The mind ... is present to itself — and likewise God (is present) — before any images are received by the senses"; a.7, ad 2: "For God himself ... is known and loved by the mind of each person to the degree that he is present to the mind"; a.11, ad 11. Cf. *Prima*, q.93, a.4, on the image of God in man, etc. This aspect of Thomist doctrine has been analyzed by M. Charles J. O'Neil, "St. Thomas and the Nature of Man," *Proceedings of the American Catholic Philosophical Association* (1951). Before that, A. Gardeil, *La structure de l'âme et l'expérience mystique*, 2nd ed. (1927), especially vol. 2, pp. 94-121.

27. Cf. Gardeil, *La structure de l'âme*, vol. 2, pp. 95 and 111, on the three moments of the soul's understanding of itself and their "dynamic interrelationship." St. Anselm, *Monologion*, ch. 67: "Most appropriately, therefore, the mind can be said to be its own mirror, in which it contemplates, so to speak, the image of its highest essence which it cannot see face to face" (PL 158:213b). St. Augustine, *Soliloques*, bk. 1, ch. 1, n. 4: "O God, who made man in your image and likeness, which image a man who knows himself recognizes" (PL 32:871).

28. Master Eckhart, *Of the Kingdom of God*: "Courage, noble soul! Reflect upon yourself, reflect on the splendor you bear within you: are you not honored above all other creatures by your resemblance to God? Disdain all that is small, for you are created for what is great!"

29. Cf. St. John Chrysostom (PG 60:411-414); St. Augustine, *De spiritu et littera*, ch. 12, n. 19 (PL 35:2064); St. Prosper of Aquitaine, *De vocatione omnium gentium*, bk. 4 (PL 51:651); and the commentaries of Lyonnet, *Quaestiones*, pp. 97-98, 101-102.

30. St. Augustine, *De Trinitate*, bk. 15, ch. 24, n. 44: "Therefore they who see their mind, in the manner it can be seen ... and yet do not believe or understand it to be an image of God; see a mirror indeed, but see so little of Him through a mirror, who must be seen through a mirror now; that they do not even know the mirror itself, which they see, to be a mirror, that is, an image" (PL 42:1091). Cf. ch. 7, n. 14 (col. 1067).

1

The Origin of the Idea of God

There are many theories to account for the origin of the idea of God, and in the course of the last century or so they have greatly increased in number. Most of them explain nothing or, without realizing it, disintegrate the idea they set out to explain. The most diverse intellectual disciplines are confused one with another, and the *a priori* consideration which governs them all is that they are concerned with an illusion. At the very beginning we find atheism, which continues to guide their steps; little wonder if we find it at the end of the journey. Indeed, the more or less explicit formulation of the conclusion is that the very idea of God must be rejected because we know "the mechanism by which humanity constructs the idea, and that mechanism is an illusion." But that is, in fact, to beg the question.

It is said that man deifies the heavens. Let it be granted. But where, exactly, did he find the idea of the divine which he applies to the heavens?[1] Why do we discover the same spontaneous movement wherever we look at our kind? Why that impulse to deify, whether it be the heavens or some other thing? Again, the word "god," we are told by the philologist, simply means "the luminous heaven of day." Agreed. But why exactly should the

---

1. Coming after the study of others, but with greater completeness and precision, Mircea Eliade has shown, in his *Traité d'histoire des religions* (1948), how, in reality, it is in one and the same act — initially indivisible and not following upon a false induction — that primitive intelligence perceives the sacred, or the divine, or whatever name man gives it, by means of the sensible object which serves him as a spontaneous symbol of the sacred (whatever the mental process might be which leads to this sort of perception). It is the phenomenon which Eliade analyzes under the name of "hierophany" and which, correctly understood, suffices to destroy "naturist" pseudo-explanations.

"luminous heaven of day" become man's god? Yet there are many people who do not even perceive the question this raises.[2]

Those who maintain that one may, in the strict sense of the word, speak of the genesis of the idea of God — whether they conceive of it as ideological or sentimental, individual or social, and regardless of whether it is totally illusory or relatively well-founded — all deny, implicitly at least, the idea of God. They deny it by tracing it back to *something else*.[3]

"It is not very easy to see," Mircea Eliade writes, "how the discovery that the primal laws of geometry were due to the empirical necessities of the irrigation of the Nile Delta can have any bearing on the validity or otherwise of those laws."[4] We can argue here in the same way. For it is really no easier to understand how the fact that the first emergence of the idea of God may possibly have been provoked by a particular spectacle, or have been linked to a particular experience of a sensible nature, could affect the validity of the idea itself. In each case the problem of its birth from experience and the problem of its essence or validity are distinct. They are problems of a different order. The problems of surveying no more engendered geometry than the experience of storm and sky engendered the idea of God. The important thing is to consider the idea in itself; not the occasion of its birth, but its inner constitution.

If the idea of God in the mind of man is real, then no fact accessible to history or psychology or sociology, or to any other scientific discipline, can really be its generating cause.[5] No observable "process" suffices to account

---

2. Again, it is based upon a similar sophism that evolutionism thinks to explain the gradual passage from the naturalistic character to the moral character of belief in the divinity, a sophism clearly denounced by C. Renouvier, *Philosophie analitique de l'histoire*, vol. 1 (1896), p. 61.

3. Such a one, among many others, is Emile Durkheim, of whom M. Merleau-Ponty very rightly remarks (*Sens et Non-sens* [1948], p. 177) that he "nominally defines the religious by the sacred, then shows that the experience of the sacred coincides with the moments of the totem society's greatest cohesion, and concludes that the religious life, at least in its elementary forms, and no doubt in its higher forms as well, is nothing other than the way in which society becomes conscious of itself." Such a one is also Sigmund Freud, when he explains "the genesis of the monotheistic idea" and the "historical and psychological conditions of its formation": *Der Mann Moses und die monotheistische Religion*; study edition: *Fragen der Gesellschaft. Ursprünge der Religion* (1934-1938), pp. 455-581. Or again, A. H. Krappe, *Die Entstehung der Mythen* (1952): "Animism is the single and necessary basis of theism."

4. *Le Chamanisme* (1951), p. 239, note.

5. In his *Analyse de l'entendement humain*, D.-J Garat wrote: "When one notices

for it. And in that sense it has no genesis — no more than geometry, to stick to the same example, has a genesis. That does not mean that it cannot be inferred — quite the contrary. It means that it cannot be reduced to the result, itself deceptive, of some empirical transformation. It is quite possible that as it unfolds in consciousness it may be dependent upon particular circumstances; it may be determined by particular circumstances or provoked by some sign or other. A particular phenomenon may be specially fitted to awaken the mind and act at the initial shock. It is quite possible, for example, that "the first conception of the word of God, as a cosmic power," may have come to our ancestors through the mediation of "a natural phenomenon, the storm: might it not be that the grumbling of the thunder suggested the powerful and awe-inspiring voice of God?"6 Many

---

that a vast number of divinities — before which the human race lived for centuries, prostrate and trembling — are born from hieroglyphic writings, one is terrified at the power of signs." Beneath the style and science of a particular era, one can recognize here a sophism which keeps repeating itself. Here Garat shows himself the "brilliant sophist," as one of the men who knew him best described him (Sainte-Beuve, *Chateaubriand et son groupe littéraire*, 2nd ed., vol. 1 [1872], p. 62, note; and Saint-Martin, in "Causeries du Lundi" [June 19, 1854]). If he had only wanted to speak of *divinities* (plural), his explanation could have been discussed on the level of scientific observation, without it being necessary to reject it *a priori*. But if he intended, as it truly seems, to explain thus the *genesis* of the very idea of *the divinity* (singular), then it was on his part an *ignoratio elenchi* (ignorance of the proper way to refute an argument). How many other examples there have been! Even Wellhausen attempted an explanation of monotheism based upon the effect of language on thought. The same sophism, resulting from the same *ignoratio elenchi*, is found more recently in Julian Huxley's "Religion as an Objective Problem," *The Uniqueness of Man* (1940), which permits the author to conclude: "The advance of natural science, logic and psychology has brought us to a stage in which God is no longer a useful hypothesis" (p. 281). He sets especially great store on the discoveries of psychology: ". . . the analytic exploration of his own mind by man must not be so advanced that he can no longer project and personify the unconscious forces of his Super-ego and his Id as beings external to himself"; but in the end, there comes a day when "the analysis of the human mind, with the discovery of its powers of projection and wish-fulfillment, its hidden subconsciousness and unrealized repressions," makes every idea of a God as distinct from man useless. That day has arrived: "A faint trace of God, half metaphysical and half magic, still broods over our world, like the smile of a cosmic Cheshire Cat. But the growth of psychological knowledge will rub even that from the universe" (p. 283). One always finds it difficult to encounter such banalities under the name of a noted scholar.

6. M.-E. Boismard, O.P., *Le Prologue de saint Jean* (1953), p. 111: "One can see a remnant of these primitive ways of thinking, more or less transformed into poetry, in Psalm 29, which is a hymn to the Lord of the storm. . . ."

other hypotheses could be formulated, some more, some less probable, some well supported, others less so, which, moreover, need not be mutually exclusive, and in fact are often complementary. It is possible, and by no means without interest, to analyze certain conditions, certain processes in the discovery of God, and this is where the historian, the ethnologist, and the psychologist abound in useful observations, although they are, for the most part, too partial. But however fruitful these researches, they cannot in any case enlighten us upon the essential question. For let us not repeat the sophism of "looking for principles in origins."[7]

There are, indeed, ways without number which do lead to God; and there are also diverse ways, ways which are certain and universally valid, along which to provide a rational basis for the idea of God. For one can "attain *he who is* starting from no matter what objects of which one can say that they *are*,"[8] and of which one must say in the same breath that they *are not*. On a very different level from the level of empirical processes, there are indeed proofs of God. And that is why, strictly speaking, there can be no genesis of the idea of God.

"If we consider things in their genesis we obtain a perfect understanding of them."[9] St. Thomas's words apply here with quite special force. For — and this St. Thomas shows very clearly — it is impossible to have such intelligence of God. The idea of God can neither be explained as an illusion whose causes have been fully understood nor as a construction of the mind.

There has been much discussion recently as to whether the objective affirmation of God belongs to "logical thought" or "mythical thought" — by which people often mean "to the realm of reason or imagination" or, as might also be said, "to truth or to the world of illusion." Perhaps insufficient attention has been paid to the fact that logic, too, has its illusions, and that it is tempted to extrapolate in the realm of the imaginary; and that logic

---

7. Cf. Jules Lachelier, *Vocabulaire philosophique*, under the entry "Origine": "Origin can only be used of a beginning in time, an initial fact. A metaphysical cause . . . should not be designated by this name. . . . One should say *beginning*."

8. Étienne Gilson, *Le Thomisme*, 4th ed. (1942), p. 119 (Eng. trans. *The Christian Philosophy of St. Thomas Aquinas*, p. 83).

9. St. Thomas, *In Polit.*, I, 2.

may become too "reasonable" to find in truth him who is above reason.... Is the God of rationalism "the true God"? Is its idea of God really solid and rational?

In reality the authentic affirmation of God — which is something much more than an affirmation — belongs in the first instance to the deepest operation of thought, which is not itself either "mythical" or "logical," although it is normally obliged to borrow the procedures of logic in order to express itself, and makes use of imagination to give itself body, in such a way that its spontaneous constructions reveal a structure analogous to the structures of myths. Perhaps, if we are to take all these elements into account, we should do better to describe it with a word of which modern abuse ought not to be allowed to deprive us, namely a "symbolic"[10] affirmation or even, to use another and older term beloved of the Fathers, "anagogical."[11]

---

10. The words "symbol" and "symbolic" in relatively recent times have been the object of such abuse in an anti-intellectual and anti-realist sense that in fact one hesitates sometimes to reintroduce them into traditional language and thought, where they nonetheless have their place. Not long ago Sertillanges wrote, in *Les grande thèses de la philosophie thomiste* (1928), p. 80 (Eng. trans. *Foundations of Thomistic Philosophy*, p. 89), that in our explanation of the knowledge of God, "we are not regressing back to symbolism; because what we say about God is not, for us, solely figurative, it is not arbitrary, it is not subjective; rather it is founded on truth, for it corresponds to a true relationship, a relationship perfectly defined from our side, although it is not so defined from the other; an essential relationship, although it refers its human term to that which has no essence.... From the moment that our attributions are well founded, all the while aiming at the Unnameable, there is no symbolism; there is formal truth, no matter how miserably feeble...." He goes on to say: "Symbolism is not a doctrine, it is a shade of agnosticism" and "disguised agnosticism" (p. 11). It goes without saying that we reject the word if it has such a meaning! See also A. Gardeil, in *Revue thomiste* (1904), pp. 70-73. On the contrary, Ch. de Moré-Pontgibaud, "Sur l'analogie des noms divins": "When it is a question of divine things... the symbol presents itself as a means of knowing, certainly not exclusive, but normal, and thus one can say that the proper and natural field of symbolism is revelation" (*Recherches de science religieuse* [1954], p. 344, n. 17).

11. This is what Jacques Maritain calls "ana-noetic intellection": *Les degrés du savoir* (1932), p. 445. Someone has said that this allusion to the Fathers of the Church was abusive, because "despite, or rather because of their pastoral and apostolic concern to turn the heart of men toward God," they "took great care to cast the least possible discredit on the transcendent value of our human concepts." We wish to take the same care as they did, and even, if it must be said, more care than some of them. For it is to understand them poorly to believe that one would never find in any of them various

All attempts to find a "genesis" for the idea of God — like the attempts to "reduce" it to something else by explaining its genesis — err in some respect or other. The idea of God is a unique idea, distinct from all others, and it cannot be fitted into any system. It strikes down like a flash of lightning, and can be seen cutting through the history of humanity; it plays havoc with the laborious syntheses of ethnologists and historians, and upsets the evolutionary schemes and the erudite "physiologies of religion." Once the intelligence reaches maturity, the idea of God germinates spontaneously.

But however indestructible it may be from then on, it does not immediately shine forth in all its brilliance. And equally it is very far from being so fully and peacefully established in the mind that it holds undisturbed sway. On the contrary, one is tempted to think that, like the seed sown in the Gospel, it fell among thorns and thistles and was quickly stifled by the incredible proliferation of myths. Or else, if it bears fruit, it seems as though the fruit were so closely intertwined with the luxuriant vegetation of the wild seed that there was no longer any way in practice of removing the latter without uprooting the former. Insofar as religion co-exists in this way with a myth, it lends the latter a power of seduction which is, in the end, turned against religion itself. The gods thus secretly nourished by the idea of God are parasites and prevent the true God from emerging. . . . Hence the "deluge of idolatry"[12] that covers the face

---

expressions which are excessive in their imprecision. And so we had avoided citing this or that text which could have caused their actual thought on the matter to be misconstrued. See, for example, St. Jerome, *In Ecclesiasten*, 5, 1: "Let us know our own weakness, for as far as the heavens are above the earth, so far is our conjecturing separated from the nature of the thing itself. . . . He who wants to speak of many things concerning the divinity, falls into foolishness. . . . Therefore our words should be few, for even those things we think we know, we see through a glass darkly, and what we think we grasp we understand as we do a dream . . ." (PL 23:1052). Or St. Hilary, *De Trinitate*, bk. 1, ch. 19: "There can be no comparison between God and earthly things, yet the weakness of our understanding forces us to seek for illustrations from a lower sphere to explain our meaning about loftier themes. The course of daily life shows how our experience in ordinary matters enables us to form conclusions on unfamiliar subjects. We must therefore regard any comparison as helpful to men rather than as descriptive of God. . . ." However, the context shows with sufficient clarity that one would certainly err in taking similar declarations in an agnostic sense.

12. Bossuet, *Elévations sur les mystères*, 7e semaine (*Oeuvres*, ed. F. Lachat [1862], ch. 7, p. 135).

of the earth. So that in order to attain to religion pure and undefiled, it seems as though we had to sacrifice all these gods, instead of purifying them or testing their worth, and retaining those whose claims prove authentic. Man frees himself from superstition through atheism[13] ... only to fall once again into superstition. Or else ... or else.... There seems no limit to the hypotheses man can construct. How, then, can he break out of the circle? Whichever way he takes, his reason is faced with difficulties and with a thousand illusions to overcome before he can emerge triumphant! And in most cases how great is the uncertainty and how many are the errors! And even in the cry of monotheism itself — so rationally well-founded after all — one can often detect a certain lack of assurance:

"O stay of the earth, and you who are enthroned above it, whoever you are, thought can approach you only with difficulty. Whether you are Zeus, or the Supreme Necessity, or the human spirit...."[14]

... Unless, that is, God himself intervenes to break the fatal circle and elects a trusted servant who is charged with the task of announcing him to his brethren.[15] Which, as the author of the Epistle to the Hebrews tells us, may happen "at sundry times and in diverse manners."[16]

It is only natural that the idea of God should be, at one and the same time, ready to emerge and yet menaced with suffocation; for mankind — made in the image of God, though sinful — while destined to grope its way slowly up, is nevertheless obsessed from the first moment of its awakening by a call from above. From the very beginning two tendencies have been at work to retard and deflect man's natural impulse towards

---

13. Is this not the case, in practice, with Buddhism? Its founder, no doubt, does not deny the gods, but declares them all incapable of assuring the salvation of men; they themselves need to be saved, and the Buddhas are above even the greatest of the gods.

14. Euripides, *The Trojan Women*, ll. 884-886.

15. Cf. Vatican I, the Constitution *Dei Filius*, ch. 2, *De revelatione:* It is indeed thanks to this divine revelation that those matters concerning God which are not of themselves beyond the scope of human reason can, even in the present state of the human race, be known by everyone without difficulty, with firm certitude and with no intermingling of error" (Acta Concilii Vaticani, ch. 250). (Eng. trans.: Norman P. Tanner, ed., *Decrees of the Ecumenical Councils*, vol. 2: Trent to Vatican II [Washington, D.C., 1990], p. 806.)

16. Hebrews 1:1. Cf. St. Thomas, *Prima*, q.1, a.1; *Secunda Secundae*, q.2, a.4; *Contra Gentiles*, bk. I, ch. 4; *In 3 Sent.*, d. 24; *In Boet. de Trinitate*, 3, 1; *De Veritate*, q.14, a.10.

his creator. One of these tendencies results from the very conditions in which the intelligence is obliged to work in order to triumph, little by little, over the darkness;[17] the other, according to the teaching of the Catholic faith, is the immediate fruit of an original moral deviation. Both tendencies, the natural and the perverse, supplement and reinforce one another in obstructing the royal road of the mind, and tempt it aside among the myriad labyrinthine paths of magic and myth.[18] There is the tendency to confuse the Author of Nature with the Nature through which he reveals himself obscurely, whose characteristics we cannot help employing in order to think of him; and there is the tendency to forsake an exacting and all too incorruptible God in favor of something inferior or fictitious. When these tendencies work together, the categories become lifeless and rigid.[19] The world itself becomes more dense. And what should have been a sign becomes a screen. The initial vision is dissipated almost before it is perceived . . . and the divine star disappears behind its "gross shadow":

---

17. Cf. Charles Journet, in *Nova et Vetera* (1950), p. 192: "It was normal that man should pass from a mythical or magical mentality, that is, where the imagination is in the foreground, to a rational or scientific mentality, where reason is in the foreground; in other words, reason's rule in the dark of night had to precede its rule in the light of day. See also Jacques Maritain, "Signe et Symbole," in *Quatre essais sur l'esprit dans sa condition charnelle* (1939). Cf. G. Van der Leeuw, text cited in the following note. Maurice Pradines, *Esprit de la Religion* (1941), p. 119: "No matter how strange it may seem, one can ask if magic did not for some time carry before the species the torch of reason." Under this aspect, magic reveals what a recent historian has called "paleopsychology." Here, however, we believe that only one of the two aspects of the reality is present. Cf. C. Jung, *Einführung in das Wesen der Mythologie* (1941).

18. Cf. G. Van der Leeuw, "L'homme et la civilisation," *Eranos-Jahrbuch* 16 (1948), p. 149: "The first form which clothes the consciousness is magic. The man of magic places himself in a position, all alone, against the rest of the world, which he conjures. . . . [The birth of the magical attitude] is much more important than the apogee of Greek thought, because in magic, for the first time, man withdraws into an interiority all the more powerful in that it is invisible." Nonetheless, one can grant to the arrival of magical thought its proper import, without underestimating either the arrival of rational thought, or its "apogee" in Greek thought.

19. On the ambiguity of heaven in ancient philosophies, see: A.-J. Festugière, O.P., *Le dieu cosmique*, pp. 120-250. It is only as the result of an *ignoratio elenchi* that one could write in this regard: "One would have liked perhaps to see more clearly recognized the noetic value of analogies which are solid in themselves and fully effective in their own realm: that is, the intellectual realm." Such a remark, in fact, does not bear any relationship to the object of our text.

Le feu, le vent, l'air subtil,
La voute étoilée, l'onde impétueuse ou les flambeaux du ciel
Sont regardés comme les maîtres du monde.

(Fire, wind and the subtle air,
The starry vault, the impetuous swell or the torches in the sky
Are regarded as the masters of the world.)

In the furthest recesses of our consciousness, "the glory of the incorruptible God," before it has had time to shine with all its brilliance, is exchanged for the gods of nothingness or untruth. . . .[20] Or at least the God who is really close to us has been put at a distance[21] — to remain for a long while the unknown God. Even to those who still preserve a memory of him, he becomes a forsaken God. And so it becomes necessary to rediscover him by stages, groping and fumbling and sometimes thinking that we have lost him. Even at times when the knowledge of God seems to have made decisive progress, he is still easily conceived of as an individual with human passions, or, on the other hand, as a vague and diffused Force. When we think we have exhausted the idea of God, it is no more than a sort of *materia prima*, a being as indeterminate and as close to nothingness as empty space; or else it becomes a principle wholly lacking in inwardness, an abstraction with no power of irradiation. Each new formula seems more discouraging than the last and, by reaction, provokes its contrary. The spiritual gain is never definitive, though this alone could stabilize and nourish the intellectual gain. The better is transformed into the worse, and the great force for good in human affairs is enslaved to profane ends: once again man deifies his needs, his interests, his passions, his ignorance and his follies. . . . And then what should have been

---

20. Wisdom 13:2; Romans 1:23 (with allusion to the story of the golden calf; cf. Psalm 105:19-20); Jeremiah 2:11: "And my people have exchanged their glory for that which does not exist!" Cf. Racine, *Hymnes traduits du bréviaire romain,* Monday at Lauds:

Star of which the sun is merely a crude shadow,
Sacred day, from which the day borrows its brightness.

21. Cf. Mircea Eliade, in *Témoignages* 28 (1951), pp. 22-26: "If there is one constant in the religious history of ancient man, it is . . . this *remoteness from the supreme God.*" ". . . Everywhere in the 'primitive' religions, the supreme heavenly Being seems to have lost religious relevance; he is absent from the cult, and in myth, he withdraws ever farther from human beings, to the point of becoming a *deus otiosus* (a disengaged god). . . . The divine remoteness, in reality, results in man's progressive fall into a 'religious concreteness' which prohibits him from all transcendence. . . ."

progress takes the form of negation. More often than not, the gods of fable are supplanted by the Divine instead of by the Living God. Religions and morals close in mortal combat. For man's inwardness is the fruit of his victory over the gods.... But from time to time, nevertheless, a ray of pure light filters through. The pagans themselves have their "hidden saints," and the true God chooses his prophets where he will.[22]

There are many facts which make the Marxist theory, and theories like it, plausible. The whole religious system varies and presents different characteristics according to whether man is a hunter, a shepherd, or cultivates the soil. And among unbelievers Marxists are not alone in emphasizing this sort of law. Research as a whole confirms it, and the historical-cultural school has made it the principle of religious evolution and has applied it rigorously to all forms of religion, apart from supernatural revelation. They have classified the religion of "pastoral" peoples, of those who "gather fruits," of the "hunters" and of the "planters".... Similarly, it has been observed that in a civilization where the horse dominates the economy, the gods adored are chivalric, etc.[23] It is also a fact that the gods of small states, bounded by narrow frontiers and centered upon themselves, are unlike the gods of the great cosmopolitan cities. As the social group expands from tribe to city and then from nation to empire, the cosmic consciousness is ordered and organized accordingly, and involves a series of parallel transformations in rite and myth.[24] It is perfectly true, therefore, that myths and

---

22. Some traditional texts on this subject can be found in our *Catholicisme*, 4th ed. (1948), p. 181. Clement of Alexandria, *Stromata* 5, ch. 6, 35, n. 2: the candelabra of the temple, symbol of Christ, "illuminating in various ways and by multiple fires" the men who believe and hope in him. See also Jean Daniélou, *Les saints "païens" de l'Ancien Testament* (1956). (Eng. trans.: *Holy Pagans of the Old Testament* [1957].)

23. "The sway of the equestrian god extends from Thrace and southern Sarmatian Russia in the west, all the way to the Indian empire of the Saka in the east, from whence the equestrian god penetrated into China." F. Altheim, *Alexander und Asien* (1953), p. 218.

24. Cf. Benjamin Constant, *De la Religion*, vol. 2 (1825), p. 2: "As soon as a revolution takes place in the human race, religion undergoes a similar change"; pp. 6-7: "In the same way, the isolation in which the fetish-gods used to live ceases being conceivable to the gods of small tribes gathered together in society.... They hold their gods in common; and this assembly of the gods happens necessarily as soon as the assembly of men has taken place." J. Duchesne-Guillemin, in *L'âme de l'Iran* (1951), p. 25: "The research of Georges Dumézil has established that the social organization of the Indo-Europeans — with its hierarchy of functions — was reflected in their pantheon, in the hierarchy of their gods."

rites reveal and mirror social conditions — which in their turn are closely dependent upon economic conditions — and in consequence these religions tend to lend their constraints to reinforce economic conditions. Yet, to be perfectly just, it should be noted that, for all its social abuses, religion thus envisaged consecrates the very principle of society; thanks to the social and mental coherence which it ensures, it contributes more than any other element to enabling man to live, which is the prime condition of progress.

There is, however, something else to be taken into account: the essential point. One might perhaps say that Marxism, like rationalism, is quantitatively right — somewhat in the same way that determinism is true in respect of the greater part of human action, at least as far as appearance is concerned. Historical materialism is one of those basic truths which cannot fail to convince at first sight, but which is of no help to those who desire to penetrate to the heart of the real. Where experience is concerned, do not the false and the insignificant attract infinitely more attention than the substantial and authentic? The fakes and illusions of the mind, its habitually lazy or bastard forms, its repeated failures, its standardized products, like its sudden unforeseen errors, are all plainly visible, and the observer cannot fail to see them. The area they cover is vast; they encumber the scene. Whereas the thing that counts most, the first sign of change, and the seed of things to come, is almost always rare and hidden, though its action may be widely diffused and may permeate everything. But even if it happens to be noticed, it still needs to be envisaged from within if it is to be appreciated at its proper value; by a method, that is, which has nothing to do with statistical methods and is beyond the scope of empirical observation. There is every reason to think, for example, that the Marxist analysis, applied conscientiously and as intelligently as possible twenty centuries ago, in Palestine, would have overlooked the humble fact summed up in a name: Jesus of Nazareth — as in fact the Jewish and Roman historians overlooked it. That almost imperceptible fact slipped through their nets, and if it happens to be caught in the mesh of learned explanations, it is emptied of its explosive force.

Nevertheless, there are certain broad lines which are too prominent to remain entirely concealed from any who will simply open their eyes. We are told, for example, that the cult of a God without form mirrors an age of trade with distant parts, and a banking system. Is monotheism the result, then, of the slow unification of the powers of the earth? — How are we, then, to explain the history of India, where profound systems of religious philosophy and exalted forms of adoration blossomed in a primitive economy and a politically amorphous society? And, above all, have people read the precepts of the Jewish Decalogue? (Their precise date is not, in this context, of great importance.) "Hear, O Israel! . . . I am the Lord thy God. . . . Thou shalt have no other gods before me. Thou shalt not make thee any graven image. . . . For I, the Lord thy God, am a jealous God."[25]

It does not require any special powers of observation to distinguish two kinds of "monotheistic" religion in our Western world, in spite of their multiple implications and their diverse origins.[26] The first is, at least partly, the fruit of social and political development as well as of reflection. Little by little the pantheons are formed in the image of what happens on earth. The gods are organized, a hierarchy is formed, and their very number and variety begin to suggest the unity of the divine.[27] In the end the head of the divine society grows into the supreme god, while the remaining gods are no more than his manifestations or his serfs.[28] As a nation comes to know the gods of subject nations, it amalgamates them with its own by understanding them as equivalent in a way that is at once enriching and unifying. If, perchance, there is competition, the gods of the vanquished, themselves defeated, are eliminated, unless, indeed, they are adopted by the conquerors or become demons. . . . Such, with a hundred variations, is the case in Babylon and in Egypt, among the ancient Indo-Europeans, and in the Achaemenid Empire, as in the Hellenistic world and in Rome under the Empire. . . . Can the result be said to have been all gain, politically, culturally, and for thought? For the most part, yes, and sometimes the profit was very considerable. But can it be said to mark religious progress, properly

---

25. Deuteronomy 5:1-8.
26. Already in ancient Egypt; cf. *Enseignement pour Mérikarê*, by means of obscure expressions, one discerns "the theory that the idols are . . . the expression of a single and hidden God, just as the successive waves which beat against the bank are waves of one and the same river." E. Drioton, "La religion égyptienne," in *Histoire des religions* (Brillant-Aigrain), vol. 3 (1955), pp. 38-39.
27. Cf. Maximus of Tyre: "Now there is found throughout the whole world a teaching according to which there is one God who is king and father of all things, and many gods who are sons of this god, co-regents with him. Thus say the Greeks and the Barbarians."
28. Cf. Dio Chrysostom: "Some people assert that Apollos, Helios and Dionysius are identical to one another, and simply gather together all the gods into a single force or power."

speaking? Not always, and sometimes not at all. Even in cases where anthropomorphism was transcended, the goal reached was hardly more than an abstract Divine or divinized Nature: *Aequum est, quidquid omnes colunt, unum putari: eadem spectamus astra, commune coelum est, idem nos mundus involvit.* . . .[29] (It is right that whatever everybody worships should be considered one thing: we behold the same stars, the heavens are common to us all, the same world embraces us.) The concentration of gods has not given birth to God!

In the second type of monotheism, on the contrary, the one God affirms his uniqueness with a fierce, exclusive jealousy. "There is no God but God." He is the result neither of concentration nor of syncretism, whether political or intellectual. He imposes and sanctions a new order of values. He is the God who cannot be reached by way of the gods; the path to him leads through conversion and the breaking of idols — those made with hands and those fashioned in the heart. He is the God who throws down his gauntlet to the gods of Nature — just as the unknown young David threw down his challenge to the celebrated giant Goliath. A God who must be followed, though it involves leaving the country of one's fathers behind one . . . A God who leads into the unknown. A God who scandalizes those he does not attract. And before his face "the gods of the nations" are nought but "wood and stone": vanity, nothingness, "the abomination," "sin," "filthy" and "impure," "corpses." They are the "non-gods." "Do not forsake the Lord and adore the gods of nothingness."[30] "Behold, the Lord will come on a white cloud and all the works of the Egyptians will be swept away before his face."[31] "A jealous and exclusive God, who divides everything and leaves nothing standing before him." Just now we were dealing with an easygoing Principle which justified the practices of polytheism and consolidated the dominions of the flesh, while remaining in itself the possession of a small

---

29. Symmachus, *Relatio*, n. 10. According to A. H. Krappe, *Die Entstehung der Mythen*, p. 343, it would be the discovery of the immutable laws of the cosmos by the Greek mathematicians, which would have led to monotheism, thus achieving a natural evolution whose starting point was the animist illusion. But he only illustrates his thesis with "the god of the Stoics."

30. *Secrets of Enoch*, ch. 2.

31. Isaiah 19:1. Cf. Robert Guelluy, "Dieu est Amour," *Revue diocésaine de Tournai* (1950), p. 27: "The Old Testament speaks of God not in terms of metaphysics but in terms of action. It does not ponder, like the philosophers, on the essence of the divinity, but describes what is unique in the power and demands of the Creator of heaven and earth, the God of Abraham, Isaac and Jacob. . . ."

élite of the wise. Now we find a Being in no sense abstract, though purely spiritual; a living Being who, although invisible, acts; an intransigent Being who demands that all worship should be addressed to him, and who wishes to be recognized by all men; a transcendent Being, though nonetheless powerfully personal, who overflows the boundaries of all the cities of the earth; not a cosmopolitan God, but a God who is to be, if he is not already, the universal God.

The second form of monotheism alone is charged with power. It alone is pregnant with religious progress, for it is the source of a radical metamorphosis in the theory and practice of religion. It alone can promote moral and social progress, even where it does not actually initiate it. The God of this monotheism is the only God who can be the object of faith in the full sense of the word.[32] In its encounter with the first form of monotheism, the second form makes no attempt to compromise or to compose the differences between them; it must, in the first place, be victorious over it. *Hebraeorum Deus a Romanis non receptus, quia se solum coli voluerit.*[33] (The God of the Hebrews was not accepted by the Romans, because he wished that only he should be worshipped.)

Then, perhaps, it may utilize the first form of monotheism to express and complete itself or in order to spread abroad, in that way leading the first form to its goal. Now we do not find the second form of monotheism

---

32. Cf. the analyses of St. Augustine, of Faustus of Riez, of St. Anselm (*Monologion*, ch. 76-78; *Opera omnia*, vol. 1 [1938], pp. 83-85), of St. Albert the Great and of St. Thomas on the formula "credere in Deum." See also our *Méditation sur l'Église* (3rd ed., 1954), ch. 1 (Eng. trans.: *The Splendor of the Church*).

33. St. Augustine, *De consensu evangelistarum,* bk 1, ch. 18, n. 26: "What God is this, who is either so unknown, that He is the only one not discovered as yet among so many gods, or who is one so well known that He is now the only one worshipped by so many men? There remains, then, nothing which they can possibly allege in explanation of their refusal to admit the worship of this God, except that His will was that He alone should be worshipped. . . . For the opinion of Socrates is, that every deity whatsoever ought to be worshipped just in the manner in which he may have ordained that he should be worshipped. Consequently it became a matter of the supremest necessity with them to refuse to worship the God of the Hebrews. For if they were minded to worship Him in a method different from the way in which He had declared that He ought to be worshipped, then assuredly they would have been worshipping not this God as He is, but some figment of their own. And, on the other hand, if they were willing to worship Him in the manner which He had indicated, then they could not but perceive that they were not at liberty to worship those other deities whom He had forbidden them to worship."

appearing in the great unified states at the conclusion of periods of expansion and conquest, any more than at the end of periods of profound speculation, or in the wake of economic changes. As far as can be seen from the hopeless state of the sources, the religion of Zoroaster, "the least pagan of pagan religions," a religion whose divine forces are not gods so much as the "attributes of the unique divinity,"[34] arose in one of the most remote provinces of Iran, far from the focus of culture which existed at that time in Babylon, and before the era of syncretism was opened by the conquests of Cyrus.[35] The history of Judaism and of Islam, too, belies all the theories of the development of religion, which only invoke factors which are foreign to it. Israel was a small nation with a rudimentary economy, a crude philosophy, and a civilization far less developed than that of its great neighbors, who each in turn crushed it. If Israel was quick to profit from their wider conceptions, especially during the exile, it did so for its own ends, and in order to clothe the God which it alone affirmed in more magnificent array. Moreover, it was during the Captivity, in a period of ruin and defeat, that the Israelites celebrated the triumph of their God. As for the Arabs before the Hegira, they can hardly be said to have been united. The idea of God in its highest manifestations and in its humblest forms always bursts and overflows social as well as mental categories. One may indeed say "the Spirit bloweth where it listeth."

A lasting religion must have roots, and its birth depends upon a series of conditions which are not all of them of a religious order. No Christian need be astonished at the fact, for he knows the place occupied in religion, even in its revealed form, by the idea of "the fullness of time." Supernatural is not equivalent to superficial. The divine does not exclude the human. Nor is it arbitrarily superimposed upon it. But in this sphere, once again let us be on our guard against mistaking conditions for causes.

---

34. Jean-Pierre de Menasce, O.P., "Le monde moral iranien," *Les morales non-chrétiennes* (Journées "Ethnologie et Chrétienté" [Paris, 1954]), p. 42.

35. Cf. Jacques Duchesne-Guillemin, *Zoroastre, étude critique avec une traduction commentée des Gatha* (1948). The reflection of S. Petrement also comes to mind, precisely concerning the philosophical allure of the religion of Zoroaster: "Everything is older than was thought" (cited in *ibid.*, p. 66).

In paganism, the progress of reflection tended towards the elimination of the gods. Through Christianity, faith in God has promoted the development of consciousness. Man, called by God, has come to know himself by learning to know his vocation. He has become a person forever, to himself.

If *God* is given the same name as the *gods*, it is not because of some parentage, however remote: as though, for example, the one were the perfection, the sublimation, or the unification of the many. It is in order to mark the fact that the others never had but a borrowed, or rather a stolen, existence. God comes into his own, into the rights which, ever since the day when man turned away from him, have been usurped by idle phantoms or by the forces of evil.

There are some who think that the one God is the product of a religious *evolution*. Scattered at first in a dust-cloud of sacred beings, the divine slowly takes form; a hierarchy is organized, and by a gradual process of concentration is ultimately raised into a supreme divinity, while all the other powers created by the mythical imagination become from thenceforward its servants. Then, at leisure, it is purified, spiritualized, and refined — perhaps to vanishing point.[36]

There are others, on the contrary, who hold that the one God is posited at a single stroke by a religious *revolution*. He affirms his position instantaneously in opposition to all else. An individual God who rejects the other gods. A certain conception of the divine which springs up in all its exclusiveness, in opposition to the conceptions entertained up to that time, when man has tired of them either because he no longer perceives their value or because he recognizes their emptiness.

Both theses are based upon careful observation, and each of them deserves to be given full weight, though if one considers the living God of religion rather than the supreme principle of philosophy, there is more historical truth

---

36. Concerning hellenistic monotheism, arrived at either by the tendency to give preeminence to one particular god, who becomes the ruler of gods and men (Jupiter, the highest, most excellent), or by a fusion of all the gods into a single divine principle, of which the many gods would only be different manifestations, see Dom Jacques Dupont, O.S.B., *Gnosis, la connaissance religieuse dans les Epîtres de saint Paul* (1949), pp. 330-333; Franz Cumont, *Les religions orientales dans le paganisme romain*, 4th ed. (1929), passim.

in the second theory than in the first.[37] The God of the Bible is named: he is Yahweh, and affirms his uniqueness by raising up and forming his own people, distinct from all others, by imposing a particular legislation upon them, and through his Prophets he makes a mockery of the gods made with hands. The God of the Gospels is no less personal: he is the heavenly Father, and Christians can only look upon the gods of paganism, if they treat them as having any real existence whatsoever, as demons. Nevertheless, it is true that the formative, intransigent phase, during which monotheism or monolatry is established, is closely followed by an enveloping movement, a phase during which, without allowing himself to be in any way contaminated, the victorious God takes over and uses to his advantage all that is true in the thought and worship that had gone astray. The phase of opposition is succeeded by a phase of absorption, so that the two theses would appear to be complementary rather than contradictory.

Yet neither theory goes to the root of the matter. Neither goes back to the source. In reality, the idea of the one and transcendent God does not

---

37. Edgar Quinet had explained this in a fine section of his work *Génie des Religions* (Oeuvres complètes, vol. 1 [1857], pp. 273-274): "Just as in nature an interval often occurs in the ladder of organic beings, a hiatus, which cannot be filled, so also between Osiris and Jehovah there is not only a progress of forms, an ascending motion, a regular succession: between one and the other there is a revolution. Should I say that Adonai, Elohim is nothing else but the successive development of Baal of Babylon, Adonis of Phoenicia, Hercules of Tyre? Certainly not. You may extol the genius of these gods in terms of a continual progression as much as you like, but they will never arrive, by means of any stages, at the idea of Jehovah. Correct, embellish, put the finishing touches as much as you want on Baal or Astarte: but you will never make the gods of Canaan into the God of Moses. Why not? Because these gods, incarnated in the universe, are one with it; because the earth forms their feet, the heavens their head, the stars their eyes; but nature is not even a garment for Jehovah; he can remake it, or shatter it, if he wishes. The winds are not his breath, they are his messengers. The stars are not his eyes, they are his slaves. The world is not his image; it is not his echo; it is not his adornment; it is not his light; it is not his word. What is it then? It is nothing before him." But in the course of his argument, Quinet makes a sort of natural link between the monotheism of Israel and the desert, "natural homeland of a jealous God." "Always," he says, "the desert appears on the horizon when you pronounce the name of Jehovah. . . . Humanity recollects itself; in the midst of the silence of the universe, the miracle of the God-Spirit is consummated in the heart of humanity . . ." (pp. 276-278). In *De l'origine des dieux* (*ibid.*, p. 422), he takes up the same idea once again: "Only a people isolated in the desert, foe to all the others round about, could manifest Jehovah in his eternal solitude." The idea was popular for a time, thanks to Renan (*Etudes d'histoire religieuse*, 2nd ed. [1857], pp. 66-67). It was generally forgotten that this notion was already found in Quinet, whose *Génie des Religions* was, nonetheless, a well-known book for a time.

arise historically as the result of criticism or in the wake of disillusionment. It is not the fruit of an immanent dialectic whether revolutionary or evolutionary. Nor is it obtained as the result of a synthesis, as though in answer to the need and impulse to unify the fragmentary expressions of the divine; nor is it an antithesis, as though man had become conscious at last of the vanity of his age-old gods. Neither integration nor contrast can explain it. What we take to be cause is in truth effect. The idea of the one God springs up spontaneously at the heart of consciousness, whether as a result of the exigencies of reason or of some supernatural illumination, and imposes itself upon the mind of itself, of its own necessity. In fact, the clearest instance shows God revealing himself, and in doing so dissipating the idols or compelling the man to whom he reveals himself to tear them from his heart: *Reverberasti infirmitatem aspectus mei, radians in me vehementer et contremui amore et horrore*[38] (You have beaten upon the weakness of my sight, shining upon me with power, and I shook with love and dread). First comes the "radiation," while the light and the attraction, interwoven with fear, emanate from it. The phenomenon of "reverberation" exposes the infirmity of human conceptions, and sets them in the full light of day, and the man whom God has touched is filled with horror at the thought of the phantoms which he had engendered. The faith which is born in him liberates him from superstition.

At the very beginning, then, there is an encounter, a contact, a certain apperception, or whatever term may, according to the case, be applied to it — an illumination of the intellect, vision, hearing, faith. The antithesis comes second, and the synthesis, insofar as one may use the expression, comes last.

The first moment alone, in fact, counts. There is Abraham, hearing the call which tears him from his country and his ancestral cult; and Moses, receiving the Law on Sinai; Isaiah, contemplating the majesty of Yahweh in the Temple. . . . Jesus, moved by the Spirit and conversing with the Father. In none of these cases is there any suggestion of a "dialectic," of the swing of the pendulum, the alternation of "for" and "against" — no trace of relativity. All forms of dialectic, whether historical or not, and whatever their mode, imply contrariety and negation. Whatever the spring of the dialectic, one term is always called forth by another. The swing of the pendulum does not imply the introduction of a new principle. Dialectic is a powerful weapon because it corresponds to one of the essential processes of the mind. But when it tries to engender thought, instead of organizing

---

38. St. Augustine, *Confessions*, bk. 8, ch. 10, n. 16.

it, its soul is a blind necessity. It throws no light on the inwardness of the beings which at each step, and turn by turn, it posits; or rather those beings have no inwardness; they are terms which are wholly relative to those with which they form a series. Once the idea of the living God has fallen like a seed into consciousness — whether by the light of reason or as the result of a supernatural revelation — it certainly is subjected, like all other ideas, to dialectic. In a sense more than any other idea, since it becomes the principle of perpetual "ferment" which works unceasingly in it. Nonetheless, it remains substantial and positive, and that is what ensures its victory. Far from corresponding to a phase in human dialectic, it is, on the contrary, dialectic which plays the intermediary role, linking in its process a reality already perceived and a mystery surmised, without ceasing to be sustained in its movement by a presence. . . .

Observe, again, how much more striking it appears in the concrete dialectic of history. Religious monotheism, even as we owe it to Israel and Christ — and this is true in some small measure in certain analogous cases — is illuminated by the divine source. Before being a belief, and, *a fortiori*, before becoming a tradition or an idea, it was a vocation, and remains one as long as it preserves its authentic vitality. Its formation bears no trace of the dialectical movement of *ressentiment* in the Nietzschean sense. Abraham did not find the true God by turning against the gods of his ancestors; he had to struggle in his heart to abandon them: his faith had to be a victory. Jesus did not preach the vanity of this world like the Buddha, or the vanity of the gods who canonize it, because they are the mythical form of its very substance: he proclaimed the Kingdom of Heaven in which his soul already breathes, and he reveals the Heavenly Father's love in and through his own person. In that sense, too, the Apostle's words are verified: There is only Yes in him.[39]

Mythologies have been psychoanalyzed with more or less success. More and more it becomes necessary to psychoanalyze atheism.[40] Attempts to psychoanalyze faith will always end in failure.

---

39. 2 Corinthians 1:19. Cf. Karl Barth, *Dogmatik im Grundriß* (1948), p. 42 : "Where the true God is recognized, the idols crumble into dust and He alone remains." For a comparison with Buddha, cf. De Lubac, *Aspects du Bouddhisme,* vol. 1 (1951), pp. 51-53.

40. There are no more psychological refutations of God than there are psychological proofs of God. Cf. the remarks of Edmond Ortigues on this subject, in the *Supplément* of *La Vie spirituelle* (1951), p. 461, concerning the work of Wilfried Daim, *Umwertung der Psychoanalyse* (1951).

2

The Affirmation of God

If, like St. Augustine, we use only the word "belief" to denote the acts in which the spirit adheres to truths beyond the grasp of the senses, and which the intelligence cannot as yet penetrate, we may say that the affirmation of God is always an act of faith. But then we must be more precise, and add at once that no other affirmation can compare with it in certitude. For even before it was formulated, before God was named, that belief provided the foundation of all others. All affirmations, as Descartes rightly saw, though he explained it badly, depend upon that belief, and certainty in all its forms is rooted in it. "However we set about it," Leibniz, for his part, declares, "we cannot do without the divine existence." The two philosophers, each in his own way — which it is not our present concern to criticize — had taken up the axiom enunciated by St. Thomas Aquinas: "All knowers know God implicitly in all they know."[1]

---

1. St. Thomas, *De Veritate*, q.22, a.2, ad 1. Joseph Maréchal, *Le point de départ de la recherche métaphysique*, pt. 5 (1926), p. 337: "We could therefore posit, quite rigorously, that the possibility of our subjective ultimate end logically presupposes the existence of our objective ultimate end, God, and that in this way, in each intellectual act, the existence of an absolute Being is implicitly affirmed.... But it is not enough to observe the logical implications of each contingent act of understanding; the act includes here a radical necessity, independent of the act which reveals it to us; for even our implicit affirmation of the absolute Being was necessary a priori." Cf. Hans Urs Von Balthasar, *Theologik 1, Die Wahrheit der Welt* (1985), p. 45.

It has been said: "It is obvious that the thought of St. Thomas is diametrically opposed to that of Descartes and of Leibniz, to which it has been likened." Let us say, with more moderation and truth, that the thought of these two philosophers (who differ

Every human act, whether it is an act of knowledge or an act of the will, rests secretly upon God, by attributing meaning and solidity to the real upon which it is exercised. For God is the Absolute; and nothing can be thought without positing the Absolute in relating it to that Absolute; nothing can be willed without tending towards the Absolute, nor valued unless weighed in terms of the Absolute.[2]

So it is not only in the acts which we call religious, nor in a crudely pragmatic sense, that *God is used* — to recall a well-known expression. The supreme contradiction is to use God in order to control the flux of existence, to organize chaos, to make statements, to judge, to choose — in a word, to act spiritually and not to fall into contradiction at each step, and then, simultaneously, refuse to recognize him; to think him away without whom thought would only be a psychical manifestation: the supreme contradiction is to lean upon God in the very act of denying him. That, indeed, is a judgment which denies and destroys itself, not only where its content is concerned, in itself, but by undermining its own structure and refusing the condition of its existence. No doubt the contradiction remains unseen, because it does not intervene between two objective affirmations, but between objective and transcendental affirmations; the contradiction is between the assertion expressed in words and the assertion lived by thought. It is not, consequently, a particular or logical contradiction — which is why it is always possible — but a total,

---

from one another) is manifestly different from that of St. Thomas, to which we had no intention of likening it. But those differences only make the very real analogy, at the point which we have indicated, all the more remarkable.

2. Cf. Maurice Blondel's answer to Leon Brunschvicg in *Bulletin de la Société française de philosophie* (March 24, 1928), p. 53: "The slightest sensation humanly perceived, the slightest perception directly grasped, the slightest understanding scientifically or metaphysically developed, implies a fundamental affirmation which at the very outset surpasses the entire empirical order, the entire conceptual order of our representations. Every act of true understanding, every thought worthy of the name, as elementary as one can imagine, irrefutably posits a transcendence of the spirit with regard to the immanent order of things apparently given or experienced. Therefore, before all critical reflection and in order to allow this reflection itself, there is in us the lived assertion of a reality which is beyond or above every act, every self-limiting thought. To know means always to contain, understand, dominate, pass beyond the world and the thought already understood, in order to grasp at that which is not of the world, at that which does not pertain only to our knowing." In this "lived assertion" there is an ever-contemporary and ever-triumphant principle of a critique of every naive empiricism and of all the so-called critical empiricisms.

vital, spiritual contradiction — a contradiction in the being who thinks, a sin by the spirit against the spirit.

That is how the pagans behaved when they sought sanctuary from the barbarians in Christian churches and took advantage of the security offered them by the God of the Christian in order to blaspheme his name. One would have to stop willing and thinking to have the right to deny God without contradicting oneself.[3] One would have to abandon speech.[4]

One cannot sever the mind's relation to the Absolute — the Absolute thought as real — without destroying the mind itself. One cannot do away with "that primary relation to being which the philosophers of progress and the philosophers of totality invariably ignore." Unless we are to close the door to all philosophy worthy of the name, we cannot refuse to acknowledge that "basic experience" — the presence of nonconceptual being to consciousness which is common to the philosopher and to all men.[5]

"God, being without principle, cannot be affirmed by virtue of a principle distinct from himself" (P. Scheuer).

That does not mean that reasoning — according to logical principles — in order to prove the existence of God is superfluous, but that the

---

3. Cf. Aimé Forest, *Du consentement à l'être* (1936), p. 104: "The act by which I affirm God is not a result in some way foreign to the very principle of objective affirmation; the act does nothing more than prolong this movement which it already implies in a real way. We would not say that it is God whom we know in knowing the world, but it is quite true to say, in a sense, that in the act of judgment about existence, there is found the implicit affirmation of God, for the one who searches out the metaphysical conditions thanks to which this act is possible. *Aliquid est, ergo Deus est.* (Something exists, therefore God exists.)

4. Cf. André Bremond, S.J., "Une dialectique thomiste du retour à Dieu," *Nouvelle Revue Théologique* (1834), p. 569: "As soon as I speak in a human way, as soon as I judge, I can not help but speak of God; even without being aware of it. I affirm absolutely some truth, and by the very fact of so doing, I affirm all that guarantees the absolute nature of my affirmation. Thus the only reason for my absolute affirmation must be an ontological one: the truth that God *is*." Thus the proof of God can be based on "the meaning of every living affirmation." (Commentary of André Marc, S.J., "L'idée de l'être selon saint Thomas et dans la scolastique postérieure," in *Archives de philosophie*, vol. 10 [1933], pt. 1.)

5. Ferdinand Alquié, *La nostalgie de l'être* (1950), pp. 144, 148.

thought, which is our affirmation of God, is not the conclusion of an argument. The thought which reasons comes before the reasoning. And if reasoning must perforce intervene, that is in order to show us what thought consists in or what it implies. For the reality of thought is not a fact in the psychological order, and cannot be explored by empirical observation, whatever the method employed.

This comes down to saying, once again, that the existence of God is not a truth among other truths, a particular truth dependent *in itself,* upon another, greater truth, or a more comprehensive and fundamental truth of which it is, in some sort, one of several possible applications. In other words, the Being of God is not a particular Being with its place among others, at the beginning of, or within, a series. God is not the first link in the chain of being.

Or again, we must recognize — in face of rationalism in all its forms, and all forms of contempt for the certainties of reason — that God is the reality which envelops, dominates, and measures our thought, and not the reverse. He is the reality which makes our thought at once so great and sure of itself, so absolute in its judgments and so necessarily obedient.

In short, the reality of God must be taken seriously, and the transcendence of God acknowledged with all that it implies.

If we did not have a certain idea of God — not yet seen, not objectified, not conscious, yet present to consciousness, and in fine, *not conceived* — previous to all our concepts and always present in all of them, the purification to which we subject them in order to think God correctly would ultimately serve no other purpose but the denial of everything and a final nihilism. To speak of the phases which succeed the phase of negation as "excellent" or "eminent" would then be a poor joke. For the phase of negation once conscientiously traversed would have left the mind a *tabula rasa:* it would have left nothing standing. All the terms formed with the prefix *sur* would be parrot-talk, pure logomachy, or a disguised return to the original affirmation such as it was before the critique was instituted.[6]

---

6. This danger can never be removed once and for all. St. Thomas Aquinas was conscious of it. For him, too, "it is indeed in an atmosphere of mystery that analyses unfold in which negation triumphs, being less favorable to illusion than superlatives": M.-D. Chenu, O.P., *Introduction à l'étude de saint Thomas d'Aquin* (1950), p. 140. The phrase *Deus, qui melius scitur nesciendo* (God, who is better known by not knowing),

In the same way, if there were no idea of God whatsoever prior to the reasoning by which we try to provide him with a logical basis in our thought, the critique which we must necessarily make of the general form in which those arguments are set would terminate in the denial of the affirmation of God.

But the proposed hypothesis is worthless. The dual activity of the mind is not like the work of Penelope. It really does reach a conclusion. Its success is definitive. That is because the idea of God is mysteriously present in us from the beginning, prior to our concepts, although beyond our grasp without their help, and prior to all our argumentation, in spite of being logically unjustifiable without them: it is the inspiration, the motive power and justification of them all. *Omnia cognoscentia cognoscunt implicite Deum in quolibet cognito*.[7] (All knowers know God implicitly in all they know.)

---

as E. Gilson remarks, is a "classical form of Thomism" (*Société française de philosophie* [March 24, 1928], reply to L. Brunschvicg). See below, Chapter 5. Cf. Etienne Souriau, *L'ombre de Dieu* (1955), pp. 297-298: "The expression 'surexistence' is full of traps."

7. This principle of St. Thomas is likewise that of Duns Scotus (*In 4 Sent.*, bk. 1, d. 3, q.3, n. 26). Cf. the correlative principle, *Prima*, q.6, a.1, ad 2: "All things, desiring their own perfection, desire God himself." This, of course, discloses itself only to the reflection of the philosopher, and does not presuppose any direct knowledge in the spontaneous exercise of the appetite in question. The reflexive analysis is something entirely different from psychological introspection.

On the basis of this principle and all that corresponds to it in Thomism, it has been said that "taken in a new sense" — the very sense which we are trying to define here — "exemplarism is one of the essential elements of St. Thomas's system" (E. Gilson, in his reply to L. Brunschvicg, p. 197). Various commentators have tried to eliminate from this system "the slightest trace of that which is believed to be ontologism" (*ibid.*, p. 104), but wrongly. In order to avoid the appearance of error, they thus risked abandoning the substance of the truth. For, as Zigliara says: "Ontologism contains an element of truth" (*Della luce intellettuale e dell'ontologismo secondo la dottrina de'Santi Agostino, Bonaventura, e Tommaso di Aquino* [Rome, 1874], vol. 1, p. xi; cf. also vol. 2, p. 10), and it is dangerous to reduce in some way the entire study of our knowledge of God to a refutation of ontologism (as is also the case in regard to agnosticism).

There is ontologism properly so-called where, by a confusion between our idea of being and the idea of *Being*, between abstract being and *pure Being*, we find more or less affirmed some "immediate sight" of God, some "ontological vision" at the beginning of human knowledge; a sort of "intuitive perception of the Infinite" or of the objective concept of God, of which all the other concepts would only be modifications or determinations. This is verified in the four kinds of ontologism which Zigliara distinguishes, in order to refute them, following "Sans-Fiel" (*De l'orthodoxie de l'ontologisme modéré*, letter 1, p. 6): "In the first theory [the intuitive perception of the Infinite] results in the identification of man with God; in the second, it penetrates the intimate essence of God,

Such an assertion is valid of God alone. However moderately one interprets it, it is priceless. The idea of God presides over our negations and our critiques, rather in the same way that a word on the tip of one's tongue — a word one knows perfectly well, tries to recall and cannot quite articulate — will brush aside and eliminate all the other words that present themselves to the mind. The affirmation is triumphant in the midst of our negations, and the critique itself is a confirmation.

In its primary and permanent state the idea of God is not, then, a product of the intelligence. It is not a concept. It is a reality: the very soul of the soul; a spiritual image of the Divinity, an "eikon."[8]

If the mind did not affirm God — if it were not the affirmation of God — it could affirm nothing whatsoever. It would be without laws; like a

---

like the beatific vision; in the third, it is the only perception of the human spirit; while in the fourth, it is accompanied by the perception of contingent realities." Cf. one of these propositions which was condemned on September 18, 1861: "The being which we understand in all things and without which we understand nothing, is the divine being" (Denzinger-Schönmetzer, *Enchiridion Symbolorum* . . . [1976], n. 2842 [1660]), or the fifth and the thirty-seventh of the propositions condemned on September 14, 1887 (Denzinger-Schönmetzer, n. 3205 [1895] and 3237 [1927]). Cf. Chapter 3, note 35. Let us add that innatism is not ontologism, any more than the admission of an element a priori into the understanding is innatism.

8. The extraordinary importance of this notion of the image of God imprinted upon man did not escape the Fathers of the First Vatican Council. Two passages from the Acts of the council, which are from the pen of Monsignor Gasser, bear this out: *Acta et Decreta SS. Concilii Vaticani*, collectio Lacensis, vol. 7 (Freiburg im Breisgau, 1890), *Relatio de emendationibus capitis secundi constitutionis dogmaticae de fide catholica;* relatio R. D. Vincentii Gasser:

Seventh amendment: If we say that God is known with the light of natural reason by means of created things, that is, by means of traces which have been imprinted upon all creatures, much less do we exclude the image which was imprinted upon the immortal soul of man: similarly, the metaphysical argument is not excluded . . ." (col. 132).

Fiftieth amendment: The Reverend Amender would like this addition (in the canon): "from man made in his image and likeness"; and furthermore, would like the addition to appear for this reason, because most assuredly God can really be known by means of the mirror of created things; that is, not only by means of traces of God imprinted upon created things, but much more by means of the image imprinted upon the immortal soul of man. But while this reason is the very best, the Deputatio nevertheless has decided that this amendment is not to be admitted, because it is the custom of the Church not to add reasons to canons, but simply to condemn the error with precise words" (col. 149).

world deprived of its sun. It could no longer exercise any rational activity, and could only sink back into the dark limbo of obscure psychical subjectivism. It could no longer judge. It would have lost its light, its norm, its justification, its point of reference, the one thing which can serve as a foundation for all else.

That does not, of course, mean that we do not have to prove God. It does not mean that the existence of God is obvious from the word "go." Reason rises to the Absolute from the relative. And what supports and directs its steps is, from another angle, the goal of its journey. What explains and justifies knowledge must be established by knowledge. And in order that we should recognize it, that which is at the base must appear at the summit.

Where belief in God is concerned, I cannot rest content with a doubtful argument, and an inconclusive proof is as repugnant to my moral sense as it is offensive to my intelligence. The importance of the matter at stake is no reason to be easygoing; on the contrary, it obliges me to be more strict. But on the other hand, if I were more clear-sighted, a mere suggestion, a mere hint would suffice: for in fact I bear the proof within me. Before expressing it with a greater or lesser degree of learning and critical acumen, I am conscious of its role as fulcrum. I raise my mind to God as I breathe; in each case by virtue of the same necessity. There is, however, this twofold difference: where the body is concerned there is no escaping the necessity to breathe; whereas in the case of the spiritual life, it brings its own light with it; whereas, by an incredible paradox, while the darkness in which the body is enveloped does not prevent it from breathing with perfect regularity, the light which accompanies the respiration of the spirit is not sufficient to make it recognizable, and the mind can, without doing away with it altogether — which would mean death — at least disturb and trouble its breathing.

If, to strengthen my belief in God, I find it necessary to have recourse to external means, that is not because my intellectual certitude is in the smallest degree unsettled. If the objection put to me is valid at all, then I know that it is only valid because I am lacking in skill. I have never really entered the labyrinth in which I am supposed to have been trapped.

And then I know, too, that the intelligence is not the whole man. An intelligent man does not regard himself as pure intelligence. All the appeals to custom, to tradition, to authority, to the positive teaching of religion, to the gestures repeated since childhood — recourse to the "mechanism" — are not meant to compel reason nor to supplement it, but to protect it against the vertigo of the imagination. Their real purpose is to calm the child who, according to Plato, lives on in all of us. And the only people to be scandalized are, in the words of St. Augustine "those who do not know how rare and difficult a thing it is for the fleshly imagination to be subdued by the serenity of a devout mind."[9]

Metaphysical truths, however rigorously they may have been deduced, do in fact leave the door open to an element of doubt. Even those who are most forcibly struck by them "are afraid, an hour later, that they may have been mistaken" — in any case, they are not satisfied with them. Not that these truths are established on weak foundations or that the intelligence pure and unalloyed does not confess itself convinced by the proof. But when their demonstration is over the recollection of it, this is not always strong enough to repel the assaults of contrary impressions. Their light may, perhaps, shine in an abstract heaven: but it is meant to be felt — *est enim sensus et mentis*[10] — not simply proved; to be possessed, embraced, and not merely perceived in the dim distance, draped in a pale and superficial clarity. Now the proof imposes these truths, but it does not give them to us.[11] The certainty it confers is not given to us as a possession. It is well, indeed, that man should be able to prove his immortality to his own satisfaction. But for an immortal being, how can that proof be more than a *pis aller?* However rigorous we assume the proof to be, it is powerless to disperse the sense of unreality which accompanies it even in a clear light. The more we feel the proof as proof, the more conscious we become of the misery of the human

---

9. St. Augustine, *Contra Epistolam Manichaei*, ch. 2, n. 2 (PL 42:174); *De Trinitate*, bk. 4, ch. 1: "Their own figments have satisfied them, not your truth, which they reject and shrink from and so fall into their own emptiness. I am certainly aware of how many figments are born in the human heart, and what is my own heart but a human heart? But for this do I pray to the God of my heart, that I may not vomit forth into these writings any of those figments for solid truth . . ." (PL 42:887).

10. St. Augustine, *Retractationes*, bk. 1, ch. 1, n. 2 (PL 32:585-586).

11. Some people have misread this passage to mean: "we do not have any proof of [these truths]," which would make us contradict ourselves. It seems obvious that the abstract proof of a real object does not give us possession of that object. If the object itself were given to us, if we really possessed it, then what need would there be for proof?

condition which obliges us to resort to it, and which remains after it has been provided.

And when we turn our minds to God, the infinitely pure Being "who lives in inaccessible light," the consciousness of our misery is only sharpened, and that sense of unreality weighs more heavily still upon the mind. How can we be satisfied with a proof where God is concerned — God who is above all essence, all names, and all forms, whom nothing ultimately can represent, though all things indicate him[12] — God who because of his perfect "actuality" and his plenitude cannot be directly conceived by objective reason except as bare existence whose reality is both intimate and impossible to grasp, and that no "introversion" can ever yield us as a lasting possession.

> *Ubi est lux inaccessibilis, aut quomodo accedam ad lucem inaccessibilem? . . . Numquam te vidi, Domine Deus meus, non novi faciem tuam!*

(Where is the inaccessible light or how can I approach the inaccessible light? . . . I have never seen you, Lord my God, I have never known your face!)[13]

---

12. St. Thomas, *Prima*, q.13, a.2; *De Veritate*, q.2, a.1, ad 9. Cf. Psalm 17:12: "He made the darkness his covering." Charles de Moré-Pontgibaud, S.J., "Sur l'analogie des noms divins," *Recherches de science religieuse* 19 (1929), p. 491: "We see here one of the characteristics of this abstraction of transcendentals, which is the supreme effort of the intelligence: to separate out an idea whose content is determined not by the forms of representation which limit it, but by the amplitude of the tendency to which this idea, in the intelligible order, corresponds." And p. 500: ". . . a going-beyond or going-above the representation which conditions it and which itself is already confusedly an object of thought and of affirmation beginning with the representation itself." See also Joseph Maréchal, *Le point de départ de la recherche métaphysique* (as cited in Chapter 3 below, note 59): ". . . God, transcendent, can neither be represented by our concepts, nor even intimated as the limit toward which the generalization of these concepts would tend. . . ." See also Chapter 5, note 34. However, this does not mean, as Maréchal has also shown, that our representation itself has no significant value (*Le point de départ . . .* , bk. 5, p. 323, etc.). It is a "significant representation": J. Defever, S.J., *La preuve réelle de Dieu, étude critique* (1953), p. 52; cf. pp. 53, 124-125, 138-139, and p. 80: ". . . The transcendence itself of the affirmation is based once again upon a finite representation. Therefore we only signify the nature of God by means of and by going beyond a representation which does not really fit him, that is, by means of inadequate images, whose essential meaning God eminently fulfills, but whose representation itself one must carefully negate, and along with it, its limits, determinations, quiddity. . . ."

13. St. Anselm, *Proslogion*, ch. 1 (PL 158:225c). St. Bonaventure, taking up a development of St. Anselm in *Proslogion*, ch. 16: "Truly, O Lord, this light in which you dwell

Haec lux est inaccessibilis, et tamen proxima animae etiam plus quam ipsa sibi. Est etiam inalligabilis, et tamen summe intima.

(This is the inaccessible light, and yet it is even closer to the soul than the soul itself. It cannot be grasped, and yet is most intimately present.)

We are always dreaming of the impossible. We should like a truth that was not abstract and a reality that was not empirical; a fact that had all the characteristics of a law; a verification which would at the same time be the answer to a need; an ideal satisfaction which was also a real possession. On these terms only could we have perfect peace of mind. But in fact we always swing between the two poles. The duality is insurmountable to our divided nature. Unity always slips the grasp of that compound of sense and reason. No sooner do we think we have seized it on the wing than it falls apart, and universal unity is not concrete unity. What in fact we attain is not merely, because of its inadequacy, the starting point of a new inquiry: it is always a fresh disillusionment. *Cur non te sentit, Domine Deus, anima mea si invenit te? An non invenit, quem invenit esse lucem et veritatem . . . ?*[14] (Why does my soul not perceive you, Lord God, if it finds you? Or does it not find you, whom it finds to be light and truth?)

---

is inaccessible, for truly there is nothing else which penetrates this light, so as to look upon you there. Truly therefore, I do not see this light, because it is too much for me, and nonetheless, I see something, I see by means of that light; just as what the weak eye sees, it sees by means of the light of the sun, which light it is not able to look upon in the sun itself" (PL 158:235c-d).

14. In the *Proslogion,* ch. 14, St. Anselm explained very well this kind of disappointment, which, though recurring, is nevertheless not discouragement. In the first place, he addressed the soul, to reassure her: "Have you found, O my soul, what you were seeking? You were seeking God, and you found Him. . . . For if you did not find your God, how is it that He is what you found, and what you understood to be Him with such certain truth and such true certainty? And if you did find Him, why is it that you do not perceive what you found?" Then, he addresses God Himself: "Why does the soul not perceive you, O Lord God, etc. . . . ? Why is it so, O Lord, why? . . ." (PL 158:234d). Here we are dealing with quite a different matter than "this psychological malaise which one easily experiences when faced with the most rigorous metaphysical proofs," malaise about which it has been written that "true wisdom consists in reacting against these unjustified impressions and these demands of the carnal man" (Fernand Van Steenberghen, "Le problème philosophique de l'existence de Dieu," *Revue philosophique de Louvain* 45 [1947], p. 313).

Are we moved by a figment of our imagination? By no means. There is one instance in which the impossible is not a phantom. But God alone, operating in a realm beyond sense and beyond reason, can bring about the synthesis, though it is always partial and fugitive here below. The unique Presence shines in the night of the senses and in the night of the reason, in the night that remains dark.[15]

Why is it that the mind which has found God still retains, or constantly reverts to, the feeling of not having found him? Why does that absence weigh on us even in the presence itself, however intimate it may be? Why, face to face with him who penetrates all things, why that insurmountable obstacle, that unbridgeable gap? Why always a wall or a gaping void? Why do all things, as soon as they have shown him to us, betray us by concealing him again?

The temptation is to succumb to this scandal and to despair in proportion as one had formerly thought to have found him: a temptation to deny the light, because the veil becomes opaque once again, or because we are blinded; a temptation to relax once we have made the effort which, as always, led us back to the starting point. In some cases, the opposite temptation pertains, that of easy shortcuts; this is the illusion of those who persuade themselves that they have only to tear aside the flimsy veil for the Presence to appear, in the belief that, provided they turn their gaze inward and fix it upon the luminous center which illuminates all their thoughts, they will enjoy the sight of God; the illusion that it suffices to be in order to possess Being.... The temptation in this case is to underestimate the obstacles, to imagine that serenity is easily acquired, and to confuse the faint clarity of being with the divine light....

Why, O Lord, these ambiguities? Why those hesitations and oscillations of the mind? Why those contradictory motions of the soul?

> ... *Cur hoc, Domine, cur hoc? Tenebratur oculus ejus infirmitate sua, aut reverberatur fulgore tuo? — Sed certe et tenebratur in se et reverberatur a te. Utique et obscuratur sua brevitate, et obruitur tua immensitate. Vere et contrahitur angustia sua, et vincitur amplitudine tua....*[16]

---

15. It is quite clear that we are not dealing here with a natural intuition of God, which would be, so to speak, right from the start, a natural or necessary accompaniment of the human spirit. On the contrary, even mystical and supernatural gifts never attain more than a partial and fleeting anticipation....

16. St. Anselm, *Proslogion*, ch. 14.

(Why this, O Lord, why this? Is the eye darkened by its own weakness, or blinded by your light? — Without doubt it is darkened in itself and blinded by you. Indeed, it is obscured by its own littleness and overwhelmed by your immensity. Surely it is contracted by its own narrowness and overcome by your greatness.)

It is sometimes said that the existence of God is "probable"; but this really has no meaning. On what could that probability be based except, like any other probability, upon a more general certainty of the same order? But God is alone in his order, and the place which he occupies in knowledge is unique. The probability of God ought therefore to be based upon the previous certainty of his existence. You might as well say that our own existence is probable. . . .[17]

Probability has no meaning outside the empirical realm. It has no sense except with reference to a particular object, an object, that is, which forms part of a group or class: one fact among others. Now, God does not form part of our common experience. God is not a fact, any more than he is an "object." The reality of God is not that of an event. Nor is God a particular case, the particular application or the realization in a particular instance of a general truth, or of a universal principle existing prior to him. As the ancients said, "Being is extraneous to kinds";[18] God is unique, "God is not in a genus."

And so, in order to respect the mystery in which our knowledge is steeped, even where its most intimate certainties are concerned, we may

---

17. We are using these words "probable" and "probability" with the contemporary meaning that they have in French, and not, of course, with the Latin meaning of "capable of being proven" and "capacity for being proven."

18. St. Thomas, *De Potentia*, q.8, a.3: "God cannot exist in any genus . . ."; *Prima*, q.3, a.5; q.6, a.2, ad 3: "He is beyond genus . . ."; *Contra Gentiles*, bk. 1 ch. 25 and 32. St. Bonaventure, *Itinerarium mentis in Deum*, ch. 5: "Being itself is outside of every genus." Zigliara, *Oeuvres philosophiques*, French trans., vol. 3, p. 77. Joseph de Finance, *Etre et agir dans la philosophie de saint Thomas*, pp. 95 and 148-149. A.-D. Sertillanges, *Les grandes thèses de la philosophie thomiste* (1928), p. 67: "There is no genus which can pretend to encompass God, to contain God, not even the false genus of being, the idea of which is not homogeneous, and which, nonetheless, in a certain manner, contains all." Renouvier was mistaken when he reproved Scholasticism (and it is well known what a prominent place this reproach has in his thinking) for making God the *genus generalissimum* [all-encompassing genus] of being (*Histoire et solution des problèmes métaphysiques* [1901], ch. 25, p. 177). See below, Chapter 3, note 37.

say that the life of the spirit rests upon a belief, and that at its root is a certain kind of confidence, or better still an "anticipation."[19] It is better to acknowledge the sense of unreality which, in the condition of our terrestrial existence, even the most rigorous use of reason very often serves to strengthen.... But these various notions are not opposed to the notion of certainty, and have nothing whatsoever to do with the notion of probability.[20]

The probable may also mean what is "likely." But who could describe the Being of God as "likely"? On the contrary, if we are content with analogies and appearances, if we only listen to ordinary reason and ordinary judgment, what could be more unlikely? What could be more baffling, from whatever angle one approaches it? No, I do not affirm the Being of God, the Being which is God, because it is "likely," but in spite of its being unlikely, in spite of the antinomies I come up against in affirming it, in spite of the difficulties which continue to hold me back. But I affirm it, nevertheless, with complete assurance, not because I am impelled to do so by some extraneous impulse, but because rational necessity tells me that it is impossible that he should not be. Its light is indirect, and what it reveals is only negative; but for all that its power is such that it sweeps aside all "likelihoods." The unlikely is also the incontestable — and the latter infinitely outweighs the former.

"Certainty is that deep region where thought can only keep its balance in action."[21]

---

19. This word *prolêpsis* is dear to Clement of Alexander: *Stromateis*, bk. 4, ch. 4, n. 16, etc. Cf. Thomassin, *Dogmata theologica, De Deo;* and Joseph Moingt, "La gnose de Clément d'Alexandrie dans ses rapports avec la foi et la philosophie," *Recherches de science religieuse* 37 (1950), p. 548.

20. The author of the German translation of this book — an excellent translation on the whole — was tripped up here by the ambiguity which the words "probable" and "probability" have for those who are not abreast of the French usage of these words. Hence I am given to make an assertion which is untenable, clearly contrary to my thought as well as contrary to the entire context. In the review which he made of this translation (*Scholastik* 1 [1950], p. 129), Rev. Fr. De Vries happily pointed out this misunderstanding.

21. Jules Lagneau, "Fragments," *Revue de métaphysique et de morale* (1918), p. 169.

"Truth," Malebranche says in a magnificent phrase, "is distant, it is not palpable, and it is not a good which we feel impelled to love. It calls, therefore, for the closest attention." "But," he adds, with St. Augustine, "how can a man who is torn in all directions, struck from all sides, who is thrust back when he takes a step forward, dragged on if he steps back, and who is continually irked and ill-used, how can such a man apply himself to the matter?" For that, after all, is the condition of the spirit in the flesh. It is never — as yet — completely itself. Man can never give himself up for long to the contemplation and search for the truth without encountering obstacles.

That is why we need all the paraphernalia, the whole "machinery" with which our belief in God is protected and strengthened — and at the same time justified. They do not exist to remedy defective proofs or supply rational certainty, but simply to allow or facilitate in some measure the "closest attention." The task itself continues to be necessary, because "prejudices always return to the charge, and drive us out of positions we had already occupied unless we entrench ourselves securely and guard our positions vigilantly." Those "solid entrenchments" do not distort the truth, they save it. Thought, in that way, is preserved from "mental vertigo"; it is not enslaved but freed.

Freedom, the supreme prerogative of the spirit, is respected even in our most unshakeable certainties, whenever they concern an object that surpasses us. It is respected, then, in the supreme certainty, the firmest and most solidly grounded of all, of the existence of God. Indeed, it is only then that freedom exercises its full powers. For the human mind, in spite of a temporary dislocation, is not at bottom divided against itself. Its faculties are not mutually exclusive. It is untrue that the two faculties of knowing with certainty and of willing freely can only be exercised at each other's expense, or by subjecting one to the other, as though a free certainty were a half certainty or only half free. On the contrary, they enhance one another in proportion as their object is exalted, and tend to meet in unity. They are never more closely united than in the affirmation of God.

The affirmation of God in the subject who makes the affirmation is not only essentially and fundamentally free in Spinoza's sense, *qui sola ducitur ratione*, with the freedom which belongs to all spiritual activities, nor is it only free in the higher sense of being autonomous and possessing the initiative which freedom requires in order to fulfill itself.²² It is also free in the sense that it possesses that humbler, empirical, and everyday freedom which is always struggling to adapt itself to circumstances, forestalling surprises, striking root in daily life, and using if need be, without shame, all the little tricks that prudence suggests and that common sense recommends.

The first of these freedoms is the very condition of true knowledge, the freedom of the subject whose judgment cannot be "compelled by any external cause whatsoever."²³ The second is indispensable to the affirmation of God, the keystone of knowledge. The third may be useful or necessary at any moment in substantiating our reflective affirmation which maintains us in the truth of our own nature.

22. Any reasoning which progresses from the premises to the conclusion implies an initiative, a free act in the reasoning itself — not to supplement it or bend it in any way, but simply to give it the necessary impulse without which there could be no progress in thought.

23. Cf. Descartes, *Fourth Meditation:* "These past days, examining whether something truly existed in the world, and knowing that from the very fact that I was examining the question it followed quite clearly that I myself existed, I could not prevent myself from judging to be true something which I grasped so clearly — not that I found myself forced by any exterior cause, but simply because from a great clarity which was in my understanding there followed a great inclination in my will." Although they understand freedom very differently from one another, Descartes and Spinoza are in agreement in recognizing its role in judgment.

In *La liberté cartésienne,* Jean-Paul Sartre has a good commentary on this text, while emphasizing the voluntarist character of the thought of Descartes: "In the ecstasy of understanding, there is always the joy of knowing ourselves responsible for the truths which we discover. No matter who the teacher is, there comes a time when the student is entirely alone in front of a mathematical problem; if he does not discipline his spirit to grasp the relations, if he himself does not produce the speculations and the schemas which are then applied like a grid to the problem under consideration and which unveil its principal structures, and if he does not bring about a decisive illumination, then the words remain dead signs, everything is learned by rote. Thus, I can perceive, if I examine myself, that knowing is not the mechanical result of a pedagogical process, but that it has for its origin my single will to be attentive, my single application, my single refusal of distraction or hurry, in a word, my entire spirit, with the radical exclusion of all exterior actors. This, then, is the first intuition of Descartes: he understood better than anyone else that the slightest progress of thought engages the entire thought, an autonomous thought which establishes itself, in each of its acts, in its complete and absolute independence." *Situations* 1 (1947).

In affirmation, as in the object itself, in thought as in being, nothing is isolated: everything is joined by an unbreakable chain, and one link involves all the others. From a static, abstract point of view one can and must distinguish various stages, but what happens at one level does not invariably react on other operations occurring above or below. Each individual proof has its own degree of validity; each object its own degree of evidence. We cannot hope for sound method or healthy thought as long as there is no attempt to arrange questions in a series, and so avoid calling everything in question at every moment. On any hypothesis, the natural use of reason teaches us certain truths, though others remain unknown. It allows us to rise to the knowledge of the highest of all things, the truth of the existence of God, and even in the most essential matters a sinner may reason better than a saint.

But the problem of the knowledge of various truths, or even of their respective degree of certainty, is one thing — the problem of their *ontological index* is another. In the last analysis it affects everything which the mind affirms. This question is not governed, like the previous one, by the formal logic of the intelligence (which it leaves intact) but by the real logic of the concrete being. It bears, necessarily, upon the whole as such, and what it envisages is the activity of a living spirit engaged in an adventure which itself forms a whole. And in the last analysis, the meaning which the spirit imprints upon its adventure confers a corresponding coherence and solidity upon its mental universe.

So we shall not say that the spirit cannot by itself be certain of many things; nor even, which would be quite another matter, that it cannot attain to a distinctively metaphysical certitude. But, to be more precise, we must add that the character of metaphysical certainty is still provisional, and, above all, that the being upon which it bears does not as yet possess, if one may so express it, all its density. It is essential to distinguish here in order to simplify a process which is all *nuances* in the concrete, and is composed of infinite shades of meaning; there is the period which precedes the subject's refusal or acceptance of grace; and there is the subsequent period. During the first period, ontological certitude is what it is, and there is no reason to declare it illegitimate or, rather, illusory. After the refusal, those epithets take on meaning — and need to be carefully analyzed. For although it may then be possible to describe the ontological certainty in question as illegitimate or illusory, that does not mean calling it illusory in itself — since the nature of the intelligence has not changed — but because from then on it is vitally contradicted.[24]

---

24. In the spirit which denies God, truths and values are "not only left up in the

Man is a spirit created in the image of God. No degree of perversion can uproot that essential characteristic and inalienable prerogative. Man cannot alter the fact that the *image* is in him.[25] But if he tries to destroy it by every means in his power, if he deliberately goes against his vocation as spirit, he inevitably introduces contradiction not only into his intelligence — which may continue to function as before — but into his very being, setting his intelligence and his life in contradiction. And as long as that contradiction is not resolved, it deprives him in principle of the right, or rather of the possibility, of saying *it is*, and of giving those two monosyllables the full force which goes to the very root of things.

Far from arresting thought at the pure representation of a thing, to be followed soon after perhaps by the affirmation of the irrational, the judgment of existence gives thought its impulse, and frees it to advance by stages to a recognition of the metaphysical absolute. But far from making us forget the real, that movement of thought recalls us to it, and in a sense we only affirm God metaphysically in order to be more certain of the existence of creatures.[26] In fact, the metaphysical explana-

---

air, but positively deprived of that which could ground them: Descartes was not wrong in thinking that the lucid atheist would not have the right to be a geometrist; because even though geometry is not immediately and in itself a knowledge of God, the denial of God compromises even geometry at its root, in suppressing the very source and the final guarantee of every truth" (J.-M. Le Blond, "Le chrétien devant l'athéisme actuel," *Etudes* [1954], p. 299). Nonetheless, it remains that "the truth, for him who rejects it or refuses to live by it, is obviously not the same as for him who is nourished on it, but it still is; although entirely different in the one case and in the other, the reign of truth is not more affected in the one than in the other" (M. Blondel, *L'Action* [1893], p. 438).

25. St. Augustine, *De Trinitate*, bk. 10, ch. 12; bk. 12, ch. 7; bk. 14, ch. 4 and 8.

26. It is a pleasure to reread a fine passage of Gratry, where a similar consideration of the acceptance or the refusal of supernatural revelation is treated from a different starting point. This passage could have been placed in the historical dossier of the idea of Christian philosophy. Although expressed somewhat too simply, it invites us to a meditation which is still valid (*De la connaissance de Dieu*, 9th ed. [1918], vol. 1, pp. 35-37): "The submission of the human spirit to the spirit of God is not the destruction of reason, it is the final perfection of reason. . . . It is the human spirit grafted on to the spirit of God, if it can be put that way. Reason then bears fruit that it in itself was not able to bear, and as the poem says (Nature is speaking here): *She admires those fruits which are not her own*. Such fruit comes from the spirit of God, having become precisely that principle which make human reason fertile, while, all the same, conserving its own principles. . . . When human reason is attached to God by faith — as history shows —

tion always comes to us as a victory over representation of the real which is purely abstract and without depth.[27]

The negativity of the consciousness, which ought not to be underestimated, is an obverse which requires an inverse. If the *for itself (pour-soi)* means separation from self, a negative power, it is because its true being, to which it aspires, has not been given to it. The capacity to say no, and to reach beyond all determination, would hardly be intelligible unless it expressed an orientation towards a higher form of being, a call to plenitude, the absence of which is in fact a distinctive mark of the consciousness. . . .

Our consciousness, certainly, is not fullness of being. It would not arise in a complete being as an unaccountable nothingness. It is in an incomplete and lower being that it expresses aspiration towards further being. It is in the experience in which the life of the spirit is inaugurated that I become inadequate to myself. The self can neither join itself nor equal itself. It is continually obliged to choose what it wishes to be, and its existence means giving itself that being in significant acts.

That transcendence, which constitutes our personal consciousness, . . . imposes upon all men the duty of having . . . a philosophy. The necessity of a philosophy and the presence of an absolute in every judgment are two ways of affirming the same necessary aspect of human consciousness. Indeed, that is not as a rule contested. The difficulties . . . begin as soon as we try to understand the nature of that absolute and the real character of the philosophy. . . .

No doubt, it will be said, the human mind cannot do without some notion of the whole; the mind needs to posit the idea of absolute truth. But should we conclude that that truth exists independently of it? That subsisting truth, it will be said, is really only an illusory projection into

---

over and above the new and sublime realities which spring up, the natural strength of reason grows, its own principles bear their most sublime natural fruit, mixed with the divine fruit. When, on the contrary, reason breaks the covenant which is always offered to every spirit in every age, this refusal, this turning of reason upon itself alone, this isolation and this sacrilegious denial, exhausts even its natural strength, and leads reason from one denial to another, and finally to the denial of itself, an intellectual suicide which is called Sophistic. . . ." These last words can be compared to the famous "Nothing is" of one of the characters in Claudel's *la Ville.*

27. Aimé Forest, *Du consentement à l'être,* pp. 107-108.

being of a category indispensable to the play of thought. The idea of the absolute plays the part of the scaffolding which thought uses in order to construct itself. And the scaffolding which was at first larger than the construction must subsequently be eliminated. But it is difficult to speak in these terms, for the idea of truth cannot just be added to thought in an optional way. Thought is consubstantial with truth. Thought is not constituted in itself prior to the idea of truth; it is the birth in consciousness of the need for truth. It is not a secondary or contingent aspiration of the mind; the aspiration is mind itself, which is only the capacity or function of truth. It is impossible that the absolute should not be, because my mind only exists through it. The mind denies it in a judgment which is only valid because it affirms the absolute. That by which my mind acquires its being cannot fail to exist.[28]

If our concepts, by themselves, uncorrected by analogy, are only suited to the world of experience, then we must say as much and in the same degree of our reasoning insofar as it is merely the organization of our concepts.

It will be said, no doubt, that duly selected and corrected, our concepts can be adapted to transcendental reality. That is true. We are indeed obliged to use them although in spite of everything they remain unworthy of so noble a usage.[29] But for that to be true it is necessary, in the first instance, for that reality to be posited; it must, *in a sense,* have been thought implicitly.

If we apply this reasoning to the subject in hand, it is only when the affirmation of God is first posited — an affirmation which is still implicit, implied in each of our judgments on existence or judgments of value, and in consequence co-extensive with our whole spiritual activity, an affirmation congenital to the mind — that we can try to rejoin our affirmation in our conscious life, turning it into logical form by way of reasoning: just as it is only when we are in possession of the idea of God contained in the implicit affirmation that we can attempt to form some representation of it by the only way open to us: the way of concepts. That is the first, subter-

---

28. Gabriel Madinier, *Conscience et signification* (1951), pp. 62-67. On the "spell of negation" and the philosophies of negation, see Aimé Forest, *La vocation de l'esprit,* pp. 15-42.

29. Cf. St. Augustine, *Sermo* 241, ch. 7, n. 9 (PL 39:1498); *Contra Adimantum Manichaei discipulum,* ch. 11 (PL 42:142), etc.

ranean, phase of the mental life, unperceived but definitive. God must be present to the mind before any explicit reasoning or objective concept[30] is possible, and this is necessary if they are to perform their indispensable task with reference to him; he must first of all be secretly affirmed and thought.[31] Before he can be "identified" by a conscious act, there must exist a certain "habit of God" in the mind.[32]

---

30. In order to avoid exaggerating or misrepresenting the sense of this paragraph, the words "before any objective concept," i.e., before any representation, any objective grasp, should be clearly noted. For "the innateness of the natural light must not be confused with the innateness of its content" (E. Gilson, *La philosophie de saint Bonaventure*, 2nd ed., p. 297, n. 3). But one may try to bring out the significance, apart from any content, of this innateness of the natural light. And since the confusion is frequent, let us repeat that it is, nevertheless, not an objective knowledge, any more than an *appetitus naturalis* or *innatus* would be an actual desire, objective, deliberate, and conscious.

31. Something analogous likewise takes place on the level of conscience, whether dealing with natural knowledge or even the knowledge of faith. Cf. Gabriel Marcel, *Du refus à l'invocation* (1940), p. 231: "Reflection and history seem to me to converge on this assertion: that the idea of proof is inseparable from a reference to a certain previous affirmation, which one had been induced, later on, to call into question, or more exactly, to put in parentheses; it is the parenthesis that needs to be taken away." Among the historical examples to which he makes allusion, Gabriel Marcel could have included that of St. Thomas Aquinas. Aquinas, as Chenu tells us (*Introduction*, p. 72), "calls into question" the existence of God in order to furnish a rational proof of his existence, starting from faith first of all, a faith which is always present (which does not mean that logically, the rational demonstration depends in any way upon the act of faith; and which, on the other hand, is not the same thing as the Cartesian "methodic doubt"). The same thing can be said for Duns Scotus, *De primo rerum omnium principio*, ch. 1, a.1. Quoting this last text whose "fullness" he praises, Etienne Gilson does not present it as something unusual, but on the contrary regards it as "the method of Christian philosophy": *L'esprit de la philosophie médiévale*, 2nd ed. (1944), pp. 51-52; cf. *The Spirit of Mediaeval Philosophy*, p. 52. Nevertheless, whatever may be true concerning these analogous cases, here we are only concerned with the entirely implicit affirmation contained in the act of judgment.

32. H. Paissac, O.P., "Preuves de Dieu," *Lumière et Vie* 14 (1954), pp. 101-102: ". . . When the act of being is identified as God, reasoning is already involved in the consciousness. . . . The habit of identity can be recognized as the habit of God, if we can speak this way, *after* the use of reason, which demonstrates the existence of God. After this use of reason, and in the light of the certitude acquired by demonstration, the spirit is able, by turning back to itself, to recognize in fact that the habit of the first principles of my thought is equivalent to the habit of God. Indeed, this is the law of every habit: it is impossible to be aware of it *before* having experienced the act to which it corresponds. The habit of God has this particular quality, rigorously unique in the

If there is a truth "towards which everything in us aspires and conspires, a truth which is lived before it is known, a truth that we can perceive with certainty even before subjecting it to the discipline of proofs and the control of concepts — because it is connatural to us — then it is, without a doubt, the knowledge of God."[33]

If we consider the affirmation of God where alone it exists in act, where alone it is really made, in the concrete intelligence which is at the same time a particular subject, in the responsible person that is, then the affirmation of God can be seen to be an act which is unlike any other. There is something in it of the ontological argument, and something of the wager; though it is neither the one nor the other. It expresses the most luminous evidence and attests the most obscure truth.[34] Of all our acts, it is the most free and the most necessary. It is the most enduring of affirmations and the most personal of all engagements.[35]

The more pure the light, the less it compels us.[36]

---

life of the mind, that is, *to be possessed by the spirit before every act* [emphasis mine]: this habit is a gift of God, it pertains to the very nature of the created spirit, and makes of it an 'image of God'. . . ."

33. J. Maréchal, in *Nouvelle revue théologique* (1931), pp. 195, 204: ". . . The conceptual analysis also 'demonstrates,' that is to say, exercises a rational, thoughtful control, but it does not create."

34. Cf. J.-H. Newman, *Apologia pro vita sua*: "Of all points of faith, the being of a God is, to my own apprehension, encompassed with most difficulty, and yet borne in upon our minds with most power" (pt. 7, General answer to Mr. Kingsley).

35. These oppositions derive, as the reader will have perceived, from the fact that this affirmation may be envisaged either impersonally, in the intelligence as such, or as a concrete act of the human being, as a "decision of thought."

36. One could have written this before, in general, to underline paradoxically the intrinsic character of the light of what is true: "What is true doesn't force us as much as it obliges us." Cf. Jean Lacroix, "Le problème de Dieu," *Le Monde* (Feb. 18, 1956).

3

The Proof of God

Many people regard the existence of God as a matter of opinion; or if they consent to speak of certainty at all in this connection, they add, by way of excuse, that it is a question of feeling, an exclusively personal certainty. I would affirm, rather, that God is the object of proof. On this point the Catholic Church has expressed herself more than once, helping the reason of those who have confidence in her to regain its self-confidence, and encouraging reason to face the danger which threatens it in our day: "the abdication of metaphysics." The movement which carries us to God beyond the "visible and invisible" creation on which it rests is not just an impulse of the heart, accompanied at the most by an intellectual opinion. However personal it may be — and should be — in each one of us, that movement has a universal value. A *de-monstratio* could trace its itinerary, analyze its essential mechanism, indicate the source and distinguish its stages, which are valid for all minds.

But just as there are different kinds of objects, so there are different kinds of proof. Provided a proof is not limited to developing the content of a concept, provided it marks a real progress and attains a radically new object, then the dynamism of the intelligence which elaborates the proof implies finality. The mind is then "commensurate" with the object in question. It is specified by that object beforehand. There is nothing accidental in the link between them. That is to say: by virtue of the something "new" which it brings, an object of this kind is already present to the mind with a mysterious presence, a presence in germ as it were. Then, when it is grasped as the term of a logical process, when it is caught in the network of objective forms, it is, in a sense, "recognised." To demonstrate, in this instance, is "to realise." One "discovers" what already was.

This is specially true of the proof of God. The finality essential to an intelligence which penetrates a new domain is then doubly unique. For in every other case, in fact, we are aiming at an object belonging to our own world, the world of experience, even if it is still beyond the grasp of our experience. But when, on the contrary, it concerns God, with reference to whom the very words "object" and "existence" assume a transcendental significance, it concerns the Being who is the source of my being, and who is "more I than I myself." How far above all others, and how much more intimate! In this instance, then, the procedure which accounts for the dynamism of the proof is a presence which has a stimulus and a profundity which are all its own, a sanctuary, the sign of God upon me, and that which makes me a spirit.[1] And at the same time, that which makes a person of me and makes me responsible. That is why the strongest of proofs depends more than any other — not of course in respect of its abstract form, but where its power of concrete persuasion is concerned — upon "good-will." For there is always more at work than the impersonal functioning of an intelligence. Charity and purity of vision are inseparable at this point from loyalty and honesty.

Furthermore, there is no essential heterogeneity between the spontaneous movement of the soul towards the recognition of God's existence and the rational analysis of the philosopher. Faced with the former, people are inclined to speak of instinct, heart, feeling, intuition: equivocal terms, all of them, which attempt to express the dynamism of the intelligence, its ultimate source, the unity of its movement, and

---

1. Cf. the beautiful text of St. Thomas Aquinas, *Contra Gentiles*, bk. 3, ch. 54, which is dealing with a somewhat different problem, but which can nonetheless apply here; for the reasoning in the given instance has a wider application than the immediate context: "The divine substance is not beyond the capacity of the created intellect in such a way that it is altogether foreign to it, as sound is from the object of vision, or as immaterial substance is from sense power; in fact, the same divine substance is the first intelligible object and the principle of all intellectual cognition. But it is beyond the capacity of the created intellect in the sense that it exceeds its power." Cf. Louis Lavelle in the preface to *L'existence de Dieu* (1951), p. 10 (the French trans. by Régis Jolivet, of M.-F. Sciacca, *L'Esistenza di Dio*, in *Filosofia e Metafisica* [1950]): "All the more reason when it is a question of the existence of God, who is infinite being, must it be said that our thought moves in him from the very first step; not that our thought could ever reach him, if one assumes that it was at first separated from him."

at the same time to evoke the richly concrete and delicately sensitive region through which the light of the spirit makes its way. The philosopher's work is critical: he seeks to purify, to analyze, or sometimes to rectify or complete; but, above all, he analyzes and decomposes that unbroken movement into its logical components and tries to check and verify them. It is rare for him to pursue his studies beyond the itinerary, to the heart of the dynamism, to that central and secret point where reason and will originate. No doubt he is acutely conscious that logic is no longer an adequate instrument of analysis; that one should go further, make suggestions, ask questions, and help the mind to a fuller awareness of itself; that one ought to "reveal," while always fearing to disturb, its latent content: a delicate task which he regards as beyond his competence. And then, perhaps, if it ceases to be a purely professional question, so to say, if the problem touches him personally, it is possible he will hesitate, fearing obscurely to meet not only a subject of analysis, but God himself, not merely to discover the "author of nature," of the whole of nature, — but as a living man, to encounter the living God, utterly unique and insistently at work in all men. *Non enim fecit Deus et abiit.* . . .

(V. Fontoynont, S. J.)

Where the proof of the existence of God is concerned, the simplest classic form is, in itself, always the best.[2] It provides the permanent scheme, which survives all the superficial technical adjustments which each thinker, each age and every school find it necessary to introduce. It continues feeding the thought of those who think they can do without it — for "the proof which every man needs in order to attain full certainty is so easy and so clear that one hardly notices the logical process which it implies."[3] That is what Fénelon calls "a sensible, popular philosophy open to any man free from passions and prejudices."[4] In principle, as well as for the straightforward, honest mind, "the merest glance reveals the hand that has made

---

2. Cf. Régis Jolivet, "A la recherche de Dieu," *Archives de philosophie* 8 (1931), p. 85: There is a "simple, common and universal form" of the arguments, "accessible to all"; cf. p. 149 re the argument from motion: "so simple and so evident in its general structure."

3. Scheeben, *Handbuch der katholischen Dogmatik,* vol. 2: *Gotteslehre* (Freiburg, 1948), p. 15.

4. Fénelon, *Traité de l'existence de Dieu,* pt. 1, ch. 1, n. 2.

everything."⁵ Movement, contingence, exemplarity, causality, finality, moral obligation: the eternal categories are the starting-points open to man; they are always to hand and always resist his critique; they are as contemporary as man and his thought.⁶ *Ecce coelum et terram: clamant quod facta sint.*⁷ (Behold the sky and the earth: they cry out that they are made.) Or quite simply: *Aliquid est, ergo Deus est.* (Something exists, therefore God exists.) "The whole School is agreed that nothing further is necessary."⁸

But if the spontaneous proof which springs up in this way is to impress reflective thought to the fullest possible extent, it will call for unceasing modification, and the resulting commentary will inevitably take the form of a justification, in some respects critical and never quite the same, by the nature of things. This "learned" form of the proof, "designed in the first instance to forestall and answer objections," implies a continual effort, constantly renewed, to adapt it to changing conditions.⁹ The need to adapt the proof will seem strange only to a man who has never dreamed of what is implied by the uniqueness of the case. "The sublime and simple operation"¹⁰ which leads to

---

5. *Ibid.*, n. 1.

6. The reader will have noted that I am here opposing the Kantian criticism and all that follows from it.

7. St. Augustine, *Confessions,* bk. 11, ch. 4, n. 6 (PL 32:811); *In Joannem,* tract. 106, ch. 17, n. 4 (PL 35:1910). Cf. Wisdom 13:1, 9.

8. André Bremond, *Une dialectique thomiste du retour à Dieu,* p. 561.

9. Régis Jolivet, "A la recherche de Dieu," p. 85: ". . . The classic proofs of God are simpler, more obvious, less contentious, and although 'metaphysical,' they assert themselves, in their essential elements, with a sovereign power. Their learned form, designed above all to respond to objections or to forestall them, is not the common form, that which acts immediately on the spirit and brings it to belief. . . . That is why the most 'subtle' and most captious objections . . . usually do not succeed in shaking the belief of the true believer: the simple and clear schema of the demonstration is incorporated into the spirit beyond and in spite of all the aporia of the clever. . . ."

10. A. Gratry, *De la connaissance de Dieu*, vol. 1, pp. 45-46: "If there are true proofs of the existence of God, these proofs should be accessible to all men. For the light of God enlightens and should enlighten every man coming into the world. . . . It is necessary to seek the origin and the reality (of the proofs) in some common and daily operation of the human spirit; then, once this sublime and simple operation has been found, it suffices to describe it and to translate it into philosophical language. Afterwards its scientific value will be demonstrated." This does not eliminate the importance and the necessity of more technical considerations, in their own place, as we indicate in the text. Cf. Gratry's observation that "there is no reason separate from the higher attraction which seeks to elevate it" (*ibid.,* vol. 2, p. 279).

As for the particular way in which Gratry conceived of this "sublime and simple

God remains fundamentally the same. The changes in technique, in perspective, and in presentation do not affect the proof itself.[11] God in his eternity dominates the incessant flux of creation, and in the same way the idea of God in us dominates the fluctuations of our intellectual life, imposing itself through those fluctuations with the same unalterable power. The great minds that have spoken about God are all our contemporaries.

Kant tried to prove that the "transcendent" use of causality was illegitimate, but the causality he had in mind was a narrow, scientific category, the specialized category of causation which rules the universe of Newton. Shaped for the ordering of phenomena, it exhausts its virtue in doing so. Kant's causality is, of course, only one example among many. In fact, modern Western philosophies "are singular in one respect: the world they start out from is," as a general rule, "the world constituted and constantly modified by the sciences."[12] There is nothing surprising in the fact that this world is impotent, by itself, to provide a foundation for thought and sustain the movement of thought to the end. For that to be achieved, it would be necessary to dig down beneath the artificial, methodological categories of science to the great natural categories of reason. Then it might be possible to begin discussing the real question: on the one hand the negative critique, the view that the natural categories are illusory; and on the other hand a reflective effort to justify them and purify their spontaneous use.[13]

---

operation," it seems to call for greater precision, which can be found below, supplied by R. P. Maréchal. In this regard, one might also call to mind the enthusiastic article of P. Ramiére, "Du procédé dialectique," in *Etudes de théologie, de philosophie et d'histoire*, vol. 2 (1857), pp. 85-130. See also Louis Foucher, *La philosophie catholique en France au XIXe siècle . . .* (1955), ch. 8, pp. 197-236; B. Pointud-Guillemot, *Essai sur la philosophie de Gratry* (1917).

11. This is why it was possible to say that the proofs of God "are not so much an invention as an inventory, not so much a revelation as an elucidation, a purification and a justification of the fundamental beliefs of humanity" (Maurice Blondel, *La Pensée*, vol. 1, p. 392).

12. Ferdinand Alquié, *La nostalgie de l'être* (1950), p. 151: "We know how much the physics and logic on which Kant meditated influenced his critique."

13. In order to free ourselves technically from criticism, the most useful work is certainly that of Joseph Maréchal. Cf. *Le point de départ de la métaphysique*, pt. 5 (1926), p. 452: "The transcendent principle of causality expresses this complementary and simultaneous revelation of objective contingency and the eminent perfection which measures it." Cf. pp. 450-451; J. Defever, *La preuve réelle de Dieu, étude critique* (1953), pp. 28-40.

Behind the apparent variations, the skeleton of the proof always remains the same.[14] The proof is solid and eternal: as hard as steel. It is something more than one of reason's inventions: it is reason itself.

All the objections brought against the various proofs of the existence of God are in vain; criticism can never invalidate them, for it can never get its teeth into the principle common to them all. On the contrary, that principle emerges more clearly as the elements with which the proofs are constructed are rearranged. That is because it is not a particular principle which the mind can either isolate and sift so as to determine its limits, or reject out of hand: it forms part of the substance of the mind. It is not a path which the mind can be discouraged from pursuing to the end, or one from which it can turn away, afraid of having taken the wrong road; path and mind are merged together. *The mind itself is a moving path.*[15]

14. Many authors have noted this without, however, explaining things in the same way. Cf. Pedro Descoqs, S.J., *Praelectiones theologiae naturalis,* concerning the five "ways" of the Summa of St. Thomas: "It seems to us that all the arguments can be reduced to one, and involve the way of efficient causality as the only proof in the order of scientific discourse" (vol. 1, p. 353; vol. 2, p. 15). H. Paissac, *Preuves de Dieu,* p. 88: "The proofs of God radiate from a single center: the affirmation of causality."

15. Cf. Charles de Moré-Pontgibaud, "Sur l'analogie des noms divins," *Recherches de science religieuse* (1954), pp. 510-511: ". . . This fixity in direction; this intrepidity in the climb toward an end which is naturally inaccessible; this ease in spontaneously embracing, in the unity of the same perspective, and in a prodigious succinctness, resemblances so unlike one another that they thoroughly exclude every strict proportion and every common measure; this boldness of reasoning which progresses without fear of dizziness on the path of the middle analogic term, by its negations imperturbably avoiding wrong paths and false trails to the right and to the left; which reasoning, having a great fear of those who measure this climb by one of the ordinary paths of our spirit, 'goes to the limit' and easily places the Infinite as the goal of its path, or more precisely refers to Him in its affirmation, while it needs reason thus reflected upon in order to justify and speak precisely about this route, undertaken with such laborious effort; — all this would doubtless be perilous and would be ill-conceived, if it were a matter of passing from one particular idea to another particular idea, but it is normal and legitimate if, in so doing, we follow only the fundamental and constant inclination of our understanding, under the direction of the first cause, toward the only and total source of reality and intelligibility."

Causa essendi, ratio intelligendi, ordo vivendi (the cause of being, the explanation of understanding, the pattern of living). All thought, like every being, and like every act, needs a principle and a term.[16] The mind did not set itself in motion, and its movement presupposes a direction; that is to say, a fixed point. The purely gratuitous is the purely absurd. One cannot do with the economy of God.

If, as many people think, man's adoration of God were his adoration of humanity itself, he would adore it as nature or as an ideal; that is to say, as something realized or realizable. In either case, the object proposed would be no more worthy of adoration than the transcendent God such as he has been imagined to be and, so imagined, subjected to criticism.

If the divinity were conceived as a pure ideal, never capable of realization, always becoming and never necessarily existing, by what right could it still be called "humanity"? And in what sense could so elusive a term be called intelligible — or adorable?

These are three attempts to evade the living God, ways of escape into mystification.

God is not the first link in the chain, the first of a series in the sequence of causes and effects which constitute the world.[17] God is not "a point of

---

16. St. Augustine, *De civitate Dei*, bk. 8, ch. 4: "... so to admit that in Him are to be found the cause of existing, the ground of understanding, and the pattern of living: of which three things, the first is understood to pertain to the natural, the second to the rational, and the third to the mortal part of philosophy. For if man has been so created as to attain, through that which is most excellent in him, to that which excels all things — that is, the one true and absolutely good God, without whom no nature exists, no doctrine instructs, no exercise profits — let Him be sought in whom all things are secure to us; let Him be discovered in whom all things are certain to us; let Him be loved, in whom all things are right for us" (PL 41:228-229). Cf. ch. 10, n. 2 (PL 41:235). *Contra Faustum Manichaeum*, bk. 20, ch. 7: "... From God we derive the beginning of existence, the principle of knowing, the law of loving. From God all creatures, rational and irrational, derive the nature by which they live, the activity of sensation, the motion of the appetitive power. From God all bodily creatures derive their subsistence in extension, their beauty in number, and their order in weight" (PL 42:372).

17. Cf. H. Paissac, *Preuves de Dieu*, pp. 90-94: "If God is simply one object among all the others, or the first link of a chain; if, for example, the complexion of a human face is explained by the nature of the cells, which in their turn are explained by the

origin in the past": he is "a sufficient reason in the present" (in the past and in the future as well, and during the passage of time).[18] How many objections would disappear, how many misunderstandings would vanish, if that simple truth were understood!

~

God is not merely the principle and the term, at the beginning and at the end: the Good of every good, the Life of all living things, the Being of all beings,[19] he is also at the heart of all things. *In illo vivimus, et movemur, et sumus.*[20] In him we live and move and have our being. But for that

---

arrangement of the chromosomes, which are explained by God, God is not God. At least, the existence of the true God has not been demonstrated. . . . From the fact that there is causality *in* the world, it does not follow that there is a causality *of* the world. Kant is right, if one tries to establish an exclusively scientific proof of the existence of God, that is, if the cause represents 'the phenomenon which produces another phenomenon.' . . . (Only in metaphysics) is the cause no longer simply 'the phenomenon which produces another,' but that which supposes or requires an existent which is not identified with its act of existing. . . . (Now) 'one cannot go to infinity,' says St. Thomas. And we understand what he means: it is not a question either of a chain, or of a convoy, as if one could not bear the burden of counting an infinity of cars or of links in a chain, but one must exit from the series, at one point or another. . . . One could go to infinity in the order of scientific explanation. But one must exit from this order: one can not climb up to infinity and find there a definite cause. There must be an end, that is, a final cause or a first cause. Not a first number at the end of a more or less long series, but an *Other,* in the strictest meaning of the word, a First in the sense that it surpasses all the others, and no longer is part of the rest, being of an entirely different order. If an image would be useful to illustrate this, one can easily picture the single car of a passing train — not the indefinite series of cars that precede it, nor even the motor driving the whole length of the train; but more simply, more definitively, the current of electrical energy in the cables and dominating the entire length of the train."

18. Etienne Gilson, responding to Léon Brunschvicg, in *La querelle de l'athéisme* (Léon Brunschvicg, *De la vraie et de la fausse conversion,* p. 228). It is enough to recall that St. Thomas admitted the possibility of a world created *ab aeterno,* that is, a world in which innumerable series of causes and effects would succeed each other indefinitely without beginning or end, only to find himself forced to admit that he could not commit the confusion which is the beginning of so many objections to the most classic proof of the existence of God. There must be a prime mover, as Aristotle in effect already said, not because it would be necessary to have a first term in any sort of (temporal) series, but because there must be a first cause in a (hierarchically ordered) series of causes.

19. St. Augustine, *De Trinitate,* bk. 8, ch. 3, n. 4: "The good of every good" (PL 42:949). Pseudo-Dionysius, *Of the Divine Names,* 1, 3 (PG 3:589). St. Bernard, *De consideratione,* bk. 5.

20. St. Paul, Acts 17:28. Cf. John Scotus Erigena, *De divisione naturae,* bk. 1, n. 2; bk. 3,

presence of the Absolute at the heart of the relative, of the Eternal at the heart of movement, everything would return to dust.

Becoming, by itself, has no meaning. It passes away and vanishes without really becoming at all: it is another word for the absurd. But without Transcendence, that is to say, without a present Absolute installed at the heart of the reality which is in the process of becoming, not depending on it, but working within it, drawing it on, polarizing it, making it really advance, there could only be unending becoming — unless a catastrophe were to come to put a violent end to everything, and the absurd were at last to rediscover its true nature, so to say, by becoming unequivocally nothing....

All becoming is caused by Being. All becoming is turned towards Being. Becoming can only be thought by Being.

The idea of Progress, which magnifies and in some sort hypostatizes Becoming, is one of the emptiest ideas which men have ever forged. Progress deified, it has been truly said,[21] is not only "a race without a rudder," but a race without an end; or rather a race that gets lost without really being run at all. If you do away with the winning post, you do away with the direction. The result is "to create an abstract 'beyond' that shimmers before the eyes of a distraught individual, a will-o'-the-wisp that flies away at his approach."[22] It is tantamount to doing away with progress. "To do away with absolute perfection is to do away with any idea of becoming perfect." There can be no real improvement where there is "neither axis nor goal"; no real progression except by "reaching the limit." If there is becoming, if progress is possible, then one day there must be attainment (or let us say achievement); and if there can be achievement, then there always has been something other than mere becoming.[23]

---

n. 1 (PL 122:451-452 and 621d). M. Blondel, *L'Action*, p. 346: God "is at the center of what I think and of what I do.... To go from myself to myself, I pass through him constantly."

21. G. Van der Leeuw, "L'homme et la civilisation," *Eranos-Jahrbuch* 16 (1948), p. 170.

22. Gaston Fessard, *France, prends garde de perdre ton âme* (1946), p. 149; see pp. 133-150.

23. Félix Ravaisson, *La philosophie française au XIXe siècle*, 4th ed. (1895), p. 50. Cf. Yves de Montcheuil, S.J., "Une philosophie du devoir," *Mélanges théologiques* (1946), pp. 238-239. Jules Monchanin, *De l'esthétique à la mystique* (1955), pp. 43-44. Some philosophers have conceived for the created spirit a possible end which would consist, somehow, of not having any end at all. The one to whom God would not have offered the

"Abolish the end of the world (which is also its beginning) and there is no longer any *meaning* in things, only Chaos which makes one despair and terrifies one, and to which Tathâgata preferred *Nothingness*."[24]

On the one hand there is the absurdity of primordial chaos, the nothingness from which everything is supposed to emerge, which is said to engender being, the blind power which is supposed to bring forth the light of the Spirit: and on the other hand there is the source of Being — a certain "Point Alpha."

On the one hand there is the hopelessness and the final chaos of the ultimate defeat, of the Spirit finally overcome by the darkness of matter, unending death, or that mournful "eternal recurrence" in which all dreams finally vanish; on the other there is the Place where being recollects itself — a "Point Omega."

"I am the Alpha and the Omega," says the Lord.[25]

The intelligence, according to the philosophers of antiquity, "is in some sense everything." It is, indeed, spontaneously conscious of the fact, and whenever it attempts to articulate its dream, using the language of various systems, however strange and varied the formula in which the dream takes shape, the intelligence is always concerned to understand everything in itself. *Vult autem anima totum mundum describi in se.*[26] (The soul wants the whole world gathered into itself.)

---

divine vision, would nevertheless not be content with any finite good, but would tend indefinitely toward this vision as toward a pole which always attracts, but is unattainable. Without discussing here such a hypothesis, which is not without serious difficulties (and which finds scarcely any basis in the Thomism which it sometimes claims), it suffices for us to observe that it has nothing in common, in any case, with the idea of pure Becoming, an idea which is critiqued here as absurd. In fact, the hypothesis mentioned has to do with a universe created by God; it submits, therefore, from the very first, to a conceptual world which recognizes a fundamental ontological stability, and by the same token, the indefinite becoming about which it speaks is a directed becoming.

24. Paul Claudel, *Correspondance avec Jacques Rivière*, p. 60. Cf. Plotinus, *Enneads*, 5, 1, 6: "Everything that moves requires something towards which it moves."

25. Cf. Isaiah 41:4. Apocalypse 1:8. Cf. P. Teilhard de Chardin, *Le groupe zoologique humain* (1956), pp. 156, 162: "Universal focal point of psychic interiorization," "Absolutely ultimate principle of irreversibility and of personalization."

26. St. Bonaventure.

In other words, the intelligence cannot give up the Absolute for which it was made; but since it cannot situate or understand the Absolute, its natural reaction is to look for it in Nature, in the object that lies immediately to hand. But that kind of search must surely prevent the intelligence from attaining its end? The objective world is indefinite: an ocean without shores, where the mind is soon lost. To set sail there in the hope of someday dropping anchor "beyond physical things" is surely to abandon the real world for the realm of abstractions? True metaphysics is the science *par excellence* of the real and the concrete.[27]

And so, at first, people believe in the data of the senses: which have, after all, the privilege of being immediate. They brook no denial and survive no matter what theory. Are we not driven, in the end, to return to them? — Yet sooner or later one begins to notice that they are only appearances, or at the most the crust of reality. Then we place our trust in the entities fashioned by science; they, at least, provide these amorphous and fluid "sensibilia" with a solid shell. They, surely, impose law and order. — But in the long run even the claims of science must be reduced. On closer inspection the entities which one took to be absolute appear contradictory, or can be resolved into yet others, such as movement, for example, or the "atom" of antiquity. . . .[28] The scientific universe does not stand up to criticism any better than the sensual universe, unless it is supported by a universe of a different nature. The more successfully science and improved techniques bring the world under human control, the more does being, which cannot be brought under that control, evade us. . . . And in face of that new and apparently final defeat, the great temptation is agnosticism. But agnosticism, which was conceived as a way of saving logic at least from the wreck, proves in its turn contradictory. The position is untenable. For how can one continue to affirm an Absolute which is admittedly unknowable? It seems, in fact, impossible to avoid complete skepticism. But the intelligence can never abdicate. It cannot renounce its own formal law, it cannot cease judging, and that always means affirmation. Skepticism oppresses and undermines the mind because it introduces contradiction not only into the various contents of its various affirmations, but into the intelligence itself,

---

27. Cf. Ferdinand Alquié, *La nostalgie de l'être*, p. 17: "It is natural enough that most scholars, devoting their life to the search for objectivity, allow the exigency of their own being to lose itself in this research; but the realism which they profess is then a kind of professional distortion."

28. A-tom = un-divisible, unable-to-be-split.

into the heart of its every act. In trying to escape from that dilemma, the mind is sometimes driven to conceive (in the broadest sense of the word) a sort of *ersatz* Absolute Law. That introduces an intermediary sphere between the mind and the real halfway, as it were, between the immanent and the transcendent, a "*terra media* in which all our actions occur, and beyond which the need to know is lost in metaphysics; that is to say, in idle discussion and empty chatter concerning questions which have no possible bearing on practical life." But once again even that modest refuge proves unstable. Once again it has to be recognized that — just as the Absolute of the Senses proved contradictory — the Absolute of Law is left hanging in the air. The "eternal Axiom," by whatever name we call it, unless it is something else disguised, is ultimately the void, an abstract void without depth or mystery.

Here, surely, we have reached an *impasse*?

The original illusion is the cause of all the trouble. It arises from the uncriticized assumption that all we have to do is to perfect our knowledge of the world based upon certain primary data without bothering to reflect upon ourselves; from the blind assumption that the mind's vision is an extension of the body's vision, somehow prolonging its sight almost indefinitely, even when it seems, with the help of science, to sift the data and discover being beneath appearances; from the belief that the object, confusedly identified with being, must be amassed like a treasure, studied with a view to its usefulness and safeguarded so as to be enjoyed; in short, from the illusion that all we need to do is settle down in this world and become part of it. . . .

It is an illusion which is natural to the mind, as it is natural to man. Perhaps it is necessary; in any case, it is useful in encouraging the search for knowledge which is part of man's vocation. It is an illusion, nevertheless, which any thinking man will find the means to destroy in himself. He does so in a double way, by discovering that a perfectly adequate knowledge of this world is doubly impossible for him. For whether one calls it "knowledge" or "intuition" — according as one leans to a psychological explanation or a rationalist one — whether one conceives of it as a mysterious movement at the heart of the real as its forms dissolve or, on the contrary, as the living term of a great rationalist synthesis, as something immediate or as a construction — the ideal which seemed to activate human knowledge is a mirage.

Absolute Knowledge and the Intuition of the world are equally impossible.

Absolute Knowledge is impossible because its realization would automatically involve the disappearance of the person who is to have it. He could not become the Knowledge and the Knower. All contradictions would have been overcome and oppositions cancelled out. All laws would fit together, one into the other, until finally they were contained in a single formula. And by that very fact all particular views would have vanished, the individual would have been dissolved in the universal, multiplicity would have been reduced to unity, and the formula would no longer discover a symbol in which to express itself, nor a consciousness in which to be affirmed. On reaching the end of his Knowledge, the Knower would be "like the witch who ended by devouring her own inwards." "Nothing would remain but the unthinkable equality of nothing to nothing."[29]

An Intuition of the world is no less impossible because it would dissolve the world which it is trying to embrace. There is an infra-intellectual element in this world, but if it could be fully assimilated and exhausted by the intelligence, it would no longer be itself. The ultimate reason for this must again be sought in the subjective realm; for if the world is essentially the world of sense, that is because it is essentially indefinite; and if the world is indefinite, and therefore inexhaustible and incapable of being reduced to a single total, that is surely because it is the necessary correlative of minds which are themselves in process of becoming.[30]

---

29. Kierkegaard, *Journal,* 12 A 354 (1850). Cf. Gaston Fessard, *La méthode de réflexion chez Maine de Biran* (1938), p. 170, on the dream of absolute knowledge: "An absurd dream? — Not at all. Where the naturally metaphysical man goes wrong lies not in his dreaming along these lines nor indeed in his wishing to transform his dream into reality, but only in believing that he ever reached such an exalted peak. He thus forgets that the science of being cannot exist in that which does not yet exist. On the other hand, though, no less blame attaches to those who, in seeking to recognize the mirage of a cut and dried ontology, put a stop to a pursuit that they declare to be chimerical. They, for their part, forget that the science of being can only be dreamed of by way of what ought to be."

30. This is what F. Alquié goes so far as to name "the philosophical reaction of consciousness" to scientific thought. The resumption of this idea is altogether something other than a development or a going beyond. It is an idea for which the consciousness feels an eternal need, with a view to "situating itself vis a vis the world . . . that is offered to it by science" (*La nostalgie de l'être,* pp. 9, 40, and 151. Cf. p. 127, on "the doctrines of intuition and the systems" that "allow their common essence to appear" by leading the spirit that is in the world away from objects even while they claim "to deliver Being to it."

In brief, the world is neither Law nor Essence. The antinomies which it always produces, stimulating and awakening the movement of the mind, will never be all resolved. Although real on their own level, the laws and essences which the intelligence goes on discovering will never attain to that total synthesis which would make it identical with metaphysics, whose true and final object is not of this world. The understanding will never cease to be understanding; that is to say, an imperfect intelligence inseparable from the senses; but it is itself only a provisional substitute, an auxiliary of the spirit.

The understanding, the faculty of knowing, of science, is turned towards the outside; the mind, the spirit, must be turned inward; there must be a "recurrent critique" of thought, "conversion," "introversion," "reflection," through which metaphysics at last discovers its own sphere. "No," Malebranche protested, "I shall not lead you into a strange country, but I shall perhaps teach you that you are strangers in your own country."

The understanding is open to an infinity of objects; a sign, surely, that it is open to the infinite itself. Without being able to sum them all up,[31] we can represent things to ourselves indefinitely; does that not mean that we desire, as far as is in us, to possess God? "Acosmism" if you like; but in fact an acosmism which saves the world. Without it the world would be only "systematic illusion"; thanks to it, the world is given back its value, its density, its meaning, and its justification. It is revealed as a means, a stage — a trial. Its essentially indefinite character no longer scandalizes us, and it can, in its present guise, even slip through our hands, so to speak, and vanish without disconcerting us — a transfiguration, the approach and proclamation of a better world. We are "πάντα πῶς," it has been said, because we are "θε ὸς πῶς"; and it has also been said that we possess a "faculty for the divine"; perhaps it would be more precise to say: *intelligence* is the *faculty* of being, because *spirit* is the *capacity* for God.

The human mind may be compared to a plant. The aim of the plant, in assimilating the elements which it draws from outside, is to live, to become itself. The aim of the spirit which first of all becomes understanding in order to assimilate the sensible, is not to lose itself in the elements which

---

31. St. Thomas, *Prima*, q.79, a.2: "No created intellect can be like an act with respect to the whole of universal being; because in such a case it would have to be an infinite being. Wherefore every created intellect, by reason of the very fact that it is what it is, is not the act of all intelligible things."

offer themselves to it, nor to use them to construct a self-contained and perfect edifice of knowledge; its aim is to become itself, to live. Its life is the possession of itself — and of all things — in that dependence upon God which illuminates it.

"I am among men," says the traveller, "not among angels, and I have no desire but for what breathes in my own image."

"That is not true," answers the voice, "All your desire is for God, since the knowledge of God is your portion, and as the bee distills honey through the summer months, so your function is to contemplate the imperishable with loving eyes."[32]

> *Noli foras ire, in teipsum redi, in interiore homine habitat Veritas; et si tuam naturam mutabilem inveneris, transcende et teipsum. Sed memento, cum te transcendis, ratiocinantem animam te transcendere. Illuc ergo tende, unde ipsum lumen rationis accenditur.*[33]

(Do not go abroad, return into yourself. Let truth dwell in the inner man; and if you find your own nature mutable, then transcend yourself. But remember, when you transcend yourself, to transcend yourself as a ratiocinative soul. Direct your gaze, therefore, to where the reason's light itself is kindled.)

> *Solus Deus est, in quem nec pondus nec mensura cadit omnino, nec numerus. Unus Deus est, non habeat sui generis cui valet comparari.*[34]

(Only God is beyond weight and measure and number. God is one, and there are no members of his class with whom he can be compared.)

Everything that concerns God, everything that leads to God, everything that unites to God, is unique.[35]

---

32. Ernest Psichari, *Le Voyage du Centurion*.
33. St. Augustine, *De vera religione*, ch. 39, n. 72 (PL 34:154). Zigliara, who cites and comments on this text, is keen to show how the teaching of St. Thomas is in conformity on this point with that of St. Augustine (*Oeuvres philosophiques*, vol. 2, pp. 206-208).
34. St. Bernard of Clairvaux, *De diversis sermo* 81, n. 2 (PL 103:703b).
35. Cf. Aimé Forest, in Martin et Fliche, *Histoire générale de l'Église*, vol. 8 (1951), p. 57. Even though it was criticized by St. Thomas, the argument of St. Anselm is conducive, at the very least, to "an understanding that the problem of God is unique."

All "communion" in name or in essence between God and other beings is excluded.[36] Nothing about God or our relations with him enters "into a genus."[37] There can be no exception to that principle. The way to God, however varied in its secondary forms and however numerous the ways become, is in itself unique[38] ἅπαξ.

---

36. Marius Victorinus, *Adversus Arium*, bk. 4, ch. 23: "For everything for which a name can be articulated comes after Him" (PL 8:1129d). St. Anselm, *Monologion*, ch. 26: ". . . Therefore whenever he is in communion with others of any name or description whatsoever, then quite without a doubt a different significance is to be imputed"; ch. 27: ". . . It is the case therefore that that substance, from essential communion with which all natures are excluded, is not under the constraint of any common contiguity of substances" (PL 171:180a-b).

37. St. Thomas, *Prima*, q.3, a.5, etc. In *La Philosophie de saint Bonaventure* (2nd ed., [1943], p. 115, note), Etienne Gilson comments as follows on the article that is cited from the *Summa*, referring to the *sed contra* ("Nothing is prior to God either with respect to reality or with respect to the intellect"): "If God were in a genus, something would be anterior to him; the idea of genus is anterior, for the understanding which is classifying ideas, to that of the species contained under the genus. Now it is no more true that there is in us an idea that is logically anterior to that of God than that there is outside of us a reality which is anterior to God himself." "The divine reality is anterior to being and all its differences." (*La Sainte Trinité* . . . , by a Carthusian, 1948, p. 33.) Cajetan, *In Primam*, q.39, a.1, n. 7: "Deity or the divine thing is prior to being and all its differences: for it is above being and above the one." We cannot (and must not) make light of the legitimate arguments in which the existence of God appears only as a conclusion, for, as Gilson indeed notes, "prius secundum intellectum" (= "prior in the intellect") does not mean "prius secundum cognitionem" (= "prior in knowledge"). In other words, God for us is not the first known object. One could not, without acquiescing in an illusion, go along with the thesis proposed by those ontologists "who confound abstract being which the intelligence perceives without reasoning with the concrete being which constitutes the very essence of God, who confound, indeed, the poorest of all forms of being with infinite reality" (Xavier Moisant, S.J., *Dieu, l'expérience en métaphysique* [1907], p. 25), which is yet one more way of placing God "in a genus." My remark concerning the way which leads to God comes after this twofold observation. Cf. Chapter 2, note 18 above.

38. J. Defever, S.J., "La preuve transcendante de Dieu," *Revue philosophique de Louvain* (1953), p. 527: "The proof for the existence of God is not a proof like any other." J. M. Le Blond, "Le chrétien devant l'athéisme actuel," *Etudes* (1954), p. 301: "The proof of God is of another order, of an order that is fitted to it alone." Is this not what Maurice Nédoncelle in a happy turn of phrase calls "the short circuiting of the knowledge of God"? Cf. *La réciprocité des consciences* (1942), p. 107: "Most discussions on the necessity to recur to intuition or to reasoning in order to find God are quite futile. In this case two very distinct things are often mixed up: the immediate character and the direct character of knowledge. To know someone through a notion of him, which is indirect

Polemon, Do you believe in one God?

Certainly, he answered; I believe in one eternal, self-existing principle.

Whereas I, Callista replied, feel that God within my heart. I feel myself in his presence! He says to me, "Do this: don't do that." You may tell me that this dictate is a mere law of my nature, as to joy or grieve. I cannot understand this. No, it is the echo of a person speaking to me. Nothing shall persuade me that it does not ultimately proceed from a person external to me. It carries with it its proof of its divine origin. My nature feels towards it as towards a person. When I obey it, I feel a satisfaction; when I disobey, a sadness — just like that which I feel in pleasing or offending some revered friend. So you see, Polemon, I believe in what is more than a mere "something." I believe in what is more real to me than sun, moon, stars, and the fair earth, and the voice of friends. You will say, "Who is he? Has he ever told you anything about himself?" Alas! no! — the more's the pity! But I will not give up what I have because I have not more. An echo implies a voice; a voice a speaker. That speaker I love and I fear.[39]

Thought can never reaching being, though it fringes it with its very first steps. It would not move if it had not, in a certain sense, arrived.

The apparatus of the proofs is surely nothing but a vast *removens prohibens* — a clearing away of obstacles; all too necessary, indeed, in the carnal condition of the mind. But although its action is essentially positive

---

and symbolical, is not to know him in himself. It is merely to discover his probable presence. And that is why one of the two schools, the one with the most mystical tendencies, repulses the aid of reason or the systematic linkages of analysis. But to suppose that God is reached immediately through an escape from ourselves and the world is to be unaware of our created condition and even perhaps of what is unique in the relationship of the creature to God. Wherefore there are legitimate grounds of mistrust, on the part of those who are in favor of a discursive proof, towards the supposed intuition of God. — In reality, the method of approach which fits this problem is different from all others. The reflection that takes its point of departure in us does not thereby present an obstacle to intimacy. If the knowledge of God is possible by a kind of short circuit, it is because He is in total communion with our perspective on existence. And in no case do we have an example of such a communion."

39. J. H. Newman, *Callista*, ch. 27.

when envisaged in the framework of the intellectual life, its significance is, above all, negative if it is replaced in the larger framework or the greater depth of the perspective of the spirit in its concrete actuality:

> The sculptor does not make the statue.
> He removes what hid it.[40]

The ways which reason adopts on its journey to God are proofs, and these proofs, in turn, are ways. That does not deprive them of their character as proofs — incomplete though they may often be as proofs;[41] but their object, being unique among all the objects of thought, confers a special character upon them. They do not yield up their object, as other proofs do, more or less. They do not enable us to penetrate it. God alone is present to those who prove him, present in an intimate manner — as he is to those who deny him. But at the same time that presence is so beyond our grasp that he alone, among all objects, cannot be held.[42]

---

40. John Donne. Cf. Pseudo-Dionysius, *De mystica theologia*, ch. 2: "The artist proceeds in this way to make a life-size bust. From his block he chips away what keeps the pure figure that is still hidden from being seen. This cutting away makes it possible to bring the beauty that is latent into the full light of day." The idea comes from Plato, *Republic*, 10, 611c-e, and from Plotinus, *Enneads*, 1, 6, 9. Cf. St. Gregory of Nyssa, in PG 44:541d-544a, and 1069b-c. Jacques Paliard, *Profondeur de l'Ame* (1953), p. 46: "Is there any other way to demonstrate what is essential than by what counterfeits it or conceals it?" Bossuet, *Elévations sur les Mystères*, first week, second elevation, *La perfection et l'éternité de Dieu*: "The ignorant man believes that he knows change more than immutability, because he expresses change by means of an actual time and immutability by a negation of change itself. And he does not want to think that to be immutable is being and that to change is not being; now being is, and is known before the privation which is non-being" (*Oeuvres complètes*, ed. F. Lachat, vol. 7 [1862], p. 5).

41. Cf. the historical conclusions of F. Van Steenberghen on the five ways of the *Summa theologica*: "None of the *quinque viae* [= "five ways"] constitutes, in its literal purport, a complete and satisfying proof for the existence of God. The first and second need to be drawn out. The third and fifth need to be corrected and completed. The fourth way is unusable . . ." *Revue philosophique de Louvain* 45 (1947), p. 168. It is, however, perfectly allowable to debate these conclusions. On some problems of interpretation, cf. William Bryar, *Saint Thomas and the Existence of God* (Chicago, 1951).

42. Cf. Jacques Maritain, *Les degrés du savoir* (1932), pp. 445-446: "When we are dealing with things that are proportional to or connatural with our intelligence, our demonstration of them, even while it submits itself to the object, also submits the object to our grasp in a certain way, to our means of verification, which measure it, delimit it,

∽

All men know God "naturally," but they do not always recognize him. A thousand obstacles, some inward, some external, hinder that recognition. Not everyone knows that he knows God, and consequently not everyone does know him "simply." Thus, when I see Peter coming towards me — the comparison is St. Thomas's[43] — it is certainly Peter whom I see in that being coming towards me, but I do not yet know that it is he.[44]

It may be tempting to reject the comparison on the grounds that it presupposes that I already knew Peter, and that I am soon going to recognize the person I knew. Whereas in the case of God, a "proper" knowledge is to succeed to a knowledge which is still implicit. So I am not preparing to recognize him really, but to know him for the first time.

---

define it. Our demonstration takes hold of the object, touches it, handles it, judges it. This is all the more palpable insofar as it takes place by way of material processes. And perhaps the scholastics, who have received as their heritage the lofty notion of a pure science, whose very rigor and strict intellectuality have proceeded from a religious respect and a demand for purity in the face of being . . . perhaps they forget sometimes to what point the words of science, of demonstration, of proof, are charged with materiality in the usage of the moderns, since thought has turned first and foremost towards the domination of sensible nature, and since the word 'verify' conjures up nothing more for moderns than methods of measurement and laboratory apparatus. In denying themselves, as they quite rightly ought to, a degraded vocabulary, they thus risk not explaining sufficiently their own lexicon. But, in any case, they know that to demonstrate the existence of God is not to submit him to our grasp, nor to define him, nor to take hold of him, nor to wield anything other than weak ideas with regard to such an object, nor, indeed, is it to form a judgement of anything other than our own radical dependence. The process by which reason demonstrates that God exists places reason itself in an attitude of natural adoration and intelligent admiration."

See also St. Thomas, *Contra Gentiles*, bk. 4, prooemium.

43. St. Thomas, *Prima*, q.2, a.1, ad 1m: "To know that God exists in a certain common and confused way is implanted in us by nature, inasmuch as God is the happiness of man. For man by nature desires happiness. And whatever is naturally desired by man is naturally known by him. But this is not to know in an absolute way that God exists, just as to know that someone is coming is not to know Peter, even if it is Peter who is indeed coming."

44. I had written: "When I see Peter coming towards me, without yet knowing that it is he, as St. Thomas says." Someone has observed that all St. Thomas says is, "I do not know Peter in the man coming towards me, although it is Peter." I do not see an abyss of difference between the two translations. But I do take into account the words which immediately precede: "simpliciter cognoscere . . . [= 'to come to know simply']." In any case, I had no intention of putting more into the French than the very simple but instructive sense conveyed by the Latin of St. Thomas.

Of course no comparison can be perfect, and it is abundantly clear that St. Thomas's does not apply in every particular, although it would be a mistake to minimize its bearing too much. When I reach an explicit knowledge of God, I certainly do not recognize him as someone whom I had already known with the same sort of knowledge, and had since forgotten or lost to view. I did not know him consciously, as yet, in the ordinary sense of the word. Nevertheless, the extraordinary thing is that knowing God for the first time I do, in fact, *recognize him*.[45] For — to take up the illustration which St. Thomas gives at this very point — when I come to know God as the one who will make me happy, I realize at the same time that God is identified with the beatitude which I knew by desiring it, but which I placed, at first, among objects which deceived me; or rather I can now identify my beatitude with him. That is certainly recognition. And that is what always happens. I never discover the existence of God as I might discover some distant city, for example, to which I was not bound by any real tie and which I should only note as an external fact. That is what Father Jules Lebreton means when he says that "to speak of God to a human being is not to speak of colors to the blind."[46] Many men, no doubt, behave with regard to God like the blind in respect of colors, but the problems of reflective philosophy must not be confused with those of psychology or sociology; and when the blind man recovers his sight, then the moment he knows God it would be true to say that he has recognized him. For — and this is the extraordinary and really admirable thing — "the habit of God," belonging as it does "to the very nature of the spirit," is possessed by it "before any act whatsoever." That is what St. Thomas implies by his comparison, and when he explains, at the same time, that we do not know God "simpliciter" with our first knowledge, which is purely "natural" and implicit, his qualification means that in a certain sense God is, nevertheless, known; that is why, when the moment comes, it is permissible to speak of "recognizing" him.[47]

---

45. It is a similar paradox that caused St. Augustine to marvel, when he addressed Reason, exclaiming: "You who do not yet know God, how is it that you know that nothing is like God?" *Soliloquies,* ch. 2, n. 7 (PL 32:873).

46. "La connaissance de foi," *Etudes* 117 (1908), p. 735.

47. Cf. H. Paissac, *Preuves de Dieu,* ch. 2, n. 32. It is clear, moreover, that the sole text of St. Thomas recalled here would not suffice to give authority to *all* of the teaching that touches on the implicit knowledge of God.

To believe in *an eternity in the instant* — as all spiritual experience of a high order demands — without admitting that it is a participation in *eternal Eternity* is to plunge into contradiction. It involves living on an illusion without fully admitting it.

∽

One can, of course, bring the classic objection of the hundred thalers against St. Anselm's argument: existence is not a predicate, it is not a perfection of the essence. . . . One might also object that the being to which his argument leads is ultimately nothing but the thought which posits it; it would only be valid insofar as it contains the "virtuality of idealism."[48]

For, "how can that infinite, which can only be thought of as objective, exist if not as the mind's own power of transcendence? What can that unsurpassable greatness be if not the greatness of thought? And by that very fact, the thing affirmed, which does not require that thought should leave its own realm to make the affirmation, seems only to be thought affirming itself by affirming its superiority to everything. There we find being absorbed into thought." So that by reaching the conclusion that a God distinct from that thought did in fact exist, one would be realizing a particular case, and a very typical one, of the "alienation" which the heirs of Hegel are so persistent in denouncing on all sides.

That objection reveals the full significance and all the implications of the argument better than anything else could possibly do. All that is needed is that the Anselmian dialectic should be carried to the point at which it rejoins the classic "argument from contingence."

> From a strictly and exclusively intellectual point of view, the argument achieves and affirms nothing except the thought which affirms itself, and which alone can discover itself to be unsurpassable through its power of effacing all images, and destroying all representations, and of surpassing all limits. Then reflection, which becomes conscious of its unlimited greatness, is inevitably faced by an ironic ambivalence: is it other than I? Is it possible from that strictly noetic point of view to settle the question? I believe so, because the intellectual experience,

---

48. Cf. D. Parodi, "Le rationalisme et l'idée de Dieu," *Revue de métaphysique et de morale* (1930), pp. 41-42. "In the only form in which it can still be admitted by the critical metaphysics of our time, the transcendence of the Absolute can only be the creative energy of thought, realising in some way or other the consciousness of its own unity and continuity, of its fecundity and its infinite progress."

which alone is entitled to intervene at this point, is not only an experience of the triumph of reflection by which thought affirms itself superior to all else, but also an experience of the labor of reflection, of the act of pushing back and denying the limit, which always needs to be renewed. The experience is not only one of greatness, but also one of littleness . . . ; greatness and littleness are given together in their relationship which is the act itself of reflection and of transcending. But because the limit is crossed, because the unattainable is affirmed, it is impossible to forget that the transcending requires the limit and is also consciousness of the limit. From that I know that I only am through the unattainable, and at the same time that I am not the unattainable. I suffer from the greatness which is my condition and which makes me recognise my limitation. What is affirmed as being, both in the individual mind and in reality at the same time, is certainly absolute thought; but that absolute thought, which the finite spirit cannot appropriate or absorb entirely, and which the mind must therefore oppose to itself, becomes, in that opposition, the reality of thought, that is to say being itself. . . .[49]

From a strictly intellectual point of view, then, it cannot be said that the Anselmian proof contains the germ of idealism and immanentism; it is a meditation on the power and limitations, on the wretchedness and greatness of our thought taken together. It does not lead to or justify an illegitimate "alienation" of man; it shows him, by its recognition of his limitations, the secret of the only way of surmounting them.

The proof of God is incomparably stronger than any other proof, because, more than any other, it is bound up with the mind which propounds it; but it is also — as experience teaches — easier to elude, and these apparently contrary characteristics spring from the same cause. For God is not an object among other objects. If he is, he can only be the total Object and the total Truth informing the whole mind. Now in rejecting *a* particular truth, one only accepts *an* absurdity; whereas in rejecting the total Truth, one introduces absurdity itself into the mind. As long as the intelligence

---

49. Jacques Paliard, "Prière et dialectique, méditation sur le 'Proslogion' de saint Anselme," *Dieu Vivant* 6, pp. 56 and 59-60. By the same author: "Sur un aspect de la structure conscientielle, " *Actes du 3e congrès des sociétés de philosophie de langue française* (Brussels, 1947). Cf. Jean Trouillard, *La purification plotinienne* (1955), pp. 88-90.

adheres to some solid region of being, the least absurdity naturally horrifies it, since the least absurdity once recognized is enough to unsettle the inner coherence of its mental universe; whereas once the law of contrast ceases to operate, the mind finds great difficulty in "realizing" total absurdity, which is presented to it in the form of a sort of inverted coherence, co-extensive with its whole knowledge. Total absurdity infects that knowledge fundamentally but without disturbing its internal relationships. Thus the intelligence can always delude itself with its own subtleties.

The proofs of the existence of God are continuously subjected to two sorts of criticism, the details of which may sometimes coincide, though they are as different in origin as in their results.

The first of these criticisms is inspired by a strict but narrow conception of the intelligence; and if they are directed upon the proofs formulated in the past, they envisage their conceptual apparatus and their "logical forms" in a superficial way, without regard to the spirit that informs them. Criticisms of this kind are a form of historicism which becomes so literal and precise that the essentials of the doctrines which it sets out to interpret escape its grasp; it attributes a certain poverty of thought to the proof which is nothing but the poverty of its own method. . . . Criticisms of this type always lead to doubts, on the rational plane at least, about God's existence, and at the same time mutilate the intelligence itself.

The second type of criticism, on the other hand, springs from the exigencies of faith in God. It will have nothing to do with proofs which do not lead to the true God. It does not want a Cause, an End, or a Legislator whose transcendence is not assured. It is guided by the same superior instinct which motivated the proofs. It is not really a critique so much as a deepening of the proofs. It conspires with them and helps them to rectify and perfect themselves. It uncovers their real nature. It discerns and distinguishes their motivating principle. Through them the mind becomes conscious of all that is unique and complete in the various proofs, and of what gives them a force above all other proofs. Its achievement is to bring the proofs to the point at which they become one; although their expression may be marked by a particular mentality or by the state of the sciences at a particular time, the result is to bring out the supereminent and eternal validity of the activity of the mind which, without seeing God, infallibly posits his existence. That activity involves no constraint upon the mind; on the contrary, the mind cannot refuse it except by doing violence to itself and, insofar as that is possible, destroying itself.[50]

The professional who wonders "whether the proof of the existence of God can be popularized" would seem to hold that only a few specialists, technicians in the "science of metaphysics," are within their rights in affirming the existence of God with a full understanding of the issues. They alone, it would seem, are in possession of true certainty. Everybody else would be under an illusion in the matter. Intellectually, their affirmation would not be valid. At the most they might be said to benefit in the more or less remote "preparations" for the proof itself, "very useful, provided they are taken for what they are worth."

How is it that those who argue on these lines do not see that if they really believe in God they are claiming an exorbitant privilege? Or at least that they are only right from a superficial point of view?

There is, M. Jacques Maritain tells them, a "doubly natural" knowledge of God which is the fruit of the apperception of being, "much profounder than any logical process scientifically developed" because it has its roots "in

---

50. It is this meaning that would lead me to enlarge on the observation made by Chenu, *Introduction à l'étude de saint Thomas d'Aquin* (1950), p. 153: "Among the different kinds of demonstration, a completely original place must be set aside for the internal structure of certain metaphysical proceedings, such as the proof of the existence of a perfect being by means of the unequal degrees of being. This dialectic, which is at the summit of a metaphysics of participation, may certainly be expressed in the form of a syllogism. In reality the processes of the spirit are simpler and more concentrated. Here we touch on the point where the intelligence functions formally as a properly transcendent nature, and no longer as reason alone." The very depth and perfection of such a movement of spirit make for a situation where this movement is never completed once and for all. It is forever in the process of happening, just as the spirit itself is always in the process of living. It is this, it seems to me, that explains what L. B. Geiger says in a passage which is quoted by Chenu and which I as well would gladly take in a broader sense: "This process is in other respects singular in terms of another aspect, insofar as it is a departure that never fully comes to a terminal point. It must always be started again, and it is never as truly what it should be as when it creates in us the conviction both of its necessity and of its inevitable imperfection. It is a starting out that will never achieve here below the tranquillity of full possession" (*La participation dans la philosophie de saint Thomas* [1942], p. 355). But, I should add, the perfection of the proof, indeed, its sole validity, if it is true that it aims to be a proof *of God*, consists precisely of this kind of imperfection. Do we not have here a vague suggestion of the word "way," chosen by St. Thomas in his *Summa theologica*?

a single and primordial intuition."[51] Knowledge of this kind does not make the "scientific" proofs superfluous, but on the contrary it makes them possible, since that is the basic testimony which supports the proofs to which, ultimately, we must always return.[52]

There is often entertainment to be had from concentrating on certain details of our "learned" proofs, so-called. The materials used are, indeed, not uniformly solid;[53] the categories on which they rest may not always have been sufficiently well tested; the dialectical apparatus in which they are set out may be obsolete, and the subtle objection may slip through its meshes. "Sometimes [critical reflection] finds itself in the presence of a rich and profound thought which is still only implicit and unexpressed; at other times, on the contrary, it comes up against explicit formulae which claim to be authentic proofs of the existence of God, and then the formulae almost always seem vulnerable at some point or other."[54] In short, there is no guarantee that the believer who reasons will necessarily be rigorously log-

---

51. *Approches de Dieu* (1953), pp. 10, 18; cf. pp. 15-16.

52. Cf. again L. B. Geiger, "Bulletin de Philosophie," *Revue des sciences philosophiques et théologiques* (1954), p. 268: Recent works in natural theology "mark, at bottom, the abandonment of the Wolfian type of rationalism, in which metaphysical concepts must be separated as far as possible from all empirical data, and consequently also from the whole pre-philosophical life of the mind. On the contrary, it seems to us important to emphasize the whole spontaneous movement by which man rises up to God. The truly philosophical ways have no need to fear recalling their humble origins."

53. For an example taken from St. Thomas, cf. M. F. Van Steenberghen, in *L'Histoire générale de l'Église*, ed. Martin and Fliche, vol. 13 (1951), p. 254, n. 7: In the *Contra Gentiles* "the *ex parte motus* proof of God receives a development that can seem disproportionate with respect to the other ways. What is even more serious is that the explanation is still closely bound up with Aristotle's physics. These deficiencies will end up disappearing in the *Summa theologica*." Cf. M. Chossat, S.J., "Dieu," in *Dictionnaire de théologie catholique*, vol. 4, col. 932-935: "As for the argument of the prime mover such as Saint Thomas understood it, it has been a long time since it has been taught, even in the Thomist camp. . . . If the argument is taken in the sense wherein Saint Thomas borrowed it historically from the Arabs, it is not conclusive, and the criticism proffered by Scotus is decisive. . . . The Neo-Thomists, by adverting to metaphysical considerations, . . . abandon in reality the physical argument of the prime mover, just as do all the other members of the Thomistic school. . . . (The argument has only) survived in the ranks of Protestant scholasticism, among certain philosophers and well-intentioned apologists." (These reflections are, to be sure, somewhat "historicist"!)

54. F. Van Steenberghen, in *Revue philosophique de Louvain* 45 (1947), p. 166.

ical, a competent analyst, an up-to-date scholar, or a profound philosopher. Even if he reasons well, his technique may be poor. There is no reason to be ashamed of acknowledging the fact.

The point requires further consideration. Scholarly thought is in fact technical thought, and as such it is artificial in the etymological sense of the word. Now artifice, though legitimate, can always be countered, provisionally at least, by another artifice, even if a sophistical one. In order to answer the objection, greater precision and technical justifications will become necessary, while their full value may only emerge in the light of new points of view. And as a result new objections will certainly be brought forward. As Fénelon says, after making oneself "understood by the ignorant," it still remains to "answer the rash criticism of men who misuse their minds against the truth"[55] — but also to recognize the justice of new demands which may yield a positive gain. After the difficulties propounded by Locke and Hume, for example, came the difficulties, engendered by them and yet so different from theirs, put forward by Kant. Following upon these came the difficulties put forward by Hegel and so many others after him, always to some extent unforeseen — and if it is to be adequate, the answer presupposes reflections of a kind which were not previously current. And so on without end. Reason is never at the end of its tether. The dialectical chain always forges new links for itself. Mind on the march is never secure against a false step, and goes astray into many an *impasse*, but at the same time it digs down deeper within itself, and invariably discovers new sources: its life never ceases. It is an illusion to imagine it can ever be satisfied with itself.[56] And the only way of not becoming stagnant is to make the best of it. It is never possible simply to rest on the achievements of the Ancients, not even on their happiest efforts, not even if one makes every effort to assimilate their work thoroughly. That does not mean that we should disdain them or persuade ourselves into thinking that we have outstripped

---

55. *Lettres sur divers sujets de métaphysique et de religion,* Letter 2.

56. How can anyone have thought that it was perhaps "reserved for our century to arrive at fully satisfactory formulations" of the proof of God? "That," it has been said, "has nothing surprising about it if it is admitted that metaphysical knowledge in our age has for the first time reached the end of the process of its historical genesis." But that, in spite of Hegel, is precisely what one cannot easily admit. Péguy with his sound sense said: "One does not go beyond Plato." Nor, we might add, beyond St. Thomas. And on the other hand, if we are not to lose the essential, which is always threatened by new methods, new efforts must be made: the illusion noted here appears to us to add the illusion of the historical to the illusion of the definite.

them; far from it. But mere repetition is not the best way to recover their thought. The proof, in any case, remains fundamentally the same: one never gets beyond it. But the primary certainty has always to be recaptured, and in order to reestablish the simplest truths one must be prepared, in certain cases, not only for a long struggle but for unforeseen discoveries.

But meanwhile those who really believe in God will not allow themselves to be troubled. No learned objection will be able to shake their faith — whether the objection comes from the rational order, the dialectical, the psychological, or what you will. The reason for this is that the artifice developed by the learned proof is, for them, simply the elaboration and the rational organization of a permanently subsisting proof, at once simpler and more fundamental, a proof which is natural, spontaneous, and in many cases unformulated but nevertheless inscribed "in the deepest recesses of our reasonable nature," a proof which never ceases, even when the objections seem unanswerable, to engender a perfectly reasonable conviction "stronger and more unshakable than any conviction artificially formed,"[57] a proof, in fine, which is the indestructible mainspring of learned demonstration.

So, in the matter of God, whatever certain people may be tempted to think, it is never the proof which is lacking. What is lacking is taste for God.[58] The most distressing diagnosis that can be made of the present age, and the most alarming, is that to all appearances at least it has lost the taste for God. Man prefers himself to God. And so he deflects the movement which leads to God; or since he is unable to alter its direction, he persists in interpreting it falsely. He imagines he has liquidated the proofs. He concentrates on the critique of the proofs and never gets beyond them. He turns away from that which convinces him. If the taste returned, we may be sure that the proofs would soon be restored in everybody's eyes, and would seem — what they really are if one considers the kernel of them — clearer than day.

---

57. Scheeben, *Handbuch der katholischen Dogmatik*, bk. 2, *Gotteslehre*, p. 15. Cf. notes 3, 8, and 9 above. Cf. Jacques Maritain, *Approches de Dieu* (1953), p. 16: "The knowledge of God, before being developed in logical and perfectly conceptualised demonstrations, is first and foremost a natural fruit of the intuition of existence."

58. Cf. H. Geurtsen, "Les preuves de l'existence de Dieu," *Dixième congrès international de philosophie* (Amsterdam, 1948), vol. 1, p. 838: "The value of the argument does not depend upon our voluntary acceptance of it, but we consider that the inclination to accept it is the essential condition for perceiving its intellectual force."

~

"Every country has its sources of water, but the Philistine with his earthly tastes did not know how to find water everywhere. He did not know how to find reason and the Image of God in each human soul."[59]

~

At the conclusion of these two chapters devoted to the affirmation and the proof of God, in the course of which I have, at several important points, drawn on the doctrine of Joseph Maréchal and his disciples, I think it may be useful to quote two passages from his essential work, *Le point de départ de la recherche métaphysique*, bk. 5. These two passages sum up and provide a foundation for what precedes, and will help explain part of what remains to be said in the following chapter, "The Knowledge of God."

The Perspective Opened on the Internal Finality of the Intelligence as a Foundation for Our Analogical Knowledge

... But the objection springs up again as we dispose of it: all our concepts, according to the Thomist doctrine, are originally concepts of material quiddities: the contingence of created being — as revealing the divine transcendence — is given to us neither in the representation which these concepts contain, nor in their abstract and universal form: the former is only a diversified relation to the phantasm, the latter a process of objectified generalisation, which does not go beyond the level of being to which the representation belongs. There is no trace, it would appear, of a "transcendental relation" in the objective concept, such as would be metaphysical contingence of finite being.

One must admit the objection if the concept is only representation and mere generalizing abstraction. How, in fact, could the absolute and transcendent term of the contingent relationship, God, reveal itself, even by means of analogy, in finite representations or in the mere generalization of them? Does not St. Thomas tell us that the culmination of our knowledge of God is "to know that he exceeds everything that we could conceive about him"? The transcendent God cannot therefore be represented by our concepts, nor even guessed at as the limit towards which the generalization of

---

59. Origen, *In Gen.*, homily 13, n. 3 (PG 12:232-233).

our concepts tends. We should only become conscious — it would appear — of the radical contingence of created objects by escaping their finitude, by becoming conscious of the absolute super-eminence of their principle over all other possible objects of our thought. But what might that consciousness be if it is neither an intellectual intuition, nor an analysis of an intuition of the senses, nor the abstract consideration of a material form — and on what could it rest?

Thus we are faced with postulating, in our objective knowledge, something more than the static reception and the abstractive analysis of "data"; we are driven to postulate a movement of thought continually carrying us "beyond" what can be represented by concepts; to postulate a sort of metempirical anticipation which would show us the objective capacity of our intelligence to expand infinitely until it surpassed all limitation of being. Apart from that there can be no analogical knowledge of the transcendent. To explain and safeguard it we are therefore led to place ourselves on the path of the *dynamic finality* of our minds; for it is only the intelligence's "internal finality" that can enable it continually to surpass the present object and indefinitely pursue a greater object . . . (pp. 184-185).

The reader will not have failed to note a certain resemblance between this interpretation of the transcendent principle of causality — which we believe to be traditional — and the metalogical procedure of Jacobi and Gratry. According to these, the apperception of a finite object involves the affirmation of the Infinite, latent in the depths of our intelligent nature in a virtual state. That affirmation need not necessarily be perceived, but would exist in the very nature of our objective thought, or at any rate a careful analysis could reveal it.

Is the doctrine of Jacobi, or at any rate that of Gratry, true in essentials? Or is it false? We prefer to say that it is incomplete and ambiguous.

Something at the heart of our particular apperceptions must determine or necessitate the affirmation of the Absolute; otherwise we shall never be able to demonstrate analytically, starting from finite objects, the existence of the Infinite. But here, it would now seem, is the point at which a distinction becomes essential: the affirmation of the Infinite either is or is not — as implicit affirmation — a *constitutive* condition of our apperception of particular objects.

If it is not, if it is only a concomitant or a subsequent condition in relation to the primary object of our understanding, the finite object, it would imply only an act of "rational faith" in the transcendent absolute on the occasion of each of our appreciations and by virtue of a subjective necessity; the transition to the infinite would be a real "a priori synthesis," natural, legitimate even, but not justified by a genuinely speculative or scientific necessity; the understanding might, in fact, avoid the transition without becoming involved in logical contradictions.

But if it is, if, that is, the affirmation of the Infinite is a logical condition which preceded and really constitutes the apperception of finite objects, then, certainly, we can neither deny it nor withdraw it without flagrant contradiction. But it would be necessary to add, under pain of slipping into ontological intuitionism, that the transcendent affirmation which is the dynamic constitutive condition of the object thought of, has nothing in common with a "vision of objects in God" nor with an "innate idea," even a virtual one in the Cartesian sense. Purely implicit and "exercised" in the apperception of finite objects, it can be made explicit only dialectically, by reflection and analysis.

Let us try to guess what Jacobi or Gratry meant and perhaps incorrectly expressed. All that we need to conclude from the alternative given above is the following: if we opt for the first answer, in other words, if we leave the implicit affirmation of the divine Absolute outside the intelligible structure of the finite object, we shall be opposing Kant's agnostic conclusions with the simple fact of our instinctive impulse of the reason, an impulse — how ironical! — which Kant is the first to proclaim; on the contrary, if we opt for the second term, then we shall have embarked in practice on an absolute and radical refutation of Kantian agnosticism, starting from the methodological exigencies of the *Critique* itself. (Pp. 452-453)

4

The Knowledge of God

The universe through which God reveals himself is not only his work: it is his creature. It is not merely a thing which God in his omnipotence made out of nothing; and for that very reason it is a being which exists and lives only on the life and the being which it is continuously borrowing from its Author. Or rather — since the classical metaphors of "loan" and "source" are either too feeble or too strong — the universe lives and exists only in God. *In Eo vivimus et sumus.*

God is "his own being," but he is also "the being of all."[1] He is incomprehensible, inaccessible, and at the same time familiar and close to us. "The root and principle of every creature," he is the Being present *par excellence*.[2]

---

1. Pseudo-Dionysius, *Celestial Hierarchy*, 4, 1: τὸ γὰρ ε ἶναι πάντων ἔστιν[= *to gar einai pantōn estin;* "for he is the being of all"] (PG 3:177-178). John Scotus Erigena, *De divisione naturae*, bk. 1, n. 3 (PL 122:443b); n. 72 (518a). St. Bernard, *De consideratione*, bk. 5, ch. 6, n. 13: "Again what is God? — Without whom nothing exists. Just as nothing can exist without him, so he cannot exist without himself. He exists for himself no less than he exists for all things. And thus in a certain manner of speaking he is alone, for he is both his own being and that of all things" (PL 182:796a).

2. St. Thomas, *Prima*, q.8, a.1: ". . . it must be the case that God is in all things, and in an intimate way." John of St. Thomas, *Cursus theologicus, In Primam*, q.43, dissert. 17, a.3-4-11. St. Bernard, *In Cantica sermo*, 4, n. 4: "He is all in all, He who governs all, and nobody other than He owns anything in his own right. In Himself He dwells in inaccessible light, and his peace surpasses all conception. There is no way to estimate his wisdom, and his greatness has no limits. And man cannot set eyes on Him without dying. But all of this does not mean that He is far from each of us, He who is being of all being and without whom everything is mere nothingness. What is even more wonder-

God comes to us on all sides through the world; it is his Being that comes to solicit our attention. We ought to be able to meet him anywhere and recognize him everywhere. Whether we consider the "great world" or the "little world," the cosmos that surrounds us or our own spirit, everything real that comes within our orbit is by the whole of itself, and first of all by virtue of its existence, the symbol and the sign of God;[3] not an artificial sign of some kind or other, deliberately chosen and valid by convention, but a natural and, for us, a necessary symbol. It is an ontological sign which we cannot discard or emancipate ourselves from. God is not seen directly or apart from a sign; but God can be seen everywhere, through the world, however obscurely. Every creature is, in itself, a theophany. Everywhere we find traces, imprints, vestiges, enigmas; and the rays of the divinity pierce through everywhere.[4] Everything is drenched in that unique Presence. Everything becomes transparent "to a pure gaze and a steady eye."[5] If our knowledge, like our ignorance, troubles our contemplation, if our mind's eye cannot see beyond the outer shell of the world, if we are open to nothing sacred — or if, on the contrary, the world seems "full of gods" — that is because our sight is blurred. It is only too

---

ful, nothing is at once more present than He is and also more ungraspable [*incomprehensibilius*]. What indeed is there that is more present to each being than his own being? And what is there, moreover, that is more ungraspable to each being than the being of all? Most certainly, when I say that God is the being of all, I do not intend to say that all are what He is; but all are from him, and by him, and in him . . ." (PL 183:798a-b).

3. Cf. Godfrey of St. Victor, *Microcosmus*, c. 40 (ed. Philippe Delhaye [1951], p. 61), etc.

4. Pius IX, *Letter to Bishop de la Bouillerie* (Castel-Gandolfo, 30 July 1864): "[For the blindness of men who have forgotten God] there is no better remedy than to present to souls the light of the Creator as reflected in material creation. Rewakened and recalled by the work to a consideration of the worker, they will come to understand that the Creator is more powerful than the creature, and will come to know how much the one who governs created things surpasses them in beauty. . . . This is a difficult task, which requires a profound knowledge of Sacred Letters and a perfect understanding of the multiple meanings to be found therein (whether it is the Holy Spirit himself who provides these for us or whether we must seek them in the learned interpretations of the Holy Fathers). For these meanings teach us, under the appearance of material objects, to discover more that is of a spiritual and heavenly significance. . . . May the beaming rays of the Godhead, to use a phrase of St. Bernard, which burst forth from all of this creation that is so various and so beautiful in all its diverse forms, strike the eyes of the blind . . ." (In Bishop de la Bouillerie's *Symbolisme de la Nature*). Notice how the Pope's pen yokes together two sets of symbols, from nature and the Bible.

5. Paul Claudel.

true; the world conceals God more than it reveals him. Things have become opaque. And yet it remains true that the Creator "has scattered the reflections of his divine perfections upon his creatures, and that thanks to those visible lights we are able to know, by analogy, the splendours of the inaccessible Creator."[6] *Invisibilia Dei per ea quae facta sunt intellecta conspiciuntur.*[7] (The invisible things of God are made known by the things which are made.)

"O Thou who appearest through every form and structure without adhering to them or being confounded with them!"

From this it follows, in the first place, that the knowledge of God which comes to us through the external world is itself, in a sense, a revelation:

---

6. Théodore de Régnon, S.J., *Etude sur la Sainte Trinité*, vol. 3 (1898), p. 458.

7. St. Paul, Romans 1:20. St. Augustine, *Confessions*, bk. 7, ch. 17, n. 23; ch. 10, n. 16; bk. 9, ch. 10, n. 24. Hugh of St. Victor, *Didascalion*, bk. 7, ch. 4: "For the whole sensible world is like a book, as it were, written by the hand of God, that is to say, created by divine power, and each of its creatures are like forms, devised not by human effort, but rather established by the divine will in order to make manifest the wisdom of the invisible things of God, etc." (PL 176: 814b). Baldwin of Canterbury, *Liber de sacramento altaris:* Creatures are "mystical likenesses, as it were, in which the invisible things of God are caught sight of" (PL 204:744d). Robert of Melun, *In Rom.* 1, 20. St. John of the Cross, *Spiritual Canticle* (ed. Dom Chevalier, p. 51), etc.

Such texts indicate a long tradition of thought and exegesis. It would be, in fact, to limit the sense of the Pauline assertion if we were to exclude from it what may be called the symbolic or exemplarist element, seeing in it only an indication of a proof of existence. Cf. Origen, *De Principiis*, bk. 1, ch. 3, n. 1 (ed. Koetschau, p. 49), etc. It is not only in the ancient tradition, but also among quite a few of the great theologians of the thirteenth century and in particular in the work of St. Thomas (cf. "Abyssus abyssum invocat," above, note 12) that we find that symbolism "maintains and enhances the resources of religious intelligibility around knowledge and learning. We have, indeed, a curious coupling of Aristotelian theory regarding the sensible with the mystagogy of Dionysius. It was not until the Cartesian period that symbolism was ejected from theology and reserved for the use of mystics" (M.-D. Chenu, *Introduction à l'étude de saint Thomas d'Aquin,* pp. 48-49). Cf. Albert Béguin, *L'âme romantique et le rêve*, 2nd ed., p. 51: ". . . Cartesian and post-Cartesian philosophy had triumphed over this 'analogical' and 'symbolist' knowledge, which, after it had been expelled from any meditation on higher things, proceeded to return to the hidden stream of superstition and occult teachings, where it seems that human thought must every so often be invigorated in order to correct the pure rationalism whither its inclinations easily sweep it along." Alas!

For the meaning of the word "symbolism," reference should be made to the explanations given above in Chapter 1, note 10.

The greatness and the beauty of creatures
Make us, by analogy, contemplate their Author.[8]

It is an objective revelation just as natural reason is in itself, as we have seen, a subjective revelation. There is a double and unique natural revelation, a gift of the sign and of the capacity to interpret it, a gift of the book and of the capacity to read it. For it is not my mind which first rises from the world to God: it is God who first descends, in some sort, through the world to my mind. However spontaneously it may come to me, the proof comes only in the second instance. The proof is my construction, but the sign which precedes it and already contains it, which allows it, provokes it, sets it in motion, and always overflows it, is given me by another. In all truth, God *makes me a sign*.[9] The first language he uses to communicate with me is his creation. Being created by the Word, everything which comes from him is a word and speaks of him. It is for me to attend and to answer — but the initiative is not mine.

By that very fact, such knowledge of God the creator, though always mediated, is not entirely indirect. To borrow a word from St. Augustine,

---

8. Wisdom of Solomon 13:5. This is a text that has been repeatedly adverted to and commented on, notably by Leo XIII in the encyclical *Aeterni Patris* (*Acta Leonis XIII* [Rome, 1881], p. 268). Cf. St. Thomas, *In Rom.*, ch. 1, lectio 6. St. Hilary, *De Trinitate*, bk. 1, ch. 7 (PL 10:30). Angelus Silesius, *The Cherubic Pilgrim*, bk. 2, n. 48:

> The hidden God makes himself familiar and knowable
> On the part of his creatures, who bear his stamp.

See also bk. 4, n. 164b, and bk. 5, n. 86.

9. God manifests his wisdom through his visible creatures as by so many signs — just as one man communicates his thought to another by the signs of language: St. Thomas, *In Epist. ad Romanos*, ch. 1, lectio 6. St. Maximus Confessor (PG 91:1328). Cf. M.-E. Boismard, O.P., *Le Prologue de Saint Jean* (1953), pp. 111, 113, 114: "The first phase of divine revelation by the Word was the work of creation; the Bible, indeed, teaches us that the world was created by the Word of God, and that is why . . . the Bible can say, as well, that creation was a revelation. . . . Creation is thus the work of the Word of God, and it is for this reason that it is also a revelation, for God, in speaking, can only call forth himself. The world carries in itself the reflection and the image of the Word by which it was created. . . . In creating the world, God has thereby infused in it a message that men should be able to read. . . . But in fact, as the author of the biblical book of The Wisdom of Solomon and Saint Paul both affirm, this first divine 'revelation' ends up in failure and defeat, etc." Cf. Hans Urs von Balthasar, *Theologik 1. Wahrheit der Welt,* 2nd ed. (1985), pp. 105ff. It could also be said, if we recur to an old word that is nowadays no longer in use, that the world is a "signature" of God.

one might call it *contuitio*. God, in a sense, invests me with his signs, and I perceive him in his creation — until such a time as I can see his creation in him. But that knowledge is always obscure[10] owing to the weakness of my intelligence,[11] though it is nonetheless concrete, in principle, even when it follows the paths of logic and abstraction, because it is the knowledge of a *Presence*. Reasoning by itself, supposing that the initiative were entirely mine, reasoning to which I was not provoked, and which was not the result of a stimulus or an essential impulse, would give me only a completely indirect and wholly abstract knowledge. It would supply me only with a pure concept, taking the place of an *absent* being — or rather an absent thing. Yet in fact, the true God reveals himself as present under cover of the abstraction which derives from me.

Indeed, if, *per impossibile,* God were present in me only as a pure abstraction, in the form of a concept, then granted that any representation of God is totally inadequate, it might be asked how I could possibly avoid agnosticism.[12] Several people have asked the question without finding the answer. On such a hypothesis, my knowledge would be empty. But in fact the hypothesis is empty. For *there is always more in the concept than the concept itself,*[13] and that is what the critics of the concept forget, as well as

---

10. St. Bonaventure, *In Hexaemeron,* collatio 13, n. 14: "The whole world is a shadow, a way, the trace of a footprint, and is a book that is written from the outside. For in each and every creature there is a gleam of the divine exemplar, even though this gleam is thoroughly intermingled with darkness. Wherefore it is just like a patch of shade, as it were, mixed with light" (Quaracchi, vol. 5, p. 386).

11. St. Thomas, *De Veritate,* q.5, a.2, ad 11m: ". . . the weakness of our intellect, which is not capable of receiving from creatures all that information about God which creatures manifest concerning him."

12. As can be seen, the phrase is not in the indicative, and does not refer to the real. It expresses a hypothesis, which it declares at the same time false and impossible. In the language of the schools, we should say it is a *videtur quod non* [= "it does not seem that"], which is bound up with the answer to it. One must apologize for giving such explanations, which are unnecessary for most readers.

13. In this way the whole conceptual order can be found truly justified. The value of this conceptual order would, on the other hand, be compromised if it were to be seen only as a kind of atomic entity, cut off from the deep currents of the intellectual life. For this would mean rendering oneself incapable of establishing it in the realm of the absolute. Once again, this had been acutely seen by Joseph Maréchal, when he spoke of the "transcendental necessity that is implicit in the whole concept" and when he added: "It would be impossible to justify this transcendental analogy of being if the dynamic background on which the formal content of human thought, which is so infinitely diverse, were not recognized. . . . To recognize in each of these concepts, as a

many of its defenders. That is what enables me to understand that the knowledge of God remains concealed beneath the need to criticize any representation of God. All the negations which accumulate and appear to be purely destructive are, in the end, at the service of an affirmation both stronger and purer than they. If God conceals himself, it is in his very presence. His transcendence does not mean that he is exiled from the world; it is the exact opposite of an absence.[14] Every creature reveals him by virtue of the being it borrows from him, crying out that it is not he. Such is the mystery which, in spite of its obscurity, is always a light; the emptiness which it demands of us is the form of his Fullness.[15]

---

condition of its partial truth, a requirement of truth, which infinitely surpasses all possible conceptual expressions, is to lay the foundations of a general theory of analogy and of a metaphysics of transcendence" (*Nouvelle revue théologique* [1931], pp. 193,197). The sentiments of André Bremond ("Une dialectique thomiste du retour à Dieu," p. 575) are quite similar, colored as they are by the vivid humor with which he is graced: "Unless ontology admits, at the outset, of that dynamism of being or if it does not discover it, at least, along the way, it is doomed to be a mere aggregation, rather than a ballet, of anemic categories. To what end would these categories take the trouble to dance?"

See also, from another point of view, Etienne Gilson, *Le Thomisme*, 4th edition, p. 65: If the universal concept of being "is the opposite of an empty notion," it is so by reason "of all the judgements of existence that it recapitulates and that it connotes, but even more so on account of its permanent reference to the infinitely rich reality of the pure act of existing." We find analogous remarks, albeit less precise, in Théodore de Régnon, *Etude sur la Sainte Trinité*, first series (1892), p. 21. Is there really any need to specify that in all these texts, including our own, there is no question of anything supernatural?

14. Cf. Chenu, *Introduction*, p. 161: "Which is to say in this case how different, both technically and spiritually, the God of Aristotle and the God of St. Thomas are, inasmuch as there is a difference between the Aristotelian proof of the prime mover, ontologically absent from everything else, and the Thomistic way which wends towards the *Ipsum Esse subsistens* [= "Being subsisting in itself"], whose presence the being of things reveals by its very deficiency."

15. Etienne Gilson, *Le Thomisme*, p. 11: "In positing his immovable Prime Mover as a Thought which thinks of itself, Aristotle had guaranteed the purity of the supreme Action by enclosing it in the splendor of divine isolation. Aristotle's God is not simply 'separate' insofar as he is ontologically distinct from everything else, but rather insofar as he is ontologically absent from everything else. The only mode of presence to things which is proper to him is the desire that these things experience and that moves them towards him. Now this desire for God is their desire. It *is* indeed a desire for the being that they experience, not for the being that is their end term. Things are completely otherwise in the world of St. Thomas. There the relationship of things to their principle achieves a degree of depth that could not be expressed in the language of Aristotle or

Patet quam ampla sit via illuminationis, et quomodo in omni re quae sentitur sive quae cognoscitur, interius lateat ipse Deus.[16] (It is clear how broad is the way of illumination, and how, in everything that is perceived or known, God himself lies hidden.)

∞

The hidden God, the mysterious God, is not distant and absent: he is always the God who is near.

∞

Unable to think of God as he is, we take the course, which is as wise as it is humble, once it is properly understood, of conceiving him as like ourselves. We take the qualities which we attribute to him from our relation to him, and as those relations are real, what we say is true, although as definitions they are inadequate to the point of being worthless.[17]

---

even in the language of Plato. It is through its very existence that the universe of St. Thomas is a sacred universe, and thus a religious universe." And also page 144: "It is this world that is the world of Saint Thomas Aquinas, a world wherein it is a marvellous thing to have been born, wherein the distance which separates the least of beings from nothingness is quite properly speaking infinite, a sacred world, which is imbued right down to its most secret and intimate roots, with the presence of a God whose sovereign existing saves it permanently from nothingness.

16. St. Bonaventure, *De reductione artium ad theologiam*. St. Anselm, *Monologion*, ch. 13: ". . . It is a necessity that, just as nothing was made except through his creative, present essence, nothing should thrive except through the saving presence of the same" (PL 158:161a-b). St. Augustine, *De Musica*, bk. 6, ch. 13, n. 40: "Since, therefore, (the soul) is nothing of herself, whatever being she possesses comes from God; even while she remains in her own order, she is invigorated by the presence of God with respect to both her mind and consciousness. And so she enjoys this good deep within herself."

17. A. D. Sertillanges, O.P., in *Saint Thomas, Somme théologique, Dieu*, vol. 3, p. 343. Cf. p. 340: "God is unknowable in the sense that our words and conceptions do not in any way define him. They do not convey anything which is in him such as we would convey it. They do not exceed, as a meaningful value, the affirmation of his very necessity and the ineffable fulness which allows him to play, in all those indefinable realms, the role which belongs to him who is ultimately Necessary, Prime, and Sovereign. Nevertheless, God, who is thus unknowable in himself, is not thereby unknowable in every way. The conceptions that we form about him are not arbitrary. These conceptions are proper to him by reason of a certain relationship, one that is *definite on our part*, between the derivative by-ways from which we draw our concepts and the supreme Source. . . ." Thus, every name that is given to God expresses "the necessary postulate of a true

It is a wise course, and the knowledge it gives us is true knowledge, because the course we follow is inspired by a deeper thought and because our knowledge is lit by a more secret light.

Those who uphold immanence deny transcendence, whereas those who believe in transcendence do not deny immanence. Indeed, they grasp the idea of transcendence sufficiently to understand that it necessarily implies immanence. If God is transcendent, then nothing is opposed to him, nothing can limit him nor be compared with him: he is "wholly other," and therefore penetrates the world absolutely. *Deus interior intimo meo et superior summo meo* . . .

The champion of exclusive immanence thus reveals his partiality. Only the champion of transcendence is impartial, like the truth itself.

The champion of immanence refuses to consider transcendence except as a spatial image dominating a thought which is thenceforward purely mythical. He really claims the exclusiveness of the *logos*. And yet unless he is prepared to end up with the absolute emptiness of being and thought he remains the prisoner of his imagination, no less than his opponent: the "inside" is no less spatial than the "outside" or the "beyond." *A priori* there is no reason, for example, to regard it as "the concave spatial aspect" of a sphere. . . . And if "height" is an imaginative concept, so is "depth." And however subtle the form, immanentism itself might well be an "inverted spatial prejudice."[18] From whichever angle

---

relationship." Cf. St. John Damascene, *De fide orthodoxa*, bk. 1, ch. 4: "Everything that we say in positive terms about God does not assert his nature, but rather asserts that which encompasses his nature" (PG 94:800). And St. Jerome, *In Isaiam* 6: ". . . Not according to that which God is, but according to that which he deigns to show of himself to his creatures" (*Analecta Maredsolana*, vol. 3, ch. 2, p. 108).

18. The objection was formulated by Leon Brunschvicg, "La querelle de l'athéisme," Société française de philosophie (24 March 1928) (text reproduced in *De la vraie et de la fausse conversion*, 1950). For him "the hypothesis of a spiritual transcendence is a manifest contradiction in terms" (p. 209). (Cf. *Transcendance et Religion*, p. 127: "On the one hand, the realism of a transcendence which is born of a *lofty* imagination; on the other hand, the idealism of an immanence which is preceded by *deep* reflection.") Gabriel Marcel made the following observation about this issue: "I cannot help fearing that this cult of interiority . . . is, in spite of everything, an inverted spatial prejudice" (p. 249). Etienne Gilson, as well, had denounced the "tiresome confusion" in Leon Brunschvicg, a confusion that had long ago been cleared up by thinkers such as St. Augustine and St. Thomas: "The hypothesis of a spiritual transcendence is only contra-

one considers the question, a critique of the imagination becomes necessary.[19]

Locales quidem excedit [Deus] temporalesque angustias, sed libertate naturae, non enormitate substantiae! [20] (God exceeds the bounds of time and space, but through the supreme freedom of his being, not through the size of his substance!)

The champions of immanence are nourished by the illusion that by "interiorizing" the faith of those who believe in transcendence, they become the ultimate interpreters of a prophet who did not see where his intuition was leading him. In that way they believe they can ensure the transition from belief to philosophy and from spontaneity to reflection. In their disdain, wedded to a comprehensive indulgence — of which the history of thought offers many an example — they imagine they can justify the believer and criticize him at the same time. They think they can transform a relative truth into an absolute truth. But the attempt, also witnessed by the history of thought, to find a new "overall" concept, a new "beyond," a new transcendence within immanence itself, an attempt which is always being renewed and is always unsuccessful, bears witness again in favor of the believer. Transcendence always has the last word. And the victory of transcendence consolidates immanence — the two ideas are "as though woven together" — though its significance is altered.

---

dictory to reason when it is the imagination that realizes it. But the constant philosophical and theological teaching of Christianity consists precisely of the refusal to accept such a realization as satisfactory" (pp. 218-219).

19. And this criticism will perhaps finally recognize that the elevation and the movement of transcendence are not so much the primary data of sensibility, subsequently transposed by a questionable analogy of an imaginative order, as values directly perceived, by means of a spontaneous ontological symbolism, in the object of sense itself. For the history and use of the words "transcendent" and "transcendental," see Jean Wahl, *Traité de metaphysique* (1953), pp. 642-649. On transcendence and exteriority cf. St. Augustine, *De diversis quaestionibus*, 83, p. 29: "Is there anything 'high' and 'low' in the universe?"

20. St. Bernard of Clairvaux, *De consideratione*, bk. 5, ch. 13, n. 28 (PL 182:805b). St. Augustine, *Confessions*, bk. 1, ch. 3: ". . . You fill up the things which you fill up by containing them. For the vessels which are full of you do not render you stable, since, even though they may be broken, you are not poured out. And when you are poured out on us, you do not lie spilled, nor are you dispersed, but you gather us together" (ed. P. de Labriolle, vol. 1, p. 4).

God is wholly within and wholly without, supereminent and yet intimate, surrounding us yet present in us.

There is nothing above him, nothing outside him, nothing without him. Beneath him, in him and with him are all things. . . .[21]

He is everywhere in his entirety, one and the same . . . penetrating all things by engulfing them, engulfing them by penetrating them. . . .[22]

---

21. St. Hilary, *De Trinitate*, bk. 1, ch. 6 (PL 10:29), commenting on the following two verses from Isaiah: "Qui tenet caelum palma pugilo" (= "Who has measured the waters in the hollow of his hand and marked off the heavens with a span" [Isaiah 40:12; RSV]) and "Caelum mihi thronus est, terra autem scabellum pedum meorum" (= "Heaven is my throne, and the earth is my footstool" [Isaiah 66:1; RSV]). St. Ambrose, *De Fide*, bk. 1, ch. 16, n. 106 (PL 16:553): "God who fills up everything, who is in no wise mixed in and confused with everything else, who penetrates everything, without being himself penetrated by anything, who is everywhere wholly complete, etc." St. Augustine, *Soliloquies*, bk. 1, ch. 1, n. 4 (ed. P. de Labriolle, p. 32). *In Psalmum*, 130, n. 12: "God is lofty within and spiritually lofty; nor does the soul succeed in touching him unless it surpasses itself" (PL 37:1712). *De Trinitate*, bk. 5, ch. 1, n. 2: ". . . presiding without a fixed situation, containing all things without a fixed state, everywhere whole and entire without occupying a place, eternal without the benefit of time . . ." (PL 42:912). *De Genesi ad litteram*, bk. 8, ch. 26 (PL 34:391). *Epistula*, 187, ch. 4, n. 14 (PL 33:837). Pseudo-Augustine, *Liber meditat.*, ch. 3: "When he is within, he is not enclosed and confined, while when he is on the outside, he is not shut out and excluded" (PL 40:924).

22. St. Gregory the Great, *Moralia in Job*, bk. 2, ch. 12, n. 20: "Indeed he remains within everything, he is outside of everything, he is above everything, he is below everything. And he is high above in terms of his power, low down in terms of his upholding of things, outer in his great trappings of majesty, inner in his delicate subtlety. Reigning on high and holding things together below, engulfing from without, penetrating from within. Neither superior on the one hand and inferior on the other; or exterior on the one hand and interior on the other; but he is everywhere in his entirety, one and the same, sustaining things by presiding over them, presiding over them by sustaining them, penetrating all things by engulfing them, engulfing them by penetrating them." Cf. bk. 5, ch. 42; bk. 16, ch. 28 (PL 75:713, 1140).

This text was often taken up and adapted in the Middle Ages. St. Isidore of Seville, *Sententiae*, bk. 1, ch. 2, n. 2 (PL 83:541). John of Fécamp, *Contemplativa oratio ad Deum Summam Trinitatem*: ". . . Thus you are inside and outside, above and below; above in terms of your reigning, below in terms of your bearing and carrying things, inside in terms of your filling up and restoring things, outside through your engulfing them; and so you are strength so that you may be outside, thus you engulf so that you may penetrate, thus you preside over so that you may carry and uphold, thus do you carry and uphold so that you may preside over. . . ." (Ed. J. Leclercq, *Studia Anselmiana*, vol. 20, p. 99.) (See also his Letter to an abbot of the eleventh century: "Unfathomable God . . . , who fill up your works both outside and inside, you reign above and uphold

    I went into the higher part of myself, and higher still I found the Kingdom of the Word. Impelled by curiosity to explore still further, I descended deep into myself, and yet I found him deeper still. I looked outside, and met him far beyond everything exterior to me. I looked within: he is more inward than I myself. — And I recognised the truth of what I had read, that we live and move and have our being in him. . . .²³

    "The function of art," Léon Bloy wrote, "is to fashion gods." It is the function, too, of thought, and of the higher realm of human activity which is that of the "poet."

    But in addition to the *poet* who fashions the gods, there is also the *prophet* who receives the revelation of God. The sculptor of idols who gives

---

from below. . . .") St. Anselm, *Monologion*, ch. 14: ". . . He himself is [the creating and nurturing essence] which upholds and surpasses all other things, enclosing them and penetrating them" (PL 158:1, 161c). Hildebert of Lavardin, *Carmina miscellanea*, 71:

> Alpha and Omega, great God . . .
> Above everything, below everything;
> Outside of everything, within everything:
> Within everything, but not contained,
> Outside of everything, but not excluded,
> Above everything, but not raised up,
> Below everything, but not underlying.
> Wholly above in your presiding over;
> Wholly below in your upholding;
> Wholly outside of in your enfolding;
> You are wholly within in your filling up.
> Within you are never abridged,
> On the outside you are never expanded,
> Above you are supported by no one,
> Below you are wearied by no one. . . .

(*Oratio devotissima ad tres Personas sanctissimae Trinitatis ad Patrem* [PL 171:1411]). Hermann of St.-Martin, *Tractatus de Incarnatione Christi*, ch. 1 (PL 180:12d). William of Auxerre, *Summa*, bk. 1, ch. 15 (fol. 34b). St. Albert the Great, *In Sent.*, d.37, a.21 (*Opera*, vol. 26, p. 251). Alexander of Hales, *Summa theologica*, vol. 1, pp. 68, 71, etc. As early as Seneca in his *Naturales Quaestiones* 1, praef. 13: ". . . he keeps up his work both inwardly and outwardly."

23. St. Bernard of Clairvaux, *In Cantica*, sermo 74 (PL 183:1141).

form to the gods is balanced by the iconoclast who refuses to allow God to be immured in a form. There is the intellectual who organizes his thoughts into a body of thought, and there is the mystic who rejects them as they take shape, or rather from whom they are gradually withdrawn.

This opposition between different types of men is surely one of the fundamental aspects of the conflict between Hellenism and Judaism which can be followed down to modern times. But it is also an opposition within man himself which cannot be resolved, a tragic but fruitful confrontation. Here it is impossible to make a definitive choice without sacrificing something essential. The poet is a man who "has dreams" and who "declares the visions of his heart," who is always in danger of becoming a "false prophet" if he proclaims them as truths received from above.[24] Nevertheless, the prophet needs the poet — and is a poet himself in his own way — because man cannot receive anything into his mind without collaborating with his own thought: even the object of revelation must, after all, be *conceived*. In the same way the mystic needs the intellectual because detachment from defined forms — *videntur ut paleae* — presupposes the work which constructs those forms, and the judgment which acknowledges their value. So the conflict cannot end in the victory of either side. It must be transformed into harmony. It must become a rhythm — and mirror the rhythm first sounded by the incarnation, death, and resurrection of the Savior.

> Things *mean* God; but they do not "express" him; nothing can express him but himself. Spirit, too, would express him and never succeeds. But it affirms his existence as the presence of a limit beyond our reach, towards which the world in the course of its existence is for ever in movement, a sort of marvellous obstacle which cannot yet be seen, but is announced and indicated beforehand by a signal. The spirit alone has a presentiment of its end deep within itself, for it is made for and launched upon the path to God and can become conscious of its movement. Although that consciousness hardly counts until the things of the world make their signs.[25]

24. Jeremiah 23:16-28.
25. Hubert Paissac, O.P., *Le Dieu de Sartre* (1950), pp. 75ff.

The further one gets from the *He*, the more vividly one realizes the *Thou* — and through the *Thou* its necessary correlative, the *I*. Immanence and exteriority develop together. Reflection, far from dissolving or annihilating personal being, gives it a foundation. That is the principle misunderstood by idealism, which has never conceived of any relationship except that of a knowing "subject" and a known "object."

But the exteriority thus established is not, as can be seen, something "objective": it exists within an "inter-subjectivity." It is not the exteriority of a *He* — which would soon be degraded into an *it* — but that of the *Thou par excellence*. It is not the exteriority of an object which one dominates — which can be annihilated in imagination — but that of a subject to which one gives oneself, in which one finds oneself, which one has to think of as subsistent. That subject is in truth the *Other*, in the strongest possible sense of the word: the absolute Other, the mysterious Being enclosed within itself, always beyond our grasp, the totally personal Being, "the only *Thou* which, by definition, cannot become *That*."[26] He who cannot be represented, but whose reality is all the more compelling; through the knowledge of whom we become conscious of ourselves, and through love of whom we possess ourselves; whereas, as long as one clung to the representation, it only bred an illusory "other" without inwardness, without mystery, and without real fruitfulness for the subject. Idealism was then right perhaps to reduce that "other," by absorbing the object in the subject or the world into the representation — without succeeding, however, in providing a basis for an *I*, a real personal Subject.

There is no unique subject: no personality without otherness; no consciousness turned in upon itself; no real being without intersubjectivity;[27] no real knowledge nor ontological density without mystery. And no man without God.

Are we really to believe that if "many Christians" like to see their God as the "Thou" *par excellence*, it is because they "no longer dare to say 'He,' as they do of a being"? Is it true that "by making God 'Thou' in the dialogue we call prayer, they compound with the view that the structure of our consciousness requires the presence of others, and so only appears to attain

---

26. Martin Buber, *I and Thou* [German citation = *Werke*, vol. 1. *Schriften zur Philosophie: Ich und Du*, 3. Teil (1962), p. 128.]

27. Gabriel Marcel, *Le mystère de l'être*, vols.1 and 2 (1950 and 1951).

God as part of the human"?²⁸ The criticism is too subtle and the analysis very imperfect. Why should the speaker to whom one says "thou" be "a part of the human" any more than the object addressed as "it"? Why should dialogue find its explanation in ourselves any more than representation? If there is "intentionality" in all knowledge, which modern philosophy stupidly ignored and which contemporary phenomenology is helping it to rediscover, it may well be that this "intentionality" is expressed more forcibly in dialogue which puts the subject into direct relationship with another subject. In any case, prayer — whether it is petition, adoration, or abandonment — is not just any sort of dialogue; the reciprocity which it implies does not imply equality, as the believer who turns to God in prayer knows well enough, even if he has no aptitude for philosophical reflection. In point of fact, those who speak of God — rightly or wrongly — as a "Thou" rather than as a "He" are not betraying their timidity. Even if they insist on this distinction in too exclusive a spirit, their purpose is certainly to safeguard the idea of the divine transcendence by refusing to speak of Being as "a being." When they establish the relationship of prayer with him, they affirm both their own dependence upon him and his independence of them. By refusing to immure him in the "object" their intention is clearly to liberate him from what is human.²⁹

If God is already known in some way in our knowledge of duty (even by those who think themselves unable to see him and call themselves atheists), it may be said that God is found and possessed in some way in the fulfillment of duty.

However, that can be said only upon one condition. For there are two ways of acknowledging duty and consequently two ways of fulfilling it. In order that the knowledge and possession of God which goes with the knowledge and fulfillment of duty should not remain purely implicit,³⁰

---

28. Ferdinand Alquié, "Solitude de la raison," *Deucalion*, 1, p. 188.
29. Cf. Simon Frank, *Dieu est avec nous. Trois méditations* (French translation from the Russian manuscript, 1955), p. 71: "We can only speak of someone who is absent in the third person. . . . Before the face of God we can only speak to God and not engage in reasoning about him. . . . The God of a living faith is always *my* God. 'God-with-me' is a being whom only the vocative case can express."
30. It should be noted that this does not apply to all natural knowledge of God, but solely to the knowledge in question, implied by knowledge of moral duty when it is fully grasped. The fact that there is, on the other hand, knowledge of God that is both

duty must be regarded not as a purely formal law in the Kantian sense, but as the *requirement of the Good*. Only then can there be any question of getting beyond that abstraction "the natural law" and of making room for the real God, even in the case of those who do not yet know his name.

"Independently of the realization in action of any explicitly conscious knowledge," the intelligence has therefore "a vital and non-conceptual knowledge (of God) enveloped in the practical notion — vaguely and intuitively grasped, but with all its intentional power — of the moral good as the formal motive of the first free act, and in the movement of the will towards that good, and at the same time towards the good itself." By committing himself and choosing, man "thinks of what is good and of what is evil; but by the same token he knows God without being aware of it, because by virtue of the inward dynamism of his choice of the good for the sake of the Good, he desires and loves the transcendent Good as the final end of his own existence."[31]

In doing so he transcends the idea of a "natural" God, the author and extrinsic sanction of the Law, or mere pattern of moral value. For the Good, which *ex hypothesi* the moral agent recognizes in practice as a demand upon himself, the Good to which he secretly gives his adherence, is, as we have just seen, the "Good which subsists separately," and nothing else. It is the "ultimate Good," in reality God, "in whom, whether he knows it or not, he places his last End." It is the God who *is* the last End, and therefore the God of grace.

In other words, the God who reveals himself implicitly in this way to the man of good will — still unable to name God — is the God who is not content to command man, but draws him and desires to draw him even to himself, the God, according to St. Thomas, for whom man makes his first free choice when he turns towards the good,[32] in such a way that "the first deliberate act of the will, the first act of the moral life, in the strict sense of the word, is steeped in the mystery of grace."[33] That is the God who, in

---

natural and explicit is stated by me in other contexts. On the relationship between the knowledge of duty and the knowledge of God, cf. Yves de Montcheuil, S.J., "Dieu et la vie morale," *Mélanges théologiques* (2nd ed., 1951), pp. 141-157.

31. Jacques Maritain, *Raison et raisons*, pp. 137-139.

32. That is why St. Thomas, when he speaks of the awakening of the moral conscience, considers that the choice made in this case is a welcoming or a refusal of grace, that it justifies or that it condemns: *Prima Secundae*, q.89, a.6; cf. *De Veritate*, q.24, a.12, ad 2m; *De Malo*, q.5, a.2, ad 8m; q.7, a.10, ad 8m; *In 2 Sent.*, d. 42, q.1, a.5, ad 7m.

33. Cf. Jacques Maritain, *Neuf leçons sur les notions premières de la philosophie morale* (Cours et documents series, 1951), p. 123 and p. 127: "Indeed, the child . . . who chooses

Pascal's words, "makes the soul feel that he is its sole good and that it cannot rest except in the love of him."

The greater the mystery, the more the imagination will see its irreplaceable role grow, once it is recognized for what it is.

We know, for example, that our God is a personal God. For "being has the countenance of a person."[34] There is no temptation to turn back to the nature myths of so many religions, nor to their philosophical counterparts. But once this is admitted and clearly established, it remains true that analogies from "nature" are more evocative than "personal" analogies — simply because they are more distant. They may even help to purify the analogical method. The analogy from nature is "the natural cure and the normal complement which our feeble spiritual development requires."[35]

In order to understand the importance of symbol and metaphor where knowledge is concerned, one must bear in mind the law that suggestion is in inverse proportion to the definition, and the value of an evocation is in

---

to direct his activity towards that which is good and honorable inasmuch as this is a universal Value, and who chooses, at the same time, by virtue of a dynamism that can remain unconscious in him, to direct his activity towards God as the final End, this child, I say, makes such a choice by virtue of divine grace, and he tends towards his final end by the theological virtue of charity. Thus the first act etc." By the same author: *Raison et raisons*, pp. 131-165: "La Dialectique immanente du premier acte de liberté." Charles Journet, *Vérité de Pascal* (1951), p. 191, note (according to Maritain): ". . . real but preconceptual knowledge of the Good as a refuge and salvation, that is to say, of God as Savior."

34. André Marc, S.J., *Dialectique de l'affirmation* (1952), p. 605; cf. Louis Lavelle, *De l'Acte*, p. 63: the person expresses "the deepest essence of being."

35. Charles de Moré-Pontgibaud, S.J., "Sur l'analogie des noms divins, l'analogie métaphorique," *Recherches de science religieuse* (1952), p. 182. Cf. pp. 166, 173: "The metaphor (like the symbol) is presented as manifesting the connection between an inferior scheme of reality and a superior one, which the former suggests powerfully, but does not in any way, properly speaking, contain. Between that which is represented and that which is aimed at there is at once a close relationship and a manifest heterogeneity, a harmony and a 'break', — which is witnessed to once again by the word, itself, which is full of the significance of transposition. . . . In this process our minds can draw on incomparable resources so as to become conscious of the reality of the supreme object, of the living forces that are available in order to orient ourselves to it, — but, if we used it without discernment and in the prevailing fashion, we would expose ourselves to all the confusions and all the errors engendered by this failure to make an essential distinction."

inverse proportion to the value of thought.³⁶ One must also remember that law in order to appreciate the language of the mystics. Then we shall not be disturbed by a progression which, to our logic, seems to move in reverse. "O Father, Spouse, Brother," the mystic exclaims; then, as the movement of his contemplative love reaches its term, "O deep, calm River, devouring Fire, Light of all lights!"³⁷

To be honest, one would be hard put to say precisely which of the "divine attributes" was intended by the word "light." In the first instance, no doubt, it evokes the limpid transparency of a knowledge which penetrates the whole of reality without effort — but it also qualifies the purity of an essence which the shadow of nothingness has never darkened: "God is light, and there is no darkness in him." But in addition to the qualities which may be called "external," the word "light" helps us to realize the expansive power and the radiation of a sovereign Spirit, in the absence of which all other spirits would be benighted, and in a more general way to realize the triumphant, superabounding manifestation which we call "Glory." "Light" communicates fluidity and splendor to all these aspects of infinite Being which conceptual analysis and definitions threaten with extinction; it binds them together, develops them, and enfolds them in the mystery of beatitude.³⁸

36. Cf. Frithjof Schuon, *De l'unité transcendante des religions* (1948), pp. 76-77: "The highest realities manifest themselves the most openly in their furthest-removed effect . . ."; p. 163, n. 2: ". . . the position of being an analogical polar opposite, which sensible forms enjoy vis-a-vis intellections. . . ." Certain consequences which the author draws from this principle belong to his special system. Jean Trouillard, "Le Cosmos du Pseudo-Denys," *Revue de théologie et de la philosophie* (1955), p. 56: "The most disparate symbols are the best, because they do not run the risk of arresting the soul's enthusiasm at their own level." This is the teaching of St. Thomas, *In Boethium de Trinitate*, q.6, a.2, ad 1m: "Sacred Scripture does not propose divine things to us under sensory figures of speech with a view to our intellect remaining at this level, but rather with a view to its rising from these figures to the realm of the invisible; wherefore it happens that Scripture conveys its meaning even through the figurative images of base things, so that there might be a slighter chance of one's intellect remaining fixated on such a low level, as Dionysius says . . ."; *De Veritate*, q.10, a.7, ad 10m. Cf. John Scotus Erigena, *De divisione naturae*, bk. 1, n. 67 (PL 122:512a).

37. Pierre Lyonnet, S.J., *Écrits spirituels* (1951). Cf. Pseudo-Dionysius, *De caelesti hierarchia*, ch. 15, 2: "Theology situates allegories of fire above almost all other allegories . . ." (*Oeuvres complètes*, French trans. of M. de Gandillac, pp. 236-238).

38. Charles de Moré-Pontgibaud, "Sur l'analogie des noms divins," p. 167.

O God, you are Love indeed — but Love which is different from my love! You are Justice indeed — but Justice which is different from my justice! If I am lacking in love and wanting in justice I shall inevitably stray from you, and the worship I offer you will be neither more nor less than idolatry. To believe in you I must believe in Love and in Justice, and it is a thousand times better to believe in them than simply to call upon your name.[39] Apart from them, I can never hope to find you, and those who take them as their guides are on the road that leads to you. But to adore you in spirit and in truth, and to avoid the risk of adoring myself, I must, furthermore, believe that my justice — even that justice which I conceive of without being able to realize it — is not yet your Justice, and that my love is not yet your Love. My ideal is not your reality. When I apply the words Justice and Love to you, I still do not understand you.[40] For "we know imperfectly and prophesy imperfectly," and everything remains an enigma to us — we can make an idol of Justice itself, and perhaps even of Love itself.[41]

---

39. Cf. St. Bonaventure, *In Sent.*, d.8, p. 1, q.2, concl.: "Because, indeed, he fails in his knowledge of what is the case, he thus thinks that God is what he is not, an idol, for instance, or else he thinks that God is not what he in fact is, a just God, for instance" (Quaracchi, vol. 1, p. 154). St. Augustine, *In Psalmum* 134, 4 and 5: "I call all these things good, but only insofar as they are coupled with their own names, though: the good sky, the good angel, the good man. When I refer to God, I think it better to say nothing except good. . . . It is the very Truth, it is the very Wisdom, it is the very Virtue of God" (PL 37:1740, 1742). Pseudo-Dionysius, *De divinis nominibus*, ch. 4, n. 7: ". . . The beautiful and beauty are confounded together in this Cause which recapitulates everything in its powerful unity. . . ."

40. St. Thomas, *Prima*, q.13, a.5: "When this term, 'wise', is used of a man, it in some way circumscribes and comprehends the thing signified; this is not, however, the case when the term is used of God. Rather, in this latter case, the term leaves the thing signified as something incomprehended that surpasses the signification of the name." Dionysius the Carthusian, *De lumine christianae theoriae*, bk. 1, a.20: ". . . Nor is God pure goodness in the sense that pure goodness can be known by us" (*Opera omnia*, vol. 33, p. 254).

41. This thing happens only too often. And it is from this idolatry, which is like every kind of falsehood, that falsehood in turn proliferates. "It is a pharisaism that is proper to a morality of abstract axioms, or, as is said nowadays, it is a mystification that is proper to idealism, to style oneself 'pure', whereas the more a notion is generalized and abstract, the more it is liable to be charged with resonances that are absurd and dominated by the passions." Edmond Ortigues, "Quelques ouvrages de psychoanalyse," *Vie spirituelle*, supplément (1951), p. 457.

For God is above all names[42] and all thought, beyond every ideal and beyond all value![43] A Living God!

The affirmation of God rises up from the very roots of being and thought, before all conscious acts, before the formation of concepts, conferring upon consciousness its guarantee and upon the concept its universal validity. Shrouded and secret, though necessary and permanent, it lies at the basis of all our judgments about being. It is one with the life of thinking being. It is the affirmation of God which gives the thinking being, at all levels, coherence and consistency — without which it would vanish into

---

42. St. Augustine, *Contra Adimantum Manichaei discipulum*, ch. 2: ". . . For they, who have not yet seen that no words are consistent with his ineffable majesty, shudder at these words (the wrath of God, the zeal of God . . .). Indeed they think that he must be controlled by these words, as if they are saying anything worthy of God, when they do not say them. For the Holy Spirit, who insinuates into the minds of intelligent men the very notion of how ineffable the highest aspects of divinity are, has seen fit to use even words such as these, which are wont among men to be considered a flaw, so that in this way words, even those which men think that they speak with some sense of God's worthiness, might be considered to be unworthy of his majesty, with reference to which an honorific silence is more agreeable than any human voice" (PL 42:142). Or *Sermo* 241, ch. 7, n. 9: ". . . Thus it is, nevertheless, that Scripture happily stoops to using even those phrases (that God is displeased and that God does not know), phrases which you abhor. This is so that you may not infer that those matters which you consider to be of great moment are spoken of in a worthy manner, etc. May the person, moreover, who has transcended such phrases and who has begun, to the extent that man is permitted to do so, to ponder God in a worthy manner, discover a silence that offers praise through the ineffable voice of the heart" (PL 39:1498; allusion to Psalm 65:2: "For you silence is praise").

43. St. Augustine, *Sermo* 241, n. 9: "Nonetheless, brothers, we say these things of God, because we have not found anything better that we might say. I speak of a just God, because I can find nothing better in terms of human words to express myself: for he is beyond justice. . . . Indeed you speak of a just God: but understand this as something quite beyond the idea of justice which you are wont to consider in the case of man . . ." (PL 39:1498). Cf. Isaac of Stella, *Sermo* 22, n. 5: "What is God, if he is Justice? Or what is Justice, if it is God himself? . . . But we must indeed say what we can when we wish to speak of the ineffable, about which nothing can be spoken in the right terms. We must of necessity be silent or else use borrowed terms." (French trans. by André, O.C.) Cf. St. Gregory the Great, *Moralia in Job*, bk. 35, ch. 6, n. 9: "O Lord, the sentence of your judgement shows how much our blindness is at variance with the light of your rectitude" (PL 74:754b).

dust, just as without God the world itself would vanish. *Forma mea, Deus meus.*[44]

But in order to rise to consciousness and become, on its own level, a judgment among other judgments, that fundamental affirmation must objectify itself. It does so in a thousand imaginative forms, and finally expresses itself in the definite form of a concept, the necessary instrument of human thought. But that necessary instrument, even where used correctly, is also necessarily inadequate. The Absolute, upon which our knowledge rests, now enters into the system of our knowledge. It therefore appears to be caught up in the universal network of relationships. And the Transcendent, which by definition "goes beyond" the notions elaborated by our intelligence, seems to allow itself to be imprisoned within them.

At that point the equally necessary labor of intellectual purification begins — instinctively at first and then methodically. For how, in fact, are we to save the idea of God unless we can save the idea of the Absolute and the Transcendent? As the idea of God is particularized and becomes objective, it is submitted to a negative dialectic, which is turned against all the gross elements from which it seems to take its substance.

But is there no danger that, in the end, the process of purification might empty the affirmation of meaning? Might not that be the price of not falling into idolatry? For in the last analysis "it is not as a concept that God would have us think of him, nor even as a being whose content would be that of a concept."[45] As the object takes form, Being evaporates.... "Beyond all sensible images and all conceptual determinations God affirms himself as the absolute act of being in its pure actuality."[46] Any element that can be grasped, whatever it may be and however fine the filter through which it

---

44. Cf. St. Thomas, *Prima*, q.106, a.1, ad 3m: "The rational mind is formed immediately by God, either as the image from the exemplar, inasmuch as it is not made in the image of any other but God, or as the subject by the ultimate perfecting form, because it is always considered unformed, unless it inheres in the First Truth itself." St. Augustine most often envisaged this second aspect: hence *De Genesi ad litteram*, bk. 1, chs. 4 and 5, where the subject dealt with in a special way is the wise and happy life (PL 34:249-250).

45. Cf. Jacques Leclercq, *Dialogue de l'homme et de Dieu* (1948), p. 37.

46. Etienne Gilson, *L'esprit de la philosophie médiévale*, p. 52; cf. p. 56: "Envisaged (as infinite), the Divine Being challenges the narrowness of our conceptions more than ever. There is not a single one of the notions that we have available to us that does not in some way crack under the strain, when we try to apply it to him. Every attempt at naming constitutes a limitation. Now God is beyond all limitation. Therefore he is beyond any kind of naming."

has been passed, will always be too gross to express the Being whose essence is Being, pure Being, pure "Existence," pure Act undefiled and simple, a Subject which cannot be a predicate, which must be posited "absolutely," and in respect of whom a "qualification" is a sacrilegious "restriction."[47] How, in these circumstances, can we say anything about God? How can we know anything about God? Any likeness which we think we can note between Creator and creature is at once annulled and more than annulled by a far greater unlikeness.[48] Are we not obliged to confess that "what God is remains totally unknown to us"?[49] So that when we have at last eliminated all risk of idolatry, thanks to a thorough purification, shall we not fall into agnosticism — can we avoid the feeling of becoming atheists?

As we have seen, that is mere appearance. The intelligence cannot retrace its path, and unless it lies to itself, it cannot go back upon a necessary affirmation. Although by a paradox, the effect of which we cannot help feeling, what prevents us reaching such a conclusion is precisely what produces the appearance of it. What, we may ask, is a pure affirmation? What is an affirmation which, to all appearances, affirms nothing, since it does not proceed from a subject distinct from itself, and does not bear upon any object? "He Is": how can that Fullness, if reached by analysis alone, not seem at first sight empty?[50]

---

47. André Bremond, *Une dialectique thomiste* . . . , pp. 572ff.: "Every affirmable subject is . . . attributable to the absoluteness of being, but with some notion of restriction, which is signified by the predicate; God is the sole subject that my mind posits necessarily within the absolute, absolutely, without restriction, without qualification. . . ." Cf. Etienne Gilson, *L'Être et l'Essence* (1948), p. 326. J. de Finance, *Être et Agir*, p. 351: "It is true: the word evokes in me only an incredibly impoverished *representation*. . . . But this poverty is merely the outward trappings in the guise of which there is manifested, in the conceptual sense, a dynamism whose objective amplitude is in nowise restricted." St. Thomas, *Compendium theologiae*, 1, ch. 10; I, q.13, a.11; *De Potentia*, q.7, q.2; *Contra Gentiles*, 1, ch. 22, etc.

48. Fourth Lateran Council (1215): "So great a likeness between Creator and creature cannot be observed without there being an even greater unlikeness observable between them."

49. St. Thomas, *De Veritate*, q.2, a.1, ad 9m. *Contra Gentiles*, bk. 3, ch. 49. *De Potentia*, q.7, a.5, ad 14m. Cf. *De anima*, q.2, a.16, etc.

50. In *Le Dieu de Sartre* (1950), Hubert Paissac submits the human expression of the divine Name to a penetrating criticism: "It is indispensable to give expression to a subject. It is quite necessary, without being duped by the process, to call God: He Is" (p. 80). God is neither a subject such as would distinguish himself from his action, nor an object, "but the pure Act of existing, beyond a superficial separation between subject and object. He is therefore unthinkable. Or to be more precise, in order to think of him,

The proof, once again, is not for that reason invalidated. The demands of reason remain unchanged. The affirmation continues to be the center of thought, tenuous perhaps, but tenacious.[51] It continues to rise up again and again, always necessary, always imperious, always invincible, and despite all the criticism and the scruples which seek to prevent its emergence, always prepared in the long run to engender the same process of objectivization. Being fortunately incapable of fusing within their limits any of the particular forms in which it tends to take shape, it suffices to prevent the intelligence from ever settling in the negations which follow upon them — which inevitably follow.[52] And by the same token it closes the road to retreat. The affirmation allows neither of denial nor of doubt, and cannot be called in question. There is no appeal from the judgment of reason. What is gained is a permanent acquisition.

It may seem, perhaps, as though man were destined to oscillate forever between those two poles without ever finding a haven in which to rest. Reason may remain serene with its proofs untouched; but the man who reasons is perplexed. The theoretical problem may well have been solved in principle, and all appearances to the contrary may have been overcome in theory; but the practical question remains, the fundamental question about the use of the idea of God in the spiritual life.

Then, to our astonishment, the Gift of God intervenes. It is the second gift, or the first is the gift of mind itself, of the affirmation. Then the *donum perfectum* is grafted on to the *datum optimum*. It in no way adds to the force of the affirmation or to the value of its rational foundation. It in no way supplements the proof, nor does it offer a substitute, which is not, in any case, required. Its action is of a different order: it comes to assure the

---

it would be necessary in actual fact to be him. Only in this case, in a presence rigorously immediate to the self, would the very reality of God be at once lived and known" (p. 84). "The Divine Name (He Is) . . . would not be appreciated without an area of silence and of night such as is represented by our conceptions. Thinking fit to affirm of God that he is this or that, creator or gazing eye, Other or Same, waited for and touched, we in fact bring together subtle negations which cause an emptiness in our spirit and are realized as a summons. In the last analysis God is the one who will respond perfectly to this summons" (p. 154).

51. St. Augustine, *De libero arbitrio*, bk. 2, ch. 15, n. 39: "the form of cognition is certain, although it has been quite tenuous to this point" (PL 32:262).

52. It should be noted that the oscillation is not between the affirmation and negation of God, between dogmatism and scepticism, but between the two moments of knowledge: affirmative theology and negative theology.

spirit of the tranquil enjoyment of its object, without depriving it of its original impulse, and to restore peace to the mind. And precisely because it is "of another order, supernatural," a situation which had seemed inextricable is unravelled without effort. It is as though a new dimension had been introduced. By allowing us to participate in the Life of God himself, the life of charity furnishes our idea of God with a spiritual content. Instead of interrupting or discouraging the process of purification which, on the contrary, it may even stimulate, this spiritual content helps us to pursue the work in peace; because, on another plane, it ensures at a single stroke the peaceful continuation of that work and, if one may so express it, confers an indispensable density upon the affirmation.[53]

That Gift is the Spirit of God — in fact the "Spirit of Jesus" — through whom our hearts are filled with charity. "No one, strictly speaking, knows God unless it be God alone. The Spirit enables us to know him in a certain measure, because it assimilates us to him. . . . The Spirit alone can plumb the depths of God. The Spirit alone grants us a knowledge of God which is more than radically inadequate or purely negative knowledge. The Spirit

---

53. This does not, of course, mean that the affirmation owes its intrinsic solidity to grace. The value of the affirmation in itself, in an impersonal state, so to say, is one thing; the serenity or repose of a particular mind in which the affirmation triumphs over all kinds of adverse forces is another thing. Other cases of the same kind present themselves in the intellectual life. Thus it is by an analogous process that a certain number of Christian philosophers, of whom St. Thomas is one, consolidate and clarify their affirmation of God the creator by having recourse to the mystery of the Trinity. Possessing as they do a knowledge obtained by natural reason, and without truly putting this knowledge in question again, they declare that this knowledge causes no fewer problems in its turn and that, in order to remove the antinomies which rise in the spirit as a result of it, the lights of supernatural revelation offer them assistance, which alone is fully efficacious. Cf. the last writings of Maurice Blondel, or Karl Adam, *Christus unser Bruder* (1950) And St.Thomas, *Prima*, q.32, a.1, ad 3m: "Knowledge of the divine persons was necessary to us . . . for a proper discernment about the creation of things . . ."; *Contra Gentiles*, bk. 2, ch. 3. Cf. A. R. Motte, O.P., "Théodicée et théologie chez saint Thomas d'Aquin," *Revue des sciences philosophiques et théologiques* (1937), pp. 15ff.: "Is not, moreover, one of the 'necessities' that Saint Thomas discerns from the revelation of the mystery of the Trinity the exclusion in a decisive way of emanational conceptions according to which God would act by a necessity of nature, inasmuch as it is precisely the notion of Word and creative Love which is inclusive of a mode of intelligent and free production? . . . The word *necessaria*, obviously, should not be pressed. The text, however, suggests without a doubt how difficult Saint Thomas thought it was for reason alone to eliminate these errors about creation which are at the same time errors about the Creator."

makes new men of us, men participating in the divine nature, as the Second Epistle of St. Peter makes bold to say, and gives us the only knowledge of God which is on his own level, because it is a connatural knowledge."[54]

But this does not mean that the natural laws of the intelligence are suspended. The increase in knowledge obtained in this manner is not of a rational or philosophical order. It is something more or something else: but however that may be, it is different. It is not the privilege of the scholar or the reasoner. It is a knowledge related to experience.[55] Or rather, it is worthless apart from that experience — which is wholly spiritual and beyond the reach of psychology. In one respect it is the privilege of that personal intimacy and concrete intuition which belongs to all religious knowledge, but in another respect it participates in its extra-scientific character. It is a simple, quasi-immediate knowledge, although in reality it is always analogical, *in speculo*.[56] For "he who loves," St. John says, "is born of God, and knows God."[57] "He who loves," Augustine comments, "sees love, and he who sees love sees God": *inde videmus, unde similes sumus* (there we see where we are like); and this love, adds William of Saint-Thierry, is the eye which enables us to see God: *ipsa [caritas] enim est oculus quo videtur Deus*.[58] But at the same time, that knowledge is precarious and always obscure, for it depends upon a life which is both precarious and full of "vicissitudes," and never possessed as one possesses a natural good; and because it can never catch the pure light which is shed by that life, in the prism of the concept — and indeed never attempts to do so.

Putas quid est Deus? Putas qualis est Deus? Quidquid finxeris non est; quidquid cogitatione comprehenderis, non est. Sed ut aliquid gustu accipias,

---

54. Louis Bouyer, *Le sens de la vie monastique* (1950), pp. 132ff.

55. Cf. St. Thomas, *In primum Sent.*, d. 14, q.2, a.2, ad 3m; d. 15, q.2, ad 5m; d. 16, q.1, a.2.

56. Here, in the case of love, we can apply the restatement of Augustinian thought made by St. Thomas in the parallel case of his view of truth: *Contra Gentiles*, bk. 3, ch. 47: "in the minds of men a kind of image, as it were, of divine truth." Cf. St. Augustine, *Confessions*, bk. 12, ch. 25, etc.

57. 1 John 4:7. "There is," writes Georges Lefebvre, commenting on St. Gregory and St. John of the Cross, "a certain sense of God which is the fruit of charity"; it is "that obscure and mysterious knowledge which is the presentiment of the object loved, something which is found in love itself." Thus God is known "in the very love which is directed to him by a person." *Prière pure et pureté du coeur* (1954), pp. 38ff. Cf. Clement of Alexandria, *Stromata*, 5, ch. 1, 13, n. 2: "God is love, and He makes himself known to those who love."

58. William of St.-Thierry, *De natura et dignitate amoris* (PL 184:390).

Deus caritas est, Caritas est qua diligimus.[59] (Do you think what God is? Do you think what God is like? Whatever you imagine, he is not that; whatever you can grasp in thought, he is not that. But to give you some taste of him, God is charity, and Charity is that by which we love.)

Novimus haec (de Deo). Num ideo et arbitramur nos comprehendisse? Non ea disputatio comprehendit, sed sanctitas: si quo modo tamen comprehendi potest quod incomprehensibile est. . . .[60] (This we know [about God]. Do we therefore suppose that we have understood? It is not argument which makes us understand these things, but sanctity; if indeed what is incomprehensible can be in any way understood. . . .)

Such, indicated schematically, are the principal stages in the dialectic of the idea of God, of its *concrete* dialectic in the life of the *concrete* spirit. Always supported by the first, the other four stages are engendered, follow one another, merge, conflict, and are harmonized in the ever-moving complexity of this idea which is stronger than all criticism — stronger than death.[61]

---

59. St. Augustine, *De Trinitate*, bk. 8, ch. 8, n. 12: "Let no one say: I do not know what I love. Let him love his brother, and he loves the same love. For he knows the love with which he loves better than the brother whom he loves. Behold already God is better known to him than his brother: clearly better known, because more present; better known because within him; better known because more certain. Embrace love through God and embrace God through love. It is love indeed which unites all the good Angels and all the servants of God in a bond of sanctity, and us as well, and in turn it joins them together with us, and it subdues all to itself. . . . I see charity, and I behold it in my mind's eye as much as possible, and I believe in the words of Scripture, because 'God is charity, and he who remains in charity remains in God' . . . and 'everyone who loves is born of God, and knows God' . . ." (PL 42:957-958). Let us also take note that St. Catherine of Genoa calls God "Love-God," "beatific Love" (*Vita*, ch. 10, 21); for her "what the theologians call the metaphysical essence of God is made up uniquely of pure love, that is to say, love which has purity as its essential postulate": Umile da Genova, O.M.C., "Catherine de Gênes," *Dictionnaire de spiritualité*, fasc. 8 (1938), col. 300.

60. St. Bernard, *De consideratione*, bk. 5, ch. 14, n. 30: "But if it were not possible, the Apostle would not have said: 'to comprehend with all the saints' (Ephesians 3:18). Therefore the saints comprehend. You ask how? If you are a saint, you have comprehended and you know; if not, you will learn by experience" (PL 182:805c-d). All knowledge of God is a certain kind of response to the initiative of God, and all real knowledge presupposes a certain proportion, a certain connaturality between the knower and the known; now "it is love alone . . . by which a creature can, albeit not as an equal, respond to its author, or make a mutual repayment in kind": *In cantica sermo*, 83, n. 4 (PL 183:1183b). Cf. P. Dumontier, *Saint Bernard et la Bible* (1935), p. 160, note.

61. J. de Vries, in *Scholastik* (1950), p. 129, has happily laid hold of and summarized the concrete dialectic that has been sketched herein: "On the one hand, faith in God is

Our power of affirmation is greater than our power of conception or our power of argumentation. For although the last two may be called in question at some point or other, the first remains intact and revives the others. It also enables them to reach a successful conclusion.

Hence an ebb and flow and a whole series of apparently irreconcilable conflicts — which nevertheless, provisionally at least, always find a solution. What we can least prevent ourselves from affirming almost always seems compromised in the realm of argument and concepts. The critical reason is endlessly inventive in discovering arguments against what had been most solidly established. Among those who make use of it, some are mainly concerned with our idea of God, while others attack our proofs. From a purely logical point of view it is no easy matter to show that they are wrong, since the believer is often awkward when he gives a rational justification for his belief; his philosophy may be short-winded, his analysis inadequate; moreover, his belief may oblige him at times to accept the criticisms with both hands. Yet nothing prevails against our affirmation, which always restores the value of our ideas and our proofs. Our affirmation is ceaselessly inventive against the inventiveness of criticism.

For God is *the Wholly Other* and in every sense. A process capable of leading us to other beings and to other truths could not, of itself, and as such, lead us to him, any more than the representations which fittingly express other beings and other truths can, by themselves, express him. His mystery remains inviolate even when logic has obliged us to affirm that he exists. Our reason does not penetrate into him.[62] Dialectic and representation cannot cross the threshold. But reaching out beyond dialectic and

---

placed in danger in man in all kinds of ways, but on the other hand it is thrust on his spirit in an irresistible way. . . . When the fundamental affirmation is developed with conscious thought, then there arises the danger that this affirmation might lead to the fabrication of myths that humanize the divine or indeed that the purification of the concept of God might in the end leave standing only an abstract notion of the divine, leaning towards agnosticism. Only the life of love, springing out of the supernatural order, frees man from this antinomy. That way, the value of the proof of God's existence is not denied. For it too arises from the essential orientation of the mind and soul. What it constructs is stronger than the hardest steel. Nevertheless, it can be set aside, because it concerns only reason, whereas God lays claim to the whole of our mind and soul."

62. St. Thomas, *In librum de Causis*, 6: ". . . That alone is capable of being received by our intellect which has a quiddity that partakes of being; but the quiddity of God is being itself; wherefore he is above our intellect."

representation, our spirit affirms him who, although reached by their mediation, is beyond their grasp. And that affirmation, as it passes from darkness into light, and then again from light into another darkness, always remains invisible.

As created spirits, we are impelled towards the Absolute. Many things conceal us from ourselves and tend to deflect that impulse. But deep within us it persists, waiting to be released. So that when we apply ourselves to the business of criticism, correcting the process of our thought and its products, we are being faithful to our nature and to the impulse which makes us what we are. Criticisms can neither deflect nor obstruct it: for the impulse itself inspires them, directs them, and gives them a positive meaning. And it is in that impulse that the Absolute makes itself known to us.

The philosopher and the spiritually-minded, the primitive and the civilized man, the most personal thinker and the humblest of believers, the "prophet" and the mystic, do not merely converge in their use of the word: God. If they are correctly oriented they really do meet, however partial and sometimes narrow their outlook may be, or at least they tend to meet — and in that tendency do meet — although the object about which each of them is thinking seems to be different.[63]

---

63. In a note on "La triple origine de l'idée de Dieu," *Revue de métaphysique et de morale*, vol. 16 (1908), 2, pp. 717-721, Gustave Belot distinguishes "three irreducible sources" for this idea: "the popular religious source, the intellectual and metaphysical source, and the mystical source." Then he asks himself "by what right," for example, the metaphysician borrows this word for God from the religious tradition, or "by what right" the mystic makes so much use of it on his part, seeing that there is between these three accepted meanings of the same word "no unity, even a psychological one, and no homogeneity, even a functional one." A process of reflection that was at once more modest and more pointed could have led the author to ask himself "by what right" he undertook in this way to shatter into three fragments an idea which, in spite of the diverse elements analyzed by him, took on the appearance everywhere of a singular phenomenon, at least in its ultimate aim. (And does not even he, himself, in his title speak in the singular of "the idea of God," despite its "threefold origin"?) Perhaps in such case he could have begun to get some glimmer of the idea that what he took *a priori* for the "sources" of three truly irreducible notions were in fact merely three "channels," three great ways of approach through which an idea as complex as it is singular succeeds in forcing its way through to the human consciousness. But in order to envisage this, it would, at the very least, have been necessary to entertain the hypothesis that this idea was not exhausted by its most apparent psychological or

They have one idea of God — and of the soul — in spite of its many and diverse origins, in spite of the differently formed concepts, and in spite of representations which differ strangely.

It is as though they shared a single space, one external world, although within that world there are distinct worlds of sight and smell, sound and touch. . . .

God is indeed unique! And the astonishing convergence of so many points of view, each one of them seemingly independent, is a further testimony to his uniqueness.

God of the intelligence and God of the consciousness — God of supernatural revelation and God of reason — God of nature and God of history — God of being and God of value — God of reflection and God of prayer — God of the philosopher and God of the mystic — God of the soul and God of the universe — God of social tradition and God of solitary meditation . . . so many opposites and one unity!

Infinite God and perfect God — perfect in his infinity and infinite in his perfection! God who is both Absolute and personal!

God who is unique under so many aspects; the one End approached by innumerable ways. God of my whole self! God of all men! None of the avenues which lead to you is closed, and I have no right to forbid the use of any one of them.

Voces diversae, semitae multae: sed unum per eas significatur, unus quaeritur.[64] (There are many voices and many paths, but the same thing is indicated by them and the same person sought.)

I do not believe we need think of God as a bearded old man, and I think we can form a different idea of him. It is in that direction that

---

"functional" aspects; that indeed it could have had some relationship to an absolute standard of thought; that not everything in this realm is explained in the last resort by a series of "psychological and social processes" on the basis of some sort of "mythical imagination." . . . In brief, it would have been necessary not to suppose *a priori* that the idea of God, in its most broadly accepted meaning, was illusory. . . .

64. St. Bernard, *De consideratione,* bk. 5, ch. 13, nn. 27-29, concerning the multiplicity of our observations about God, notably as conveyed by these words: "length, immensity, height, depth" (PL 182:804-805).

the sacred frontier of the spirit lies, where man, leaving his senses behind him, like Moses removing his sandals before the burning bush, and like Jesus leaving his three disciples behind him, goes to pray a little farther off, "at a stone's throw," armed solely with his heart and his intelligence. That is where metaphysical awe begins, the "ecstatic aphasia" spoken of by Plotinus. And in spite of the fact that we cannot express this idea, how much more intense, how much more vivid it is than the idea we form of an ordinary object![65]

The idea of the Good, the Prime Mover, Necessary Being, the One superior to being, the Universal Principle, Nameless and Formless Deity; God of the Patriarchs, God of Moses and Isaiah, Sovereign Lord, Judge, King of History, Father of Jesus. . . . Between each of them an abyss — and yet they are, or at least can be, the same God.

"There are many outside who appear to be inside, and many inside who appear to be outside." The words used by Origen and Augustine[66] are apt at all times. The fact that they can be misused should not be allowed to conceal their truth. And what is true of belonging to the Church is, doubtless, no less true of belief in God. One can be an atheist and profess belief in God;[67] one can be a believer and call oneself an atheist.[68] *Novit Deus qui sunt ejus.* (God knows who are his.)

---

65. Paul Claudel to Jacques Rivière, 11 May 1908 (*Correspondance de Paul Claudel et de Jacques Rivière*, pp. 158ff.).

66. Cf. *Histoire et Esprit, L'intelligence de l'Écriture d'après Origène* (coll. "Théologie," 1950), pp. 158ff. St. Augustine, *De baptismo contra Donatistas*, bk. 5, ch. 27, n. 38: "Many who seem to be on the outside are within, and others who seem to be within are outside." On this text see *Cahiers universitaires catholiques* (March 1953).

67. "There is an atheism concealed in all hearts, which is diffused in all our actions: God counts for nothing." (Bossuet, *Pensées détachées*, 2.)

68. This does not mean that all atheists are unconscious believers! Cf. Maurice Blondel, *La Pensée*, vol. 1 (1934), pp. 392ff.: ". . . And there are *truly* those who do not believe *in God*. . . . 'Belief in God' will come to pass only in the situation where, without metaphysical or magic or superstitious presumption, there is a practical recognition that God can only be reached if he yields himself, and that a person cannot have him for oneself without in the first place being his. . . . If therefore it can be said that 'there are no atheists', it can also truly be said that 'it is difficult and burdensome not to be an atheist'. . . ."

"Those who scrutinize the Majesty will be overawed by the Glory."[69]

The philosopher does well to look with suspicion upon titanic metaphysical structures. He should not imagine that he can rise, of his own power, to a genuine "science of God." He should use his critical faculties to moderate the pride of his curiosity. If, at the conclusion of his efforts, he begins to rediscover the object towards which his deepest impulse moved him, and affirms the existence of God, he is simply giving a principle of unity to all beings, a basis to his thought, an explanation of his own existence and meaning to the universe. Thus he limits himself "to putting down the only answer required by the world in question: God has not yet unveiled himself."[70] And though he may pursue his reflections beyond the proof, they will never enable him to penetrate into the divine nature. His inkling of the unknown may perhaps keep him outside it. Nor will all the wisdom of which he is capable allow him to begin contemplating God himself; he can only contemplate "the economy of his wisdom."[71]

"Lord, I do not try to reach your heights, for I do not put my intelligence on your level. But I long for a glimpse of the truth which my heart loves and believes in."[72]

---

69. Proverbs 25:27b (LXX).

70. H. Paissac, O.P., "Théologie, science de Dieu," *Lumière et Vie* 1 (1951), p. 36. Cf. Karl Barth, *Dogmatik im Grundriss* (1948), Paragraph 3.

71. Evagrius, *Gnosticos*, bk. 5, ch. 51: "He who sees the creator through the harmony of beings does not know what his nature is, but rather recognizes his wisdom. By this wisdom God made everything. I do not mean his essential wisdom, but rather the wisdom which appears in beings, the wisdom which those who are learned in these matters are accustomed to call natural contemplation. If this is the case, how foolish are those who profess to understand the nature of God himself!" Cf. *Selecta in Psalmos* (PG 12:1661c). Zeno of Verona, bk. 2, *Tract.*, 17, n. 1: "It is a religious confession of human devotion to know about God what it is licit to know; for just as testimonies of him can be searched for in the simple heart, his inmost secrets are not to be investigated through curiosity . . ." (PL 11:444-445). St. Bernard of Clairvaux, *In Cantica sermo* 62, n. 5: "not an examiner of his Majesty, but of his Will" (PL 183:1078b; cf. *De consideratione*, bk. 5, ch. 3, n. 6 (PL 182:790d); St. Thomas, *De virtutibus in communi*, a.12, ad 11m: "The wisdom by which we now contemplate God does not look immediately to God himself, but to the effects by which we contemplate God at the present time."

72. St. Anselm, *Proslogion*.

5

The Ineffable God

Infinite intelligibility — such is God.¹ The incomprehensible is the opposite of the unintelligible. The deeper we enter into the infinite, the better we understand that we can never hold it in our hands. *Quidquid scientia comprehenditur, scientis comprehensione finitur.*² (Whatever is understood by science is limited by the understanding of the knower.) The infinite is not a sum of finite elements, and what we understand of it is not a fragment torn from what remains to be understood. The intelligence does not do away with the mystery nor does it even begin to understand it; it in no way diminishes it, it does not "bite" on it: it enters deeper and deeper into it and discovers it more and more as a mystery.

At the summit of man's effort, face to face with the Being of God, the nothingness of man is brought home to him; and in the same way, as the Mystery of God allows itself to be penetrated by reason — or rather as it penetrates reason — it reveals its depths, and the light which it radiates only increases the obscurity in which the Mystery conceals itself. That does not, strictly speaking, mean that we realize increasingly "the infinite distance between God and man" — to use Kierkegaard's expression — as though God withdrew his greatness from us in proportion as the infinite grows in

---

1. For he is, to use the words of St. Gregory Nazianzen, *Oration,* 45, *in sanctum Pascha,* ch. 3 (words that are taken up by St. John Damascene, *De fide orthodoxa,* bk. 1, ch. 9 [PG 94:833], and then also by St. Thomas Aquinas (cf. below): The one who "gathers together in himself the totality of Being, like a limitless, shoreless ocean of 'ousia.'"

2. St. Augustine, *De Civitate Dei,* bk. 12, ch. 18 (PL 41:388).

us, and as we come the better to see that the divine is not "simply the superlative of the human."³ It is not really a question of distance, or at least the word only expresses one aspect of the reality. God does not retreat to the outermost edge of our horizon; he does not escape us entirely, or better still he does not let us escape him — but in this, too, he reveals himself as God, as the incommensurable, the inapprehensible, that is to say, impregnable. One can, therefore, without the least fear, enjoin reason to "understand." But with each advance and each time it discovers some new wonder in the divine Object, the desire to know and the desire to comprehend will be mortified.⁴

The exercise of "speculation," says the Carmelite, Dominic of St. Albert,⁵ "is the deepest death that a loving spirit can suffer."⁶ And the Angelic Pilgrim, Angelus Silesius, adds:

The better you know God, the more you agree
That you are less and less capable of expressing what he is.

Amictus lumine sicut vestimento.
(Clad in light as in a garment.)⁷

3. Kierkegaard, *Journals*, 11 A 48 and 679; 12 A 320 (1849 and 1850).
4. Théodore de Régnon, S.J., *Etude sur la Sainte Trinité*, vol. 3 (1898), p. 458: "[A definition] should be 'measurative'. But can reason encompass God? Can the effect circumscribe its cause? As well, the rational measure of God can only be the negation of all measure or the affirmation of incommensurability." St. Hilary, *De Trinitate*, bk. 2, ch. 7 (PL 10:57a). Cf. St. Bonaventure, *In Hexaemeron*, bk. 20, ch. 2: "Consequently that is where we find that thick, misty cloud which, though, illuminates minds that have done away with prying attempts at investigating it" (Quaracchi, vol. 5, p. 447). Cf. also the following heading of a question in the *Summa theologica* of Alexander of Hales (pars 1, inq. 1, tract. 2, q.2 [Quaracchi, vol. 1, p. 58]): "On the immensity of God insofar as the intellect is concerned, or on his incomprehensibility."
5. 1596-1634; the favorite disciple of John of St.-Samson. Cf. Henri Bremond, *Histoire littéraire du sentiment religieux en France* (1916), vol. 2, pp. 388-389. (Eng. trans., *Literary History of Religious Thought in France* [1930], vol. 2, p. 287.)
6. Cf. the expression used by Henry Suso: "Bild mit bilden us triben," which means "to drive out image with image." See P. Bizet, *Henri Suso et le déclin de la Scolastique* (1946), p. 280.
7. *The Cherubic Pilgrim*, bk. 5, ch. 41. Cf. Clement of Alexandria, *Stromata*, 5, the whole of ch. 12.

The mind which tries to "comprehend" God is not a *miser* amassing a heap of gold — a summa of truths — which goes on increasing.[8] Nor can it be compared to an *artist* returning to a rough sketch, adding to it, improving upon it, and, in the end, enjoying his work aesthetically. The mind is better compared to a *swimmer* who can only keep afloat by moving and who cleaves a new wave at each stroke.[9] He is forever brushing aside the representations which are continually reforming, knowing full well that they support him, but that if he were to rest for a single moment he would sink and perish.

"However far thought may rise, there is always further to go."

"If you have understood, then this is not God. If you were able to understand, then you understood something else instead of God. If you were able to understand even partially, then you have deceived yourself with your own thoughts."[10]

---

8. On the impossibility of getting away completely from the imagination here below in this world, one should read the quite beautiful meditation of William of St.-Thierry, *Meditativae orationes*, meditation 2: ". . . Therefore the quaking and bewildered soul stands before her God, ready to entreat him, ever holding her very self in the hollow of her hands, as if she were about to make an offering of herself to you. Quaking at the things she is accustomed to, bewildered at things that are out of the ordinary, she carries a sign of faith in you, in order to find you. But not as yet has she discovered to whom she might remit that sign. Behold her seeking your face, Lord, seeking your face, and not knowing, not at all knowing what she seeks. She loathes the phantoms that her heart conjures up about you as she would idols. She loves you, such as faith describes you to her; but her mind does not suffice for the sight of you. And when, burning with a desire for your face, offering to you a sacrifice of her piety and justice, oblations and holocausts, she is carried off, she is thrown into confusion all the more. And when she does not obtain so quickly the illumination of faith in you, who are the one to whom she has entrusted herself, she is sometimes so bewildered that she scarcely trusts herself to believe in you, so bewildered that she hates herself, because, as it seems to her, she does not love you. Far be it from her not to believe in you, seeing that she is so anxious on account of her desire for you. Far be it from her not to love you, seeing as she desires you even to the point of contempt for everything that exists, even herself! *How long, Lord, how long?* If you do not light my lamp, if you do not illuminate my darkness, let me not be rescued from this trial, nor, except in you, my God, let me step foot across this wall" (Latin ed. by M. M. Davy, pp. 64-65 and 68-70).

See also St. Gregory Nazianzen, *Oration* 28, ch. 12 (PG 26:41). And the general law formulated by St. Thomas, *Prima*, q.84, a.7.

9. St. Bernard, *De consideratione*, bk. 5, ch. 7, n. 16 (PL 182:798).

10. St. Augustine, *Sermo* 52, n. 16 (PL 38:360). *Sermo* 117, n. 5: "We are talking about God. What wonder is it, if you do not comprehend? If you do have comprehension, he is not God. . . . To touch God just a little bit with the mind is a great beatitude; to comprehend him, however, is altogether impossible" (PL 38:663). It is, I believe, to

"Whatever is understood by knowledge is limited by the understanding of the knowledge.... If you have reached an end, then it is not God."[11]

When we say that God is ineffable, it does not mean that we cannot say anything about him![12] It does not mean that there is nothing to say on the subject, or that there is nothing to be done but keep silence, or that the

---

strip the thought of St. Augustine of its force to say with X. Le Bachelet (*Dictionnaire de théologie catholique,* vol. 4, col. 1110) that in texts like these what is at issue is only the discarding of the idea of a "perfect knowledge," by which "divine knowability would find itself plumbed exhaustively." These kinds of enfeebling commentaries signal an era when the urgent peril of modernist agnosticism gave rise to a one-sided apologetics, too earnest and officious to be always adequately thought out. — Already Théodore de Régnon wrote, in *Etude sur la Sainte Trinité,* first series (1892), p. 45: "It is to do the Fathers of the Church a gratuitous injury to hedge in their teaching with so many minimizing interpretations." For St. Thomas, cf. above, ch. 4, nn. 17 and 40, etc.

Cf. *Le livre de la Bienheureuse Angèle de Foligno* (= French trans. by Paul Doncoeur), p. 140: "... When I came to my senses, I knew with very much certainty that those who are more keenly conscious of God are less able to speak of him. For it is by virtue of the very experience they have of the infinite and ineffable God that they are less able to speak of him.... Would to heaven that you understood this when you set about to preach.... For in that case you would not know how to say anything at all about God. And in such an instance every man would fall silent. And I would be very pleased to come to you at that point, saying: 'Brother, tell me a little bit about God now.' And you would not know how to say anything to anybody, or how to think of God in any way, so much would his infinite Goodness surpass you. And the soul does not lose her consciousness, any more than does the body and all its senses. One is fully conscious and in possession of all one's faculties. But you would say to the people most emphatically: 'Go with the blessing of God, for I can say nothing to you....'"

There is a similarly lofty reflection to be found in *The Guide for the Perplexed* by Maimonides: "Glory and praise to Him who is so raised up on high that, when the intelligences contemplate his essence, and when they delve into the manner in which his actions are the result of his will, their knowledge changes to ignorance, and when their tongues wish to glorify him with his attributes, all their eloquence becomes a feeble stammering." I am not going to try at this point to find out whether the teaching of Maimonides was able to take these traditional ideas into account in a wholly satisfying way. There is a restatement of the question by St. Thomas, *Prima,* q.13, a.12.

11. St. Augustine, *De civitate Dei,* bk. 12, ch. 18 (PL 41:368); *Sermo* 53, ch. 11, n. 12 (PL 38:370). Cf. Pseudo-Dionysius, *Letter to Gaius,* ch. 1.

12. St. Anselm, *Monologion,* ch. 65: "Thus, therefore, his nature is also ineffable, because it is in no wise able by way of words to be appreciated as it truly is; and it is not false, if under the tutelage of reason there can be an appreciation of his nature by way of another thing just as in a riddle" (PL 158:212b).

names which men have given him are all of them synonymous, and that one can affirm anything one likes about God, or deny everything about him, indiscriminately. Nor does it mean that everything that has been said is only provisionally or pragmatically valuable. The ineffability of God — and this is what gives it a precise and eminently positive meaning — is acknowledged *at the end* of the dialectic. Those who affirm it do not fall into an empty void. On the contrary, their affirmation is the summit of a thought-process rigorously pursued. It does not nullify the results of that effort of thought, and even in its negation it gathers its fruits.

Our ideas about God need, in fact, to be conducted with as much and more order as our ideas on other subjects. Nothing is worse than a premature "negative theology." The interplay of affirmation and negation is not a game without rules.[13] The qualities which are affirmed about God — and they are not all affirmed in the same way or on the same grounds — are only identified, as is right, when they transcend themselves and when they cancel one another out. God is not ineffable in the sense of being unintelligible: he is ineffable in the sense of being above everything that can be said of him. He is always above everything which one *must* in fact say of him at first, and which is never simply revoked subsequently: to *deny* is not to *revoke*, for it is always the same God, *semper major*, who impels us first of all to "affirm" and then to "deny" in the course of the same movement, of the same advance.

The ineffability of God is only another name for absolute transcendence. Silence comes at the end — not at the beginning.

> Have we said anything, uttered any sound, which is worthy of God? Indeed, I feel that I have said nothing but what I wished to say; yet if I have said anything, it is not what I wished to say.... And a sort of battle with words ensues. Since if what is ineffable is what cannot be said, yet what can be called even ineffable is not ineffable. This battle with words is to be prevented by silence rather than stilled by speech....[14]

---

13. See, for example, the proposition condemned in 1348: "... that the propositions, 'God is,' and 'God is not', signify the same thing in their deepest meaning is allowed in another manner of speaking." *Errores Nicolai de Ultricuria*, n. 3 (Denzinger-Schönmetzer, *Enchiridion symbolorum* ..., 32nd ed. [1963], n. 1030, p. 302).

14. St. Augustine, *De doctrina christiana*, bk. 1, ch. 6 (PL 34:21). St. Thomas, *In Boethium de Trinitate*, q.2, a.1, ad 6m: "... God is honored by our silence, not because we do not say or inquire into anything about him, but rather because we understand

In the dialectic of the three ways, which gives us access to a human knowledge of God (*affirmatio, seu positio; negatio, seu remotio; eminentia, seu transcendentia*), the via *eminentiae* does not, in the last analysis, follow on the *via negationis;* it demands, inspires, and guides it. Although it comes last, the *via eminentiae* is covertly the first — superior and anterior to the *via affirmationis* itself. Although it never assumes a definite form in the eyes of the intelligence, it is always the light and the norm, a cloud of light which shows us the path in the desert of our terrestrial pilgrimage, a hidden power which excites us to pursue objective knowledge and compels us to rectify it. . . . That is why we can enter the *via negationis* and remain in it without fear, once the necessary preliminary affirmations have been left behind. Understood in this way, the *via negationis* is only negative in appearance or negative of appearances. In other words — and more exactly perhaps — although it is negative and remains negative, it is the very opposite of *negation*.

Negativity is not negation. A "negative theology," a theology which heaps up negations, is, nevertheless, not a theology of *negation*. The moment of negativity which characterizes it does not consist in *calling in question* — any more than the movement of transcendence or of eminence implied by theology is a backward movement.

The affirmation, consequently, remains to triumph in its highest form. It triumphs by negation, which it utilizes as the only means of correcting its own inadequacy. It triumphs in negation itself, which does not annul it, but compels the affirmation to transcend itself, which is only the aspect of the movement of transcendence which can be grasped objectively.[15] It triumphs every time

---

that we are deficient in our understanding of him." Wherefore Sirach 43:30 (RSV): "When you praise the Lord, exalt him as much as you can; for he will surpass even that. When you exalt him, put forth all your strength, and do not grow weary, for you cannot praise him enough."

15. Cf. St. Thomas, *Contra Gentiles,* bk. 1, ch. 30: "His mode of supereminence, moreover, . . . cannot be signified except through negation . . . , or also through his [God's] relationship to other things, etc." *Prima,* q. 13, a. 1: "[God] is known by us from his creatures as their cause and also by way of excellence and remotion." John Scotus Erigena, *De divisione naturae,* bk. 1, n. 14: "Essence is, which is an affirmation; essence is not, which is a disavowal; it is superessential, which is at the same time an affirmation and a disavowal. For superficially it lacks negation; intellectually, though, it is heavy with negation. For the person who says that essence is superessential is not saying what it is, but rather what it is not; for he is saying that it is not essence, but that it is more than essence" (PL 122:462d).

because it comes first and because everything necessarily unfolds under its banner and sign. It is bound to triumph in the end, because in spite of all the indications to the contrary, that affirmation is, at bottom, mind itself.

The mind is not, as has been claimed, "that which denies"; it is that which affirms. The mind is neither revolt nor opposition nor refusal: it is adherence. Negations, revolts, oppositions, all the mind's refusals, insofar as they are well founded, are explained by the demands of that affirmation and adherence. And if those demands are ignored, the mind can no longer be faithful to its laws, and becomes the slave of the natural forces from which it had freed itself and from which it must go on freeing itself, by using those negations, oppositions, revolts, and refusals.

An analogy drawn solely from below leads nowhere. However negative the analogy may be said to be, one must, nevertheless, possess in some sense what one is trying to attain indirectly in the form of an aspiration or basic need. If I start from my experience, and using ideas of justice and love, try by analogy and by denying all limitations to qualify God as absolute Justice or Love, I am immediately faced by an alternative. Either the substance of my enterprise consists in a sort of extrapolation, and what is projected into an inaccessible region remains fundamentally homogeneous with the point of departure; and then we are left with a God made in our own image, and the process is typically anthropomorphic. Or else we have within us (and that in the last analysis is what we presuppose) a possibility, a law of transcendence, which makes us posit an absolute justice and love beyond our grasp. That transcending of ourselves is conceivable only if that absolute is already active within us, in some sense, from the start. The analogy must be inverted; what we, in our experience, call justice and love are only what they are because they verify or express something of this aspiration or of this presence.[16]

. . . We can now realise how far away we are from the supreme Good, for we can see justice only as freedom from guilt, and blessedness only as freedom from wretchedness.[17]

---

16. Gabriel Madinier, *Conscience et signification* (1952), pp. 88ff.
17. St. Bernard of Clairvaux, *Sermones de dedicatione Ecclesiae*, 4, 5 (PL 183:529b).

In the end we deny everything which, starting from the creature, we have first affirmed of God. Nothing escapes that law. There is no conceivable exception to it. But we do not deny everything at the same stage of the dialectic, nor for the same reasons, nor in the same way. In fact, if it is true that there is an unbridgeable abyss between the unique Being of the Creator and the totality of creatures, it is no less true that creatures participate in different degrees in the Being of the Creator. Where analogies are concerned, one cannot treat those drawn from the realm of the senses on the same plane as those drawn from the realm of the spirit, or those which are the fruit of an effort of abstraction on the same plane as those derived from personal experience. One cannot equate all forms of anthropomorphism, regardless of whether they spring from the body or the soul, etc. Furthermore, we must not merely distinguish, as did Justin Martyr, between two sorts of divine attributes, those concerning God himself and others referring to his operations *ad extra,* and treat only the names of the former as "divine names."[18] We must follow Pseudo-Dionysius in distinguishing between what is said of God without real truth and what is said of him with truth, although it is subsequently denied with more truth. And in the Augustinian tradition, we distinguish between the image and the vestige of God, more or less distant, more or less effaced. Like John Scotus, we must distinguish between the words which we apply to God — between those which are *quasi propria* and others which are *aliena, hoc est translata.* We distinguish, again, with St. Anselm, the qualities which are not better than what is not themselves *(non meliores quam non ipsae)* and those which are better than what is not themselves *(meliores quam non ipsae),* and we recall that if we are forbidden to assume that the perfect Being is something which is in some way bettered by something not itself *(aliquid quo melius sit aliquo modo non ipsum),* it is equally necessary to admit that he is really whatever is altogether better than what is not itself *(quidquid omnino melius est quam non ipsum).*[19] And following all the Schoolmen, we distinguish finally the "mixed perfections" which cannot be found in God himself at all, and the "simple perfections" which must be found differently in him than in us.

Now, the effect of these distinctions is never completely abolished, as

---

18. St. Justin, *Apol.,* 1, 3

19. John Scotus Erigena, *De praedestinatione,* 9, 2 (PL 122:390-391); *De divisione naturae,* bk. 1, 37 and 76 (480b and 522a-b). St. Anselm, *Monologion,* ch. 15 (PL 158:161-164).

though they had been purely illusory. The creative essence is more profoundly known, the more it is sought for among creatures akin to ourselves *(Tanto altius creatrix essentia cognoscitur, quanto per propinquiorem sibi creaturam indagatur);*[20] a principle which is always true. Our negations bear, in the end, upon everything, though they are always relative and have their respective bearings. They are not equivalents. And if we may be allowed a very imperfect image, they are not identical at the base, though they converge and meet at the summit. They are involved in a sort of "levelling from above." Their particular meanings remain very diverse, although taken together they converge upon the necessary affirmation that God is always *beyond.*

The degrees of participation are real and various — but "the cause which does not participate is, above all, participation."[21] The spiritual creature is like God — but "God in his total transcendence is unlike anything else."[22] "No name can name the superessential Deity, and no reason bears upon him; the Deity remains inaccessible and beyond our grasp."[23]

---

20. St. Anselm, *ibid.,* ch. 66: ". . . Therefore it is obvious that just as the mind alone among all created things is rational, and is able to rise upwards to enter into an investigation of him, so no less is it the mind alone through which the mind itself is most able to advance towards a discovery of him" (PL 158:212-213).

21. Pseudo-Dionysius, *The Divine Names,* ch. 12, 4.

22. *Ibid.,* ch. 9, 6, etc. Cf. St. Thomas, *Contra Gentiles,* bk. 1, ch. 29: "Therefore God is not assimilated to the creature, but rather the converse is the case." Auguste Valensin, S.J., *À travers la Métaphysique* (1925), p. 234: "God cannot be like a person, inasmuch as he is the Absolute to whom everything has reference, while He himself has reference to nothing."

23. Pseudo-Dionysius, *The Divine Names,* ch. 13, 3. Cf. St. Thomas, *De Potentia,* q.7, a.5, ad 14m: "This is the ultimate aspect of human knowledge, the fact that man knows that he does not know God, to the extent that he learns that what God is goes beyond everything that we think about him." In *Contra Gentiles,* 1, 30, St. Thomas distinguishes the names which "indicate absolute perfection without defect" and the names which specify a mode proper to the creature; but he does this only to add immediately: "as for the mode of signifying, every name has a defect," and yet again: "in every name spoken by us, insofar as it concerns the mode of signifying, an imperfection is found which does not fit God, although the thing signified suits God in some conspicuous way or other"; he explains this with an example: "as is clear in the name denoted by goodness and good, for goodness is significant insofar as it does not subsist, good, moreover, insofar as it is concrete." Coming at things from another point of view, he distinguishes, in *Prima,* q.13, a.2, between the names which are spoken of God *negative* [= "negatively"] and those which are spoken of him *absolute et affirmative* [= "absolutely and affirmatively"]. But he specifies that even these latter are only im-

Yet how shall we complete the process of negation and proclaim fearlessly that God is always *above all things* if not by virtue of some requirement anterior even to conceptual thought; by virtue, that is to say, of a sort of primary, unshakeable affirmation? It is that affirmation which obliges us, when the moment comes, to deny everything: and so it cannot be denied. It embraces within itself the truth in all the affirmations which it has made us reject — the truth which cannot be isolated conceptually because we are unable to conceive properly what the *modus altior* or *eminentior*, to use St. Thomas's expression, or the *modus quidam singularis*, to use St. Anselm's, can be in God. That affirmation is always the soul of our negations, and if we came to deny it the process of negation would come to a halt: then, as the result of the fixity of thought, which amounts to a denial that God is always *above everything*, we should fall, not into atheism but into idolatry, "attributing to the image what only belongs to the truth,"[24] by the very fact that we attribute to truth what only belongs to the image.

The power of negation which is in us is therefore not a negative force: it obliges us always to affirm God without ever allowing us to stop at anything unworthy of him, and in doing so reveals itself to reflection as a doubly positive power. By the principle which sets it in motion, it makes our idea of God, beneath its negative form, not simply but eminently positive.

We do not know *what God is*. . . . That may mean one of two things. It has a vulgar meaning — that of mere ignorance; and that meaning is to be rejected. But it has a second, particular meaning which refers to God alone; we do not know what God is, but we know what he is not. Or rather, we say that we know what he is because we know what he is not. The last two affirmations are inseparable. In fact, they are identical. Not to know what God is is to know what he is not. And that is a very exalted knowledge. If we refuse to apply any meaning to God which, as such, applies to creatures, we are affirming that God is distinct from all creatures: in a word, we proclaim him as God.

---

perfect representations of the divine essence. Since, moreover, they are such as they are, we ought similarly to repudiate them in order to affirm their ungraspable unity in God.

24. Nicholas of Cusa, *De docta ignorantia*, bk. 1, ch. 26.

Deus, qui scitur melius nesciendo.[25]

(God is better known by nescience.)

When we consider the problem of the knowledge of God as it presents itself to reason, starting from our knowledge of the world, it is more important than ever to distinguish very carefully between the two questions *an est* (whether it is) and *quid est* (what it is).[26] It is no doubt true that one cannot affirm the existence of a being, whatever it may be, without giving at least some sort of definition of it.[27] But strictly speaking, the definition of an essence is one thing and the determination of a role quite another. In the case of God only the latter, according to the argument, is possible, at least in a positive form, and it is not necessary to know anything more in a positive way in order that God should fulfill the role attributed to him by the argument; it is even essential not to know more.

In other words, if the *proof* of God's existence, starting from the world, is to be valid, and if it is really to be a proof of *God*, it is not, strictly speaking, indispensable to know anything about the divine essence; on the contrary, it seems indispensable not to be able to know anything. For that is the only way in which one can know something about him as distinct from all else. And if one could know something about him, in the same sense in which one knows something of the world, or of the objects in the world, then that essence would

---

25. St. Augustine, *De ordine*, 2, 16 (PL 32:1015). John Scotus Erigena, *De divisione naturae*, 66 (PL 122:510B). St. Anselm, *Monologion*, c. 26: "It is to the extent that that being which in itself is whatever, and which makes every other being from nothing, is different from that being which comes to be whatever it is through something other from nothing — it is to this extent, I say, that the highest substance is utterly separate from the things which are not the same as it is. And since it alone of all natures is in a condition to be whatever it is without the aid of another nature, how is it not uniquely whatever it is without the partnership of its own creature? Wherefore, whenever it has communion with others of some name or other, quite without a doubt a different significance must be ascribed to this" (PL 158:179-180). Cf. ch. 27.

26. William of St.-Thierry, *Aenigma fidei*, init.: "It is a religious acknowledgement of human weakness to know this one thing about God, namely that God is. For the rest, it is pious to seek out and indeed examine thoroughly his essence or nature and those secret decrees of his inscrutable judgement. Since, however, the earthly mind does not penetrate these things, it must be confessed that they are inscrutable and unsearchable" (PL 180:397b). On this subject see Jacques Maritain, *Approches de Dieu*, pp. 20-22.

27. St. Thomas, *In Boethium de Trinitate*, q.6, a.3.

in some measure enter into the categories of thought as do the others. It would "fall under a genus." From that moment it would form part of this world, and would no longer help us in any way to explain it. We would have to begin everything over again and would be travelling in a circle.[28]

But what a rich matter for reflection intelligence finds in that very contrast between a world which can be known and explained and him without whom the world would be nothing! What an immense difference between vulgar ignorance and that qualified ignorance! What paradoxical knowledge is contained in that rejection of knowledge! How much there is in the void which opens before it, and how great is the light in that obscurity! How can the intelligence fail to feel that its impotence in face of him whom it cannot define is not a sign of insufficiency but of an unbelievable increase? "That God cannot be measured is what gives me the measure of him."[29] And on the other hand, leaving the world and its explanations aside, surely the evidence accumulates in proportion as the negations grow in strength and precision, and are more clearly dictated by a previous unconditioned affirmation whose incomparable vigor cannot be otherwise expressed.

Our concepts have the power to *signify* God truly — and yet strictly speaking, we cannot *seize* God in any one of them; or rather that is how they truly signify him. God would not be God unless he were — not unknowable but — beyond our grasp.[30] He is always above and beyond all

---

28. Similar arguments will be found in A. D. Sertillanges, *Les grandes thèses de la philosophie thomiste*, pp. 48-49. For some specific details, see also below. Cf. St. Thomas, *Contra Gentiles*, bk. 1, ch. 14: "In considering the divine substance we cannot accept anything like a genus, nor can we accept his being distinct from other things through positively asserted differences.... At that point, when he is recognized as distinct from all things, there will be a proper examination of his [God's] substance. There will not, however, be perfect knowledge, since what he is in himself will not be recognized." For some specific details concerning the thought of St. Thomas, cf. H. F. Dondaine, O.P., "Cognoscere de Deo 'quid est,'" *Recherches de théologie ancienne et médiévale* 22 (1955), pp. 72-78. John Scotus Erigena, *De divisione naturae*, 1, 15: "But, as holy father Augustine says in his books on the Trinity, when we reach the realm of theology, that is to say, an investigation of the divine essence, the worthwhileness of categories is utterly extinguished" (PL 122:463b); 72: "Now at long last I understand unhesitatingly that no category is suitable for God" (518b).

29. Tertullian, *Apologeticus*, ch. 17 (PL 1:376a).

30. St. Thomas, *De Veritate*, q.2, a.1, ad 9m: "The intellect is said to know about something and what it is at the point where the intellect defines it, which is to say, when it conceives some image of the thing itself which corresponds in all its aspects to the very

that we can say and think of him: *super omnia quae praeter ipsum et concipi possunt ineffabiliter excelsus.*[31]

"The unnameable is the most beautiful of its names and sets it at once above everything else one might be tempted to say about it."[32]

---

thing. Already, moreover, it is clear from what has been said that whatever our intellect conceives about God is deficient in the representation of him. And so what is of God himself ever remains hidden to us. This is the highest knowledge that we can have of him in this life, so that we recognize that God is above everything that we think about him, as is clear in the works of Dionysius." Cf. *De Veritate,* q.8, a.1, ad 8m; q.10, a.11, ad 4m: "While we are in the state of life, we come to learn of God by an intellectual notion, not with a view to knowing him for what he is, but rather for what he is not. . . ." Cf. *Prima,* q.13, a.2.

Writing in *Le Thomisme* (5th ed., pp. 173-174), Etienne Gilson comments on the Thomist doctrine of the perfections of God: "Without a doubt it is a very precious advantage for us to know that God is eternal, infinite, perfect, intelligent, and good; but let us not forget that the 'how' of these attributes escapes us, for if any of these certitudes obliged us to forget that the divine essence remains unknown to us here below, it would be better for us never to possess them. . . . The existence of God escapes our grasp. We can thus come to the same conclusion as Dionysius the Areopagite by placing the highest knowledge that we are permitted to acquire in this life regarding the divine nature within the certitude that God remains above everything that we think of him."

It is no more true for me than for St. Thomas that this presupposes "a corrosive criticism of intellectual knowledge" or a "suspicion with regard to reason." Furthermore, it is quite true that "the whole process," contained herein, "of the concepts of God can only be explained objectively in the face of an analogy of the divine names that is close to being univocal" and that this analogy, moreover, "is not the one taught by St. Thomas after the Lateran Council." But I do not see why it has been thought possible to suppose in this instance that it has been the intention on my part to criticize the doctrine of St. Thomas, whereas, to the contrary, I was deriving corroborative support from it. There is, if you will, a "process," but the process is established (in a moderate way) by St. Thomas himself.

31. First Vatican Council, *Constitutio dogmatica de fide catholica,* c. 1 (Denzinger-Schönmetzer, *Enchiridion Symbolorum . . . ,* no. 3000, p. 587). Apart from the texts already cited, see St. Ambrose, *De fide,* bk. 1, ch. 10, n. 63: "Nor indeed can we shut up the immense greatness of divinity within the confines of our narrow discussions, for his greatness has no end" (PL 16: 543A). Or St. Augustine, *In Psalmum,* 85, n. 12: "God is not this . . . God is not that. Then what is he? I found myself able to assert this one thing only, namely, what he is not. You seek to know what he is? What eye has not seen, what ear has not heard, what has not taken its rise and entered into the heart of man. Why do you seek to learn how what has not taken its rise in the heart arises on the tongue?" (PL 37:1090). See M. Olier, *Traité des attributs divins* (cited by P. Pourrat, in *Dictionnaire de spiritualité,* vol. 1, col. 1089).

32. St. Albert the Great, *Summa theologiae,* tract. 3, q.16, ad 1m. Cf. Nicholas of Cusa, *De visione Dei,* ch. 12, n. 47: "An immensely high wall . . . separates You from all that can be expressed or thought, because You are independent of all that can be reached by the thought of anyone, whoever it may be."

In the same way, we cannot limit the operations of the mind which really lead us to God to the arguments by which it does so, if these arguments are reduced to a formula or particularized and, by the same token, reduced to some general scheme. But neither may we conclude that our arguments prove nothing or that they are useless, any more than we could, as has just been said, admit that our concepts could not signify God in truth. Without our arguments, the basic operation of the mind could not objectify itself and take shape. We should be unable to grasp it. Only, as many philosophers have recognized, the various arguments, viewed in their particular and objective formulations, never do more than express in a rational form, each in its own way, the essential movement of the mind.[33] The hidden Presence which inspires and sustains them is not such that we can disregard the need to convert it into a proof, and that is the proper function of reason. Yet reason can never capture or canalize in its "ways" more than a fraction of the abundant sap which continuously revitalizes the mind and gives it its essential movement.

That is because the hidden pulse of the mind is beyond the grasp of any analyzable logical process, just as Being is beyond the grasp of representation.[34] Or, if one prefers, it is prior to it, the "common root" and the "hidden spring" of all these processes.[35]

But even these expressions, for all their truth, are inadequate. And in fact he whom we call Being, and whom others, undaunted by the paradox, do not hesitate to call "Negation" or "Nothing,"[36] "the eternal Nothing," or

---

33. This is what Joseph Maréchal says very well in the *Nouvelle revue théologique* (1931), p. 198: "The diversity of ways or arguments indicates the diversity of starting-points in the real which is immediately accessible to the mind, which rises from them, by a process which remains fundamentally the same, to the transcendent absolute."

34. Cf. Maréchal, *Le point de départ de la recherche métaphysique*, bk. 5, p. 183: "What is it to say that God is purely and simply 'being' and that the creature is 'being' and 'essence', except that God cannot, properly speaking, be *represented* by any of our objective concepts? For all objective concepts delimit an 'essence' (and even imply a representation that has a perceptible origin)." See above, Chapter 2, note 12.

35. Charles de Moré-Pontgibaud, "Sur l'analogie des noms divins, l'analogie métaphorique," *Recherches de science religieuse* (1952), pp. 506ff.: "This same direction of thought is, as it were, the hidden spring of all the proofs of the existence of God"; it is important to consider these proofs "in their common root."

36. Cf. St. Angela of Foligno, *Vita*, ch. 4, n. 72 (*Acta sanctorum*, vol. 1 [Antwerp, 1643], p. 197): "I saw . . . in the darkness that there is a greater good which cannot be considered or understood, and everything which is capable of being considered or understood does not touch it. . . . And the soul sees nothing at all which can be

"pure Nothingness"[37] — although immediately correcting themselves — cannot, strictly speaking, be represented by the concept of being any more than by any other concept.[38] One may certainly say, and sometimes, in order to avoid leading the unprepared mind into error, one should say, that the names we give to God — the name of Being in the first place — do represent him in a way, though very imperfectly. But if we want to observe the requirements of accuracy to the very end, then we cannot avoid adding that we are unable to represent the divine essence to ourselves at all, strictly speaking, and that there is no name which, applied to God, signifies him "quidditatively."[39] *Nullum est nomen Dei, quod ipsum quidditative significet,*

---

recounted orally, or even be conceived in the heart, and it sees nothing and it sees all things in general. . . ." Cf. Master Eckhart on Exodus: "In God there is not being, but purity of being. . . . Therefore being is not congruent with God, unless you should call purity of being by such a name": *Magistri Echardi quaestiones Parisienses,* ed. B. Geyer (1931). John Scotus Erigena, *De divisione naturae,* bk. 2 (589a-c) and bk. 3 (684-685).

37. Hadewijch II, *Poème,* 1. Henry Suso, *Das Buch der Wahrheit,* bks. 1, 5, and 6.

38. Cf. Etienne Gilson, *Le Thomisme,* 4th ed., p. 150: In a "secret desire to redeem from an all too apparent difficulty the knowledge of God that Saint Thomas Aquinas accords to us," one comes "progressively to speak of analogy as a source of almost positive understandings which would permit us to conceive more or less confusedly the essence of God." However, "to make Saint Thomas say that we have at the least an imperfect knowledge of what God is is to betray his thought such as it has been expressly formulated by him many a time. For he has not only said that the vision of the divine essence has been refused us here below, he has declared in right and proper terms that 'there is something on the subject of God that is totally unknown to man in this life, with a view to knowing what God is.' To say that *quid est Deus* [= "what God is"] is something *omnino ignotum* [= "utterly unknown"] to man in this life (*In Epist. ad Romanos,* cap. 1, lectio 6) is to posit all knowledge of the essence of God, whether imperfect or perfect, as radically inaccessible to man here below. 'Saint Paul', Saint Thomas tells us, 'spoke of the *invisibilia Dei* (= "invisible things of God"), because that in God which responds to these names or reasons is one, and is not seen by us'" (Eng. trans., *The Christian Philosophy of St. Thomas Aquinas,* pp. 105-108).

39. The knowledge of God that St. Thomas accords to us, Gilson tells us once again (*ibid.,* p. 154; Eng. trans., p. 108), "does not in any way bear on his essence, which is to say on his *esse.*" This does not, of course, stop us from being able to bring true judgments to the subject of God, because the direction of the pole towards which they orient our understanding is known to us. In this way, if we cannot reach him, we can at least turn ourselves towards him and know him with certitude. Consequently, "in order to escape the 'conceptual agnosticism' to which certain people are ill-advisedly resigned, when it is a question of God, it is not in a more or less imperfect concept of the divine essence that we must seek refuge, but in the positiveness of

seu repraesentet et hac ratione merito ineffabilis dicitur.[40] "The exclusion of any definition in regard to God" is valid even to the point at which it refers to "the qualification of God as Being."[41] *Deo quasi ignoto conjungimur.*[42] If definition always involves, to some extent at least, determination, how could it be possible to determine him whose being excludes determination?[43] Let

---

affirmative judgments which take their rise from the multiple effects of God and situate, so to speak, the metaphysical place of an essence which we absolutely cannot conceive" (*ibid.*, pp. 156-157; Eng. trans., p. 458, n. 51). In this way we can, it seems, harmonize the quite categorical texts in which St. Thomas denies us all knowledge of God's *quid est* (= "what he is") with the texts in which he observes that for God, as for every other object, the knowledge of *an est* (= "whether he is") never goes without a certain knowledge of *quid est* (= "what he is"). See, for example, *In Boethium de Trinitate*, q.1, a.2, 6 and ad 2m, and likewise q.6, a.3.

40. Suarez, *Tractatus primus, de divina substantia*, bk. 2, ch. 31, n. 10. Which does not prevent his saying in n. 15: ". . . names, which represent God imperfectly for us . . ." (*Opera omnia*, ed. Vives, vol. 1, pp. 184 and 185).

41. A. D. Sertillanges, in *Saint Thomas d'Aquin, Somme théologique* (éd. de la Revue des Jeunes), *Dieu*, vol. 2, p. 383, commenting on *Sent.*, d. 13, a.1, ad 4m. Cf. p. 341: "The being which serves the function of naming God, in the expression 'He who is', is not the being of God, but the being of creatures. This will have to be remembered when one says . . . that being itself could not be attributed to God without, like all other human words, undergoing an analogical transposition."

Cf. Suarez, *Disput.*, 30, sectio 12, n. 10: "Although we recognize that God is being itself in his essence, we do not, however, properly conceive what kind of being this is, nor are we even capable of conceiving what his very being is in its essence, except, indeed, by way of negation, because his being is something which exists in actuality, that is, not by means of another, and we declare the proper perfection of that being likewise through negation, because it is infinite." J. Maréchal, *Le point de départ . . .*, bk. 5, pp. 176ff.: "Pure being excludes all superadded determinations, because it does not contain any kind of 'potency.' . . . Abstract being . . . is potential with regard to *every* determination." Cf. St. Thomas, *Prima*, q.3, a.4, ad 1m.

42. St. Thomas, *Prima*, q.12, a.13, ad 1m: "Although we do not come to learn about God and what he is by a revelation of grace in this life, and thus we are joined to him as to one unknown. . . ." *De potentia*, q.7, a.5: "It must be said that, although our intellect cannot match the divine substance, that very thing which constitutes the substance of God remains, surpassing as it does our intellect; and so it remains unknown to us. And thus this is the ultimate reach of man's knowledge about God, namely, the fact that he knows that he does not know God, insofar as he recognizes that what God is surpasses everything which we understand about him."

43. *In I Sent.*, d. 8, q.1, a.1, ad 4m: ". . . This denominative phrase, 'who is', refers to absolute being that is not determined by anything that is added on; and so Damascene says that it does not signify what God is, but signifies a kind of infinite sea of substance, which is not determined, as it were. Wherefore, when we make progress into God

us not be afraid to recognize it, in spite of ontologist temptations, in spite of our pragmatic instincts or the sneaking desire for a God who would seem nearer to us. That is one of the forms which our love of the truth must take, and it is one of the supports of our adoration. *Deus semper major.* The imperfection in our representation cannot but fail to involve,

---

through the way of removal, we first take away corporal aspects from him; and secondly even intellectual aspects, like goodness and wisdom, as they are found in creatures. And then there remains in our intellect only the fact that he is and nothing more. Wherefore he exists in a kind of state of confusion, as it were. At the last, moreover, we remove from him even that very being such as is found in creatures. And then he remains in a kind of darkness of ignorance, with respect to which, insofar as it pertains to our state of life, we are best joined to God, as Dionysius says; and this is a kind of veil of darkness, in which God is said to dwell."

Contra Gentiles, bk. 3, ch. 49: ". . . For through his effects we come to learn about God, that he exists and that he is the cause of other things, towering above other things and removed from everything; and this is the ultimate and most perfect state of our knowledge in this life. Wherefore Dionysius says that we are joined to God as if to an unknown; what God truly is remains completely unknown. For which reason and in order to show our ignorance of this most sublime kind of knowledge, it is said of Moses that he drew near the dark cloud in which God was. Cf. Exodus 20:21."

In I Tim. ch. 4, lectio 3, in fine: "The intellect is able in a twofold way to approach the knowledge of the nature of anything, with a view, that is, to learning and to comprehending. It is impossible, moreover, for the intellect to reach a comprehension of God. . . . But there is another way to learn about God, namely, by touching him. And according to this way of thinking, no created intellect touches through its own natural faculties on the knowledge of what God is. And the reason for this is that no force can investigate into anything higher than its own object, just as in the case of sight with reference to that which is higher. The proper object of the intellect, moreover, is that which something is. Therefore, whatever rises above that which something is exceeds the proportions of all intellect. In God, moreover, his being is not one thing and his quiddity (another). . . ."

Prima, q.13, a.2, ad 3m: "We cannot know the essence of God in this life according to what he is in himself, but we know him according to what is represented in the perfections of creatures." People have raised an objection about the substance of this article. In it St. Thomas deals with "the names which are spoken absolutely and affirmatively of God, names like good, wise, and suchlike." In effect he discards the opinion of those who see therein only designations of a purely negative kind, and then also the opinion of those who think that such names are used only "to signify the appearance [of God] towards created things." These names are well said of God himself, and they correspond nicely to a positive reality; nevertheless, "they fall short in representing him." In the final analysis, as Gilson explains (*Le Thomisme,* p. 200, n. 2), this text presents the same doctrine as the others, albeit in a quite mitigated form, or, one might rather say, in a less complete form.

in turn, its negation: *Deus, de quo negationes magis verae sunt*[44] (God, about whom negations are more true). But once again it must be remembered that the negation invalidates nothing except the limits of the affirmation which preceded it;[45] and once again, in consequence, the fundamentally *quite positive* sense of the necessary negation comes to light.

As for the "operation of the mind" which results in the affirmation of God, it is not, in the proper sense of the word, an operation — not in the generally accepted sense, that is, or in the first instance. In its first logical moment it is receptivity, a substantial opening of the mind, a welcome which is in the first instance passive. It is only active in a derivative way. Though here, too, the language which we use needs to be corrected or at least carefully checked. "At every moment we receive a reason which is superior to us." We participate in a Light which comes from above. Our intelligence does not grasp the Absolute — in a way which is always abstract — without first of all having been grasped by it.[46] That is what is expressed by saying, according to a tradition which goes back to St. Paul, that if we know God, even naturally, it is ultimately through "the revelation" of God.[47]

---

44. Isaac of Stella, *In Sexagesima sermo* 5: "For rather do we deny everything about him than affirm anything at all" (PL 194:1762c).

45. Jac. Alvarez de Paz, S.J., *De inquisitione pacis,* bk. 5, pt. 1, app. 3, ch. 1: "In God, as Dionysius wisely notices, these affirmations and negations are not opposed: because when, for example, we attribute wisdom to God, we grant to him that perfection by which he knows himself and all things in himself: when, indeed, we withdraw this wisdom, we deny him that limited mode of wisdom with which we conceive of wisdom" (*Opera*, vol. 6, p. 463).

46. Fénelon, *Traité de l'existence de Dieu*, pt. 1, ch. 2, n. 56. Cf. Joseph Maréchal, in the first edition of *Point de départ de la métaphysique* (Louvain, 1917): "Metaphysics is the human science of the absolute. It translates directly the seizure of our intelligence by the absolute. That seizure is not a yoke, something external, but an internal principle of life." In a note to the above, A. Hayen, the editor, remarks that Maréchal does not say "the seizure of the absolute by our intelligence." That is very significant, and forcibly expresses the idea which I have tried to emphasize at several points. Already within the compass of our natural knowledge we only "seize" God, in a manner of speaking, after we have been "seized" by him. Here we have, *mutatis mutandis,* on the level of nature and of reason, the analogue of what Saint Paul wrote in Galatians 4:9: "But now that you have come to know God, or rather to be known by God." Cf. Louis Lavelle, in the preface to *L'existence de Dieu* (1951), p. 10 (the French trans. by Régis Jolivet, of M.-F. Sciacca, *L'Esistenza di Dio*, in *Filosofia e Metafisica* [1950], p. 12): There is "a secret identity, at the heart of thought, between our activity and our passivity."

47. St. Maximus the Confessor, *Capitula theologica et oeconomica*, century 1, ch. 25:

"We must be looked at if we are to be enlightened."[48]

Signatum est super nos lumen Vultus tui, Domine![49]

When we give a thing a name we imagine we have got hold of it. We imagine that we have got hold of being. Perhaps we should do better not to flatter ourselves too soon that we can name God.[50]

"In no wise can the soul attain the knowledge of God, unless God himself stoops down to her, in order to raise her up to himself. For the human spirit would never have the strength to stay the course, so as to attain some measure of divine light, if God did not draw it to himself — inasmuch as it is possible for the human spirit to be thus drawn — and illuminate it with his own brightness" (PG 90:1093-1096). Now we see how it is possible to understand such texts (which only take up and develop affirmations that can be found in St. Irenaeus already; cf. above, *Abyssus Abyssum Invocat*, notes 11 and 12).

48. Victor Poucel. See above, Chapter 1, notes 7 to 12. Cf. Paul Demiéville, *Le Concile de Lhasa* (1952), p. 78, n. 2: "The broad meaning of the expression *fan tchao* is 'to reflect'. But through an association that goes back without a doubt to (Taoist) beliefs that assimilate the eyes to sources of light (the sun and the moon), the word *tchao* means both 'to illuminate' and 'to look.'"

49. Psalm 4:6. St. Thomas refers to this verse in his interpretation of Romans 1:20: "What is known of God is manifest in them," with reference to "the infused light of reason"; also in *Prima*, q.84, a.5; cf. *Prima Secundae*, q.19, a.4; q.91, a.2, etc. Saint Bonaventure, *In 2a Sent.*, d. 24, pt. 1, a.2, q.4; d. 17, pt. 1, a.1, q.4.

Cf. St. Robert Bellarmine, *In Psalmum* 4, 7: "The natural light of reason . . . is inscribed and impressed indelibly on us, that is, in the supreme part of man. . . . Thus there is in this supreme part a light by which we are distinguished from the beasts; and this light is derived from the Face of God, because it causes us to be in the image and likeness of God" (*Opera*, vol. 10, pp. 25ff.). Or Dominicus Soto, *In Epist. ad Romanos*, c. 1: ". . . Therefore the very light of our nature, about which the Prophet says, 'the light of your face, O Lord, is imprinted on us', he calls, and indeed most deservedly so, a manifestation of God" ([Antwerp, 1550], p. 43).

50. St. Gregory of Nyssa, *Contra Eunomium*, bk. 12: "As the Apostle says, the only name which suits God is the belief that he is above all names. For the fact that he transcends all movement of thought and that he turns out to be beyond being taken hold of by any kind of name constitutes the proof of his greatness, which man cannot express" (PG 45:1108c). Cf. Isaac of Stella, *In Sexagesima sermo* 6: "It is clear when we, who are not permitted to keep silent, are forced to speak about the supernature or word of the ineffable God, that just as no name can be devised such as expresses what is being spoken about, even so no word can be devised such as properly signifies what it is right to speak of" (PL 194:1768b).

Non ignorabatur Dei nomen — sed plane Deus ignorabatur.[51]

(He lives apart from the names which are given to him.)

~

Quid ergo est Deus? Quod ad universum spectat, finis; quod ad electionem, salus; quo ad se, Ipse novit.[52] (What therefore is God? As regards the universe, he is its end; as regards our election, he is salvation; as regards himself, only he knows.)

~

One must not say: God is not good. He is incomprehensible; but one does better to say: God is Goodness itself, and it is that Goodness which I cannot understand. One should not say: God is not the Father, he is the Abyss; one should say, "God is the paternal Abyss."[53]

~

Even if it were not possible for the intelligence to grasp the whole universe and, in one way or another, exhaust its intelligible essence — would it, in fact, be desirable? Surely it would be quite horrible. Imagine to yourself that there were no more discoveries to be made and nothing more to wonder at. Imagine there were no depths to explore! "O the desire to desire!" Zarathustra exclaims, "O devouring hunger in the midst of satiety!"[54] And the same sentiment, stripped of its Promethean romanticism, can be found in the pages of Angelus Silesius:

> The world is too narrow, the sky too small:
> Where is there room for my soul?

---

51. St. Hilary. Master Eckhart, *Sermon sur la richesse de Dieu* (French trans. by A. Mayrisch Saint-Hubert [1954], sermon 13, p. 158).

52. St. Bernard, *De consideratione,* bk. 5, ch. 11, n. 24 (PL 182:802). Cf. *De diversis sermo* 8, n. 1: "Although we call God by diverse names, at one time, indeed, Father, and at another time Master or Lord, there is no diversity in his exceedingly simple and utterly invariable nature that is the cause: but the cause is rather the manifold variability of our affections in accordance with the diverse progressions or failings of the soul" (PL 183:561a). *In Cantica canticorum sermo* 51, n. 7: "Where, I ask you, would you find words with which you might worthily mark out this majesty of his or properly pronounce upon it or suitably define it?" (col. 1028a).

53. Origen, *In Numer. hom.,* 16, n. 4; *In Joannem,* 2, 2; etc.

54. Nietzsche, *Also sprach Zarathustra* (Kröners Taschenausgaben ed.), p. 114.

The knowledge of the Cherubim is not enough for me:
My desire is to fly high above him, in the Unknown.[55]

Think of the man whose pact with Satan gave him complete knowledge. From that moment on he was imprisoned in his own knowledge: "He spent his days spreading his wings, longing to explore the luminous spheres so clearly and astonishingly revealed to him by his intuition. . . . His heart panted for the UNKNOWN, because he knew all things."[56] God alone is worthy of the intelligence, and God alone can fill it because he is inexhaustible: "Surely we have the right not to see God? . . . And in not knowing him, I recognise him."[57]

One should not speak much in this life: one can discourse upon the world, on matter and on the soul, on rational creatures whether good or bad, on judgment, rewards and penalties, and on the sufferings of Jesus Christ; but when one undertakes to consider God, not in what he has said or done, but in what he is, restraint and sobriety are to be commended.[58]

I will tell you, my dear friends and disciples, and you my rivals in the love of truth, what happened to me in my search for God.

In the belief that I should soon attain him, I pursued God with indefatigable ardour. I climbed to the mountain top; with Moses, I

---

55. Angelus Silesius, *The Cherubic Pilgrim*, bk. 1, 187 and 284.

56. Balzac, *Melmoth reconcilié* (the figure of Castanier). Cf. Albert Beguin, *Balzac et la fin de Satan*, in *Satan* (Études carmélitaines, 1948), pp. 538-547.

57. Paul Claudel, *La Ville*, second version, p. 293. (This view will be applied *mutatis mutandis* to the beatific vision.) Cf. *Art poétique*, pp. 25 and 45. Letter to Gabriel Frizeau, 20 January 1904, concerning the mysteries of the faith: "These shadows are as dear to a believing heart as the lights themselves. Who would want a truth that could be assimilated at one's first contact with it, a truth that is prostituted to every kind of prying curiosity? . . ." (Paul Claudel, Francis Jammes, Gabriel Frizeau, *Correspondance*, ed. André Blanchet [1952], p. 34). Letter to Jacques Rivière, 12 March 1908: ". . . Finally I took my leave of that hideous world of Taine, of Renan, and other manifestations of Moloch in the nineteenth century. I left that prison-house, that frightful machinery entirely governed by laws of perfect inflexibility, laws that are, to cap the horror of them, *knowable and teachable* as well." Cf. in Hans Urs Von Balthasar, *Theologik 1, Wahrheit der Welt*, 2nd ed. (1985), the beautiful chapter on *Wahrheit als Geheimnis*, p. 235: "It is the unveiling of being which is as such its most opaque veil."

58. St. Gregory of Nazianzus, *Discourse* 27, n. 10 (PG 36:25); cf. Gregory of Nyssa, *On Ecclesiastes*, hom. 7 (PG 44:731-733).

pierced the clouds; and withdrawing from the material objects among which my spirit had been dissipated, I gave myself as far as possible to recollection. But just as I began to think that I should be able to rest my eyes on God himself, and see him face to face, I found that I could hardly see, in his works, the back he turned towards me; and even that grace I only received hidden in the rock, that is to say in the Word incarnate for our salvation. I therefore learnt that this first and most pure nature was only known to itself, and that it was hidden by a veil, shrouded by the wings of the Cherubim, covering it like the Ark of the Covenant, and that only a tiny ray of its light reaches us. Whoever you may be, that is how you may become theologians (that is to say, contemplate the divinity); — even though you were Moses and the God of Pharaoh, though you were Paul himself, ravished to the third heaven, hearing hidden words; even though you were raised above those great souls and took your place among the Angels and Archangels, since even those celestial (and more than celestial) natures are further below the knowledge of God than they are above terrestrial and corporeal natures.

Let me put it another way: a profane theologian said with great subtlety that it was difficult to know God but quite impossible to express what one thought of him; but as for me, I would rather say that it is impossible to express the greatness of God in words or to give him a name, but still more impossible to understand him.[59]

If my discourse returns to some point about which I have already spoken, you should not be surprised. For I shall continue to say the same thing about the same thing, with that tremor in the voice, in the spirit and in thought, which I feel whenever I talk of God; and I pray that this same blessed and praiseworthy feeling may also be yours.[60]

Should we understand Yahweh's words to Moses to mean: "I am he who is," or "I am who I am"? Do we hear the Absolute proclaiming himself or the hidden God remaining silent? Are we presented with a definition or a refusal to define?

Let us leave the scholars to their exegetical discussions — some of them, perhaps, will add further explanations or a subtler gloss.[61] Why should we

---

59. St. Gregory of Nazianzus, *Discourse* 28, nn. 3-4 (PG 36:29).
60. St. Gregory of Nazianzus, *Discourse* 39 (PG 36:345d).
61. An exegesis of Exodus 3:13-15, together with a discussion of the various interpretations that have been proposed, can be found in A. M. Dubarle, O.P., "La signification

not retain both meanings? The first interpretation is, perhaps, difficult to justify as it stands, grammatically and historically; and at first sight the second interpretation may sound a little thin considering the solemnity of the occasion. But although they may seem to be opposed are they not, at bottom, very close to one another?[62]

The first formula is full of grandeur. As far as possible, it names God by the name which properly belongs to him, by the name "which is more rightly his than the name of God itself."[63] He is! He exists! He is Existence

---

du nom de Yahweh" (*Revue des sciences philosophiques et théologiques* [1951], pp. 3-21). To the best of our knowledge this article constitutes the best and clearest restatement that has been made of this problem. Contrary to the translation of the Septuagint, the word of God to Moses "constitutes a wilfully evasive response. It should be translated, 'I am who I am', or, 'I am what I am'. God does not consent to giving a name which would define him" (p. 11). In fact, it is not in the scene that is reported in Exodus that the first meeting occurs "between the God of Abraham, Isaac, and Jacob and the God of the philosophers and the learned" (Gilson). "This happens later, in the book of Wisdom" (p. 19). Dubarle, however, observes quite rightly that "it can happen and it does happen that, in taking up and pondering the words of an ill-understood text, a thinker succeeds in expressing a true notion, one that is in keeping with the profundity of biblical teaching" (pp. 17-18). See also the most recent article of G. Lambert, S.J., "Que signifie le nom divin YHWH?" (*Nouvelle revue théologique* [1952], pp. 897-915). And still more recently, P. Van Imschoot, *Théologie de l'Ancien testament*, I, *Dieu* (1954), pp. 15ff.: "God's response is not a refusal to confide his name . . ."; it denotes "an existence that manifests itself actively, an efficacious being rather than an absolute being"; it is the "efficacity of the being of a liberating God"; he is and acts with an absolute liberty: "he is who he is."

62. Louis Massignon, "Soyons des Sémites spirituels," *Dieu Vivant* 14, p. 87: "The words to Moses, in Hebrew, 'I am He whom it pleases me to be', are infinitely stronger and more redolent of freedom than in the Greek of the Septuagint, 'I am the present participle of the copulative verb "to be,"' and the whole Christian theological enterprise which has drawn an ontology from this verb 'to be' has been based on the initial potency and creative shock of the Hebrew." For an opposite meaning, see, for example: Adolphe Lods, *Israël des origines au milieu du XIIIe siècle* (1930), pp. 371-373.

63. St. Thomas, *Prima*, q.13, a.11, ad 1m: "The name, 'who is', is a more proper name for God than the name, 'God', both with respect to the source from which the imposition of this name arises, namely, being, and with respect to its mode of signification and consignification. . . ." Cf. Etienne Gilson, *L'esprit de la philosophie médiévale*, 2nd ed. (1944), p. 50, n. 1: "It is not a question naturally of maintaining that the text of Exodus furnished men with a metaphysical definition of God; but if there is not any metaphysics *in* Exodus, there is a metaphysics *of* Exodus, and it can be seen being formed very early on in the Fathers of the Church, whose general directions on this point the philosophers of the Middle Ages did nothing but follow and improve on." One can read A. M. Dubarle's restatement of the issue in the article cited above, note 61.

St. Augustine, *In Psalmum*, 134, n. 4: ". . . Although, therefore, even those things

itself! It expresses a "metaphysical" truth and gives, in striking and paradoxical abridgment, an abstract definition of the "Supreme Being" which sets it apart, while at the same time refusing to assign any limit to it. In a word, it isolates the Absolute of Being and its eternity.[64] *Non est ibi nisi, Est.... Quidquid ibi est, non nisi est.... Ego, inquit, sum qui sum. Magnum ecce Est, Magnum Est!* [65] (There is nothing there but "he is." ... Whatever

---

which he created do exist, the whole matter comes, nonetheless, to a comparison with him, and as though he were alone, we find him saying: 'I am who I am', etc.... He did not say, the Lord God almighty, merciful, and just ... when all those epithets by which he could have been called and spoken of as God had been removed from discussion, he answered that he was called by the name of being; and he goes on as if this were his name: 'You will say this to them, he said, He who is sent me.' For he exists in such a way that in comparison with him all those things which were created do not exist. When he is not brought into the comparison, they exist because they exist by him; compared to him, on the other hand, they do not exist . . ." (PL 37:1741). St. John Damascene, *De fide orthodoxa*, bk. 1, ch. 9 (PG 94:835). Peter Lombard, *Sentences*, bk. 1, dist. 8. St. Bonaventure, *In 4 Sent.*, bk. 1, d. 8, p. 1, dub. 8: "And thus Hilary says that being is not accidental to God, etc." (Quaracchi, vol. 1, p. 164). St. Thomas, *Contra Gentiles*, bk. 1, ch. 22: "Moses, moreover, was taught this sublime truth by the Lord. When Moses asked the Lord, saying: 'If the sons of Israel say to me, "What is his name?" What shall I say to them?' " the Lord replied: 'I am who I am; thus you will say to the sons of Israel: "He who is sent me to you" ' (Exodus 3:13-14), thus showing that his own proper name is: He who is." And bk. 2, ch. 52: "Wherefore it is the case that God's proper name is asserted to be 'He who is', because it is proper to him alone that his substance should be none other than his being" (commentary in Gilson, *L'esprit de la philosophie médiévale*, pp. 133-134).

One can compare this with the *Guide for the Perplexed* by Maimonides: "All the mystery is in the repetition, under the form of an attribute, of that very word that denotes existence.... In giving expression to the first name, which is the subject, and to the second name, which serves it as an attribute, one has by recourse to the same word declared, so to speak, that the subject is identically the same as the attribute. What we have here is an application of the following idea: that God exists, but not existence. The result is that this idea can be recapitulated and interpreted in the following way: *The Being who is Being*, that is to say, *the necessary Being*. And it is indeed this notion that can be rigorously established by the demonstrative way, namely, that there is something whose existence is necessary, something which has never been non-existent and which will never be such."

64. Herein can be recognized the two principal currents of traditional interpretation, which are summarized in the two names of St. Thomas and St. Augustine. The difference between one and the other is less than is sometimes supposed, for the Augustinian "eternal being" is not a trite and banal "being forever." Eternity indicates a quality of being, a depth, and, so to speak, a density of being which corresponds to Thomistic "Being."

65. St. Augustine, *In Psalmum* 101, sermo 2, n. 10 (PL 37:1311); *De moribus Ecclesiae catholicae*, bk. 1, ch. 14, n. 24: ". . . Because I say that he is nothing other but being

is there, is nothing but existence.... "I," he says, "am he who is." How great, how great is this word.)

The second formula is no less precious. It suggests a concrete personality which escapes us. "I am that which it pleases me to be." It expresses a solemn and sacred reserve. Without affirming the mystery of Being in itself, it sets it in relief in the simplest and most forceful way. It recalls the "irreducible distance between anything said about God and the mysterious reality to be expressed."[66] Thus it vindicates the independence of the Living God. It is the first manifesto against idolatry in thought.[67]

On the one hand, then, there is the perpetual enigma of him who hides himself in his sovereignty: "Why do you ask me my name?"[68] On the other hand, pure light, radiating in all directions, offering itself without reserve, but too pure for our gaze.

... And the two interpretations end by meeting in the idea that "He who is" cannot be designated and is beyond our reach, a secret at once disturbing and inviolable. *Nomen quod est super omne nomen.*[69]

---

itself" (PL 32:1321); *De Trinitate*, bk. 5, ch. 2, n. 3 (PL 42:912). Origen, *De oratione*, ch. 24 (PG 11:492-493). St. Hilary, *De Trinitate*, bk. 1, ch. 5 (PL 10:28). St. Bernard of Clairvaux, *De consideratione*, bk. 5, ch. 6, n. 13: "Who are you? — Nothing sounder comes to mind than *He who is;* He wanted this phrase to be the answer to a query about himself" (PL 182:795d); and *De diversis*, 4, 2: "He, moreover, who is himself the same, who says 'I am who I am', is truly the one to whom belongs the being that exists" (PL 183:552c). Duns Scotus, *De primo principio*, 1, 1, etc.

66. G. Lambert, "Que signifie le nom divin YHWH?" p. 915.

67. Cf. Romano Guardini, "Le sérieux de l'amour divin," *Dieu vivant* 11: "In this way God rejects every name and every notion that are expressible in terms of the world. But not absolutely, since in many other places in Scripture he calls himself the Living One, the Holy One, the Just One, the All-Powerful One, among other things. At this time, however, at the decisive beginning of sacred history, he says: The world, for its part, has no name for me, and as such you will accept me. Later you will be able to call me by name on the basis of experience and knowledge, but by drawing as a starting point on this conversion accomplished by the first obedience of faith."

And Edmond Ortigues, *Le temps de la Parole* (1954), p. 22: "The theophany was not a refusal to explain, but the explanation consisted of making known the enigmatic, mysterious character of the divine name."

68. Genesis 32:30; cf. Judges 13:18; Exodus 33-34.

69. This "name above every name," "above every name that is named, not only in this age, but also in that which is to come," this name that Christ receives inasmuch as he is Lord is the divine Name (Adonai), which is to say, the very name of God, the Name that cannot be spoken. Philippians 2:9; Ephesians 1:21.

Cf. St. Gregory of Nyssa, *Adversus Eunomium*, bk. 11, concerning Philippians 2:9:

∼

"Being without a mode of being is also without name."[70] The mystics have often said so, though there are two distinct ways of understanding their words.

Being "without mode and without name" does not mean undifferentiated Divinity, an impersonal Principle, an empty Unity, or a "universal Possibility". . . . It is not the Being who in himself (if one could speak in these terms) is without form and who is falsified by any attempt to conceive him; but on the contrary — *omnem conceptum excedens ineffabilis Forma*[71] (the ineffable Form surpassing every concept) — the Being who is indeterminate, not because of his poverty but because of his superabundance. Not the Being who presents nothing in itself graspable because he is as impalpable as Space: but the mysterious Being, the personal, inviolable Core, the supreme Condensation. Infinite Being whose infinity is intensive, which makes him at the same time the perfect Being. He cannot be named any more than he can be understood — because he is *above* all names. If it is true that the ultimate secret within each one of us rests in our personality, God is the hidden Being *par excellence* because he is *par excellence* the personal Being. He is he "from whom all personality derives and takes its name."

The "Supreme Someone."[72]

∼

Περὶ Θεοῦ, καὶ τἀληθῆ λέγειν, κίνδυνος οὐ μικρός.

Speak about God, but in proper terms — it entails no small risk.[73]

∼

"He simply is, because he does not have a name which could make known his essence. But he has a name which is situated above every designation that can be made by means of names. The Apostle also writes that his name is above every name. Not as something particular, to which preference is given among all the rest, but because He who truly *is* is above every name" (PG 45:873A). Cf. Paul Henry, S.J., "Kénose," in the *Supplément au Dictionnaire de la Bible*, cols. 35 and 134.

70. Henry Suso, *Das Buch der Wahrheit*.
71. Nicholas of Cusa, *De docta ignorantia*.
72. Pierre Teilhard de Chardin, *Le phénomène humain* (1955), p. 332.
73. Origen, *In Psalm.*, 1, 2 (PG 12:1080a).

"Simplicity, Mother of Being,
There is nothing in God but that it is transparent,
Nothing is seen but that it is penetrated
By this All which is in the form of nothing. . . ."[74]

You are so great and so pure in your perfection, that everything of mine which infiltrates into the idea I form of you prevents it from corresponding with you. I pass my life contemplating your infinity; I see it and cannot doubt it: but as soon as I try to comprehend it, it escapes me; it is no longer the infinite, and I fall back into the finite. I perceive enough of it to contradict myself and to correct myself each time I conceive what is less than you; but hardly have I struggled up again, than my own weight drags me down again.[75]

So let human weakness fall down before the Glory of God, and in expounding the works of his mercy let it always find itself unequal to the task. Let us labour with our perceptions, let us face obscurity in our minds, let us be found wanting in our words: it is good that it should be too little for us that we do realise something, even correctly, about God's majesty.[76]

---

74. Pierre Emmanuel, "Simplicité," in *Visage Nuage* (1955), p. 84. Cf. Maxim. Sandaeus, S.J., *Pro Theologia mystica clavis* (1640), p. 288: "That Light . . . manifests itself as a kind of Nothingness, the nobility of which compels man to take his sabbath rest from all work." Angelus Silesius, *The Cherubic Pilgrim*, 1, 121.
75. Fénelon, *Traité de l'existence de Dieu*, pt. 2, ch. 5.
76. St. Leo the Great. Cf. *Sermo* 29, ch. 1 (PL 54:226).

6

The Search for God

What is the philosopher? And what is the mystic? What is the essential difference between them, if we consider their original "intention" and take them at the root from which they naturally develop?

Should we say that the philosopher makes use of dialectic, where the mystic relies on experience? Does the mystic plumb the depths of Being, while the philosopher tries to discover how thought engenders or expresses it? Could one say that the mystic is concerned with the immediate and the philosopher with mediation?

In fact, dialectic is common to both of them. The only difference is, perhaps, that the one is mainly affective and vital, whereas the other is rational and conceptual. In each case there is experience, though the experience of the philosopher is active and that of the mystic "passive." Certainly there is no more typical dialectic than that which attempts to translate the mystical experience — or at least its tendency — into thought. The alternation of opposites is nowhere seen more clearly, more instantaneously so to speak. . . .[1] It has even been maintained that the most obviously dialectical of Plato's dialogues, the *Parmenides,* is at bottom the most mystical.

---

1. Just as in the case of those cross-hatched designs where empty and full spaces can be seen changing alternately one into the other, there is a continuous alternation of light and shade, of affirmation and negation, identity and otherness. . . . And dialectic does nothing but interpret the experience itself. Cf. William of St.-Thierry, *Letter to the Brethren of Mont-Dieu,* bk. 2, ch. 3, n. 19 (PL 184:350b-c): "Exaltation is joined to trembling, when it is understood that God humbled himself even to the point of death on the cross, in order to raise man to a likeness with Divinity."

Could it be that the mystic tends to see Being as personal, and the philosopher to conceive it as impersonal?

And yet, to judge by many of the facts, the opposite might equally well be maintained. For as philosophy and mysticism reach the summits of their aspirations, they would appear to transcend this opposition in one way or another.

Perhaps it would be possible to indicate the essential difference between them more nearly by saying that philosophy is above all the search for the *unifying One*, whereas mysticism is the search for — or the attraction of — the *one One*.[2]

The philosopher starts from the need to explain, a need which is, at least virtually, a desire for a total explanation. What he desires is to unify diversity, and at the same time to diversify the one; he requires a system of relationships which embraces everything and makes everything intelligible. His ambition is to comprehend the universe. And if in the course of his search he comes upon God — as he cannot fail to do — it will be as an explanatory principle and a support for the world, as a unifying One. *Res divinae non tractantur a philosophis, nisi prout sunt rerum omnium principia.*[3] (The things of God are

---

2. As for ascertaining how this "One" ought to be sought, how it can be found, and whether the very desire which tends towards it should not at the outset be sacrificed, or at least transcended and transfigured — in broaching these questions we find a whole other concatenation of problems into the depths of which we shall not penetrate. At this point we are speaking only of mysticism in general, in its natural roots, not of Christian mysticism. Let us state only that a Christian mysticism cannot be other than a mysticism of love, that love of neighbor in Christian mysticism is the indispensable sign of God's love, that the preferred ecstasy with regard to it is an ecstasy of actions, and that certain forms of high contemplation are utterly incapable of being in conformity with the spirit of Christianity. As Jacques Maritain has written in *Quatre essais sur l'esprit dans sa condition charnelle*, p. 144, "the truest theology of supernatural contemplation is to be found less in the theory of an *intuition* of God" than in a doctrine of "divine experience through a union of love," although the genuinely "noetic" range of the impetus towards contemplation should not be denied. Cf. St. Bonaventure, in his commentary on St. Bernard of Clairvaux, *In 2 Sent.*, d. 22, a.2, q.3, ad 4m; or *Itinerarium mentis in Deum*. See also the remarks of Etienne Gilson in his *Introduction à l'étude de saint Augustin*, 2nd ed. (1943), p. 319, n. 2.

3. St. Thomas, *In Boethium de Trinitate*, q.5, a.4: ". . . And so the things which are common to all the things that exist are treated in the context of the principles within which they find themselves placed. . . . There is, moreover, another way of investigating things of this kind, not according as they are made manifest through effects, but according as they themselves manifest themselves. . . . And in this way divine things are treated according as they subsist in themselves. . . . And this is the theology which is spoken of through Sacred Scripture."

not treated by philosophers except as the principles of all things.) When the philosopher posits the absolute, it is never the absolute absolutely, but "the absolute in relation to him."[4]

Philosophy is the work of the reason. It is a "science." But God *in himself* is not an object of "science" to natural man.[5] He can neither be comprehended nor even named. And, as St. Thomas says, we do not know "what he is": we only know "the relation of everything else to him."[6] "To deduce God from becoming," or from any other aspect of the world, "does not mean that one rises to a certain direct knowledge of God with the help of becoming; it means penetrating further into the intelligible structure of becoming itself; or, if one prefers, it means knowing God only to the extent to which he is signified by the essential 'transcendental relativity' of metaphysical 'becoming.'"[7] That suffices, in a sense, to define him. In any

---

4. Maurice Merleau-Ponty, interpreting Louis Lavelle in *Eloge de la philosophie* (1953), p. 12.

5. I am mindful that St. Thomas defined theology as the science of God (see note 3 in particular). But it should also be remembered that theology is not philosophy. Following St. Thomas himself, whose words are too clear and too often repeated to allow of any serious dispute, I maintain that, to the reason of the pure philosopher, "God, in himself, is not an object of science" — a statement which I maintain in the sense in which St. Thomas meant it, and which the context makes perfectly clear, and not in some vague or general sense, since such a statement in isolation would be equivocal.

6. St. Thomas, *De Potentia*, q.7, a.2, ad 11m and ad 1m: "We do not know what God is. . . . The being of God is the same as his substance, and just as his substance is unknown, even so is his being. . . ." "Concerning God, we discover what he is not; what, in truth, he is remains something that is utterly unknown." *Contra Gentiles*, bk. 1, ch. 30. Here we have what Xavier Moisant called "a purist theodicy": *Dieu, l'expérience en métaphysique*, p. 136.

Cf. Etienne Gilson, *Le Thomisme*, 5th ed., pp. 150-159 (Eng. trans., pp. 103-110). A. D. Sertillanges, *Somme théologique, Dieu*, vol. 2, p. 383: "Therefore we do not know at all in any wise or in any degree what God is"; or p. 330: "For Saint Thomas . . . what appears to be a judgement of nature is in truth only a qualification of God as necessary cause. That is to say, it amounts to a pure and simple affirmation of God"; and *Les grandes thèses de la philosophie thomiste*, pp. 49ff.: "This expression, 'God is', is only positive when it is considered as an expression of the insufficiency of the world and the correlative necessity of an ultimate underpinning; as a worthwhile definition, in the proper sense of the word, it is entirely negative." H. Paissac, *Le Dieu de Sartre*, p. 15: "In the same way, the pure Act of Being is beyond reason. It is arrived at by reason inasmuch as it is the real significance of the world, and that reality without which the world would not have meaning, which is to say, would not exist. But it is never held or possessed by the intelligence in a concept."

7. Joseph Maréchal.

case, it satisfies the philosopher in the formal sense of that word which we have indicated. As such he does not ask for more:

Felix qui potuit rerum cognoscere causas![8]

But that does not satisfy man. It does not satisfy the spirit. The mystical aspiration is greater, more fundamental, and more total than the demands of reason. The mystic reaches out beyond the supreme Cause and the unifying One, which is, so to say, hardly more than a function, and pursues the One itself. He seeks the One in its being and unity. And the least knowledge of that One is worth more in his eyes than the profoundest and most comprehensive knowledge of all else[9]; and for the sake of finding the One, and being united to it, he is prepared to sacrifice the whole universe.[10]

---

8. Virgil, *Georgics*, 2, 490. *In Boethium de Trinitate*, q.5, a.4. Similar texts in St. Bonaventure, *In 3 Sent.*, d. 23, a.1, q.4, ad 5m; *Quaestiones de Theologia*, q.2, resp. ad 3m; q.4, respons. ad 3m. Cf. Patrice Robert, O.F.M., "Le problème de la philosophie bonaventurienne," *Laval théologique et philosophique* (1951), p. 22. Aimé Forest, *Du consentement à l'être* (1936), pp. 107ff. Or A. D. Sertillanges, *Somme théologique, Dieu*, vol. 2, pp. 384 and 388: "This affirmation, 'God is', is a true affirmation, not inasmuch as it qualifies God on the level of being, but inasmuch as it calls for God by basing itself on being. . . . But also we do not want to define God, but rather to think of him in terms of the creature that emanates from him and that requires this mystery so as to have meaning and so as to exist." In this case God is "the remote principle postulated by a universal need," the supreme condition for the intelligibility of the universe (J. de Finance, *Être et agir*, p. 18).

9. St. Thomas, *De Veritate*, q.10, a.7, ad 3m: "The least knowledge which can be had of God surpasses all knowledge that is had of the creature."

10. This duality has been noted by Jacques Maritain in "L'expérience mystique naturelle et le vide," which has been collected in *Quatre essais sur l'esprit dans sa condition charnelle*, pp. 139ff. and 162: "What I shall try to show is that there can be, in the proper sense of the word, a natural mystical experience that prolongs and completes a metaphysical impulse. . . . But — and in my opinion it is this point which is not adequately taken into account by the school of Father Rousselot — this philosophical outstripping of philosophy, this meta-philosophical contemplation, does not pursue the natural movement of philosophy nor does it go in the same direction. . . . To the contrary it presupposes inevitably a kind of turning back in a way that is opposite to nature; and so there is the irruption of a desire that is certainly not the constitutive desire of philosophy itself, the intellectual desire for being, but a more profound desire, one suddenly liberated in the soul, and properly religious, and which is not, to be sure, that intellectual desire to see the First Cause . . . which follows on the intellectual desire for being. The desire I am now talking about is a desire that is more radical than the natural desire of the intelligence for being and than its natural desire for the Cause of being . . ."; ". . . the intervention of a natural desire that is more profound and more total than that of the philosophical intelligence for the intellectual conquest of being"

When, as a child, St. Thomas Aquinas exclaimed "I want to understand God," it was not so much the budding philosopher who was speaking as the religious genius, the contemplative, the potential mystic, the saint with an intellectual cast of mind. And insofar as his speculation led him to satisfy that desire, it is not so much the rational science, whose long career in the West he inaugurated, as one of the aspects of the "intelligence of faith" whose ideal and method had been transmitted to him by the Christian tradition.

But when, on the contrary, he insists so emphatically that "we do not know God, but only the relations of all things to him," he is speaking as a pure philosopher. From that point of view, and that point of view only, there is no reason to read regret or nostalgia into the phrase. As one of his surest interpreters writes: "In a natural theodicy it is not God who is in question as the subject of science; it is universal being, the creature. For God is only envisaged and attained as the first cause and not in himself. In other words, there cannot be a natural theology apart from general metaphysics."[11] The God of the philosophers "completes the formula of the world"[12] and fully satisfies their reason.

(p. 162). Maritain has recently returned to these problems in the fifth of his *Neuf leçons sur les notions premières de la philosophie morale* (1951), pp. 89-108.

11. Sertillanges, *Les grandes thèses . . .* , p. 75. Cf. Etienne Gilson, *L'esprit de la philosophie médiévale* 2nd ed. (1944), p. 261: The natural theology of Saint Thomas "legitimates all the ambitions of Christian hope, but at the same time it is the most modest theology that there is."

12. St. Thomas, *Prima*, q.32, a.1: ". . . The only thing which we can learn about God by means of natural reason is that which of necessity belongs to him, inasmuch as he is the principle of all things. And we have made use of this fundamental principle above in our consideration of God." Q.12, a.12: ". . . [Through effects] we can be led to a knowledge of God and whether he exists; and we can also be led to a knowledge of those things about him which of necessity belong to him, inasmuch as he is the first cause of all things and surpasses all the things that have been caused by him. Wherefore we know of his relationship towards creatures, that he is, indeed, the cause of all things; and we also know the way in which creatures differ from him, the fact that, in truth, he is not a part of the creatures which were caused by him, and that these creatures are not removed from him on account of a defect on his part, but rather because he surpasses them all."

Such already, from the point of view which presently occupies us, was the conception of metaphysics in Aristotle. Cf. G. Ducoin, "Saint Thomas commentateur d'Aristote" (unpublished thesis, Gregorian University, Biennium S.J., Rome, 1951), p. 97: "The explanation of nature constitutes the unique angle of perspective from which Aristotle considers other systems, when he wishes to elaborate his metaphysics. When it comes

And yet St. Thomas insists no less that "the intelligence naturally desires to know God in himself." What exactly is that desire? Does it express the rational need to which philosophical activity corresponds, or does it, in its own way, define the mystical impulse in its natural root? Or should one perhaps see in it the fundamental unity of both?

Let us begin by saying — without for the moment trying to decide whether the suggestion reveals a faulty analysis or a deep insight — that, in speaking as he does, St. Thomas merges the two points of view which we have just distinguished. The "desire to see God," which he regards as natural to us, is certainly, at bottom, mystical in character. It cannot be limited to a desire to comprehend the world. Nevertheless, St. Thomas tries to establish its reality in a purely rational manner, starting from the effects which the intelligence desires to know in their Cause so as to know them fully. With that in view he unfolds a whole argument in the *Contra Gentiles*, which is inspired by his faith, and which a pure philosopher might no doubt criticize as without apodeictic value[13] — and that is precisely why a certain number of his interpreters consider themselves justified in maintaining that the natural desire in question, being the desire to see God *as cause*, is not the desire to *see God* in the full sense of the word.

In brief, the argument consists in showing that human reason, the reason which is responsible for the work of philosophy, is not satisfied with knowing an effect as long as it does not know the cause. Hence that continuous movement, that permanent disquiet, that unrest which lasts until reason, moving from effect to effect and from cause to cause, at last reaches the supreme cause from which everything derives, and which, by that very fact, explains and so unifies everything.[14]

---

to speaking of the unmoved substance, it is still with reference to the sensible world that he judges and condemns affirmations concerning unmoved substances, so true is it that his first philosophy is profoundly rooted in metaphysics and the world of Nature.... The (Platonic) Ideas are not capable of explaining movement or change, and for that very reason, since they are not *causes*, they are of no interest for science."

13. Cf. Roland-Gosselin, O.P., "Béatitude et désir naturel," *Revue des sciences philosophiques et théologiques* (1929), p. 200: "The first conviction that orients his analysis and gives it a whole air of security is his faith in the word of God, which promises man the beatific vision.... Faith in the beatific vision should be considered as exercising a positive and decisive influence in the argumentation itself."

14. In addition to the well-known texts of the *Contra Gentiles*, see, for example, *Expositio in Matthaeum Evangelistam*, ch. 5: "The happiness of man is the ultimate good of man in which his yearning is quieted.... Thus that yearning will not be quieted until he comes to the first cause, which is God, that is to say, to his divine essence."

It is a solid argument. But does it, in fact, prove *all* that it sets out to prove? Is the term of the argument *formally* the term envisaged? In its desire to comprehend the universe, the intelligence cannot abandon its search until it has reached the first cause, and one can therefore say, with every show of right, that there is a congenital desire in the intelligence to know that cause.[15] But between that and saying, as St. Thomas does in effect, that the intelligence desires to know the first cause, not only as the cause of the effects which it aspires to understand — as the universal *propter quid* — but in its essence,[16] in itself and for itself, independently of its effects and of its relations with everything else, there is surely an abyss?

The mystical impulse, no doubt, bridges the abyss at a single leap. The mystic discerns the One in the Unifying cause, and when he meets the Unifying cause he adheres to the One. But can one say that his strength comes to him from the principle which first moved the intelligence to look for the "cause of causes"? Could one even say that the mystical impulse simply continues along the path of reason, that it simply goes further in the same direction? Would it not be better to recognize that the philosopher's reasoning conceals an anagogical dialectic, the inspiration of which is quite different from the general desire to know?

St. Thomas, therefore, seems to have failed in his attempt to establish continuity between philosophy and mysticism, between the dynamism of the intelligence and the desire of the spirit. The doctrine of "the natural desire to see God" is central to his thought, and he has not succeeded in completely unifying it.

No one will succeed where he has failed.[17] The attempt, strictly speaking,

---

15. Cf. Origen, *In Psalmum 2*, v. 8: "But the inheritance of rational nature is the sight of corporeal and incorporeal things, and of God who is the cause of all these things" (PG 12:1608c).

16. *Compendium Theologiae*, ch. 104: ". . . Therefore the natural desire for learning cannot be stilled in us, until we know the first cause not in any manner whatsoever, but by way of his essence."

17. About these last words it has been written: "There now, we are somewhat reassured. . . . This too facile game only half pleases us, however, for it seems to us to elicit conjecturally, in so serious a matter, a smile from Saint Thomas, who would not be a total picture of indulgence." I admit to not having penetrated the implications of this remark. As far as I am concerned, there is no room for games in this matter. I believe quite seriously (although the matter is not easy to express in formulas that are perfectly clear) that the total and complete unification of our diverse spiritual activities is not possible in our present condition, and I believe as well that it is salutary to be obliged to make an open declaration of this sometimes. Already at this point the

is no doubt impossible. The mystical impulse does not exactly prolong metaphysical inquiry; it does not repeat or extend the work, though it can animate it and, in return, be stimulated by it. The root, in each case, is different, the end is different, and the basic procedure no less so. Philosophical inquiry rises analytically from effect to cause, in virtue of a rational necessity. The mystical impulse rises from effect, perceived as a sign, to that same cause, by a movement which cannot be wholly justified by pure reason — for if it were an argument, there would be more in the "conclusion" than in the "premisses" — but which springs from a need of the spirit no less imperious in its demands than the demands of reason, or more precisely, from the magnetic attraction of Being through its signs. The philosopher may rest from his inquiries in contemplation, once the effect is fully understood; the mystic, in the end, will reject all signs — though he will never quite finish doing so — in order to rest in the contemplation of God alone.[18]

---

coherent organization of all the proceedings of reason appears very arduous, for these proceedings are quite various, are related to a great many objects, are undertaken on a great many occasions, and are under the influence of a great many points of view that are scarcely capable of being coordinated. How much more arduous would we find the perfect synergy of every intellectual effort and every spiritual impulse! In one sense, which I define as well as I can on this page, it seems to me also that this is an impossible thing to do and that the history of Christian thought bears witness to this estimate. A want of total unification, moreover, does not in any way signify a logical contradiction. And doesn't the author of the remark that I have just cited himself write almost immediately afterwards of: ". . . Three aspirations of the human soul, organically linked, *insofar as the nature of things permits such linkage,* in the doctrine of Saint Thomas"? (my emphasis).

18. On the relationship between philosophy and mysticism, if we understand them throughout in terms of their natural roots, the following page of Jacques Maritain, in *Les degrés du savoir* (1932), pp. 477ff., may be read once again: "Whether it tends towards a known or unknown God, a God loved as God or desired as a supreme truth whose name remains unknown, such a movement, such a mystical impetus animates every great philosophy, — I speak here on the part of the subject, for a person is not a philosopher if he does not love the absolute and desire to unite himself with it. But sometimes this impulse animates philosophy insofar as it tends towards an end which transcends philosophy and insofar as it does not intervene in philosophy's specification (for the latter depends purely on the object, which is of a wholly rational order here). Sometimes this impulse animates philosophy insofar as it tends towards an end that is immanent to philosophy and insofar as it intervenes in order to constitute philosophy's own proper object and to specify it. In the first case, the very purity of philosophy as such will cause, especially in the eyes of non-philosophers, the value and efficacy of this impulse to risk being masked. But at the very least, the impulse, passing into a further

There is, however, something artificial about the distinction originally established. However well-founded it may be, it posits the "philosopher" and the "mystic" as abstract beings. It distinguishes two functions of the mind. But while it is true that the functions of the mind are diverse, we must not forget that the spirit is one. The intelligence is steeped in it, and no philosopher worthy of the name would be content to remain for good and all imprisoned in his specialty, even if it were the knowledge and explanation of the whole. Philosophy is always pushing back the frontiers of thought. The philosopher is more than a philosopher, and cannot be reduced to a precise definition. His knowledge of the world is equivalently, or at least becomes inevitably, the perception of his own inadequacy. And the labor of elaborating an intelligible world does not save him from "the nostalgia of Being."[19] The greatness of St. Thomas is to have recognized this. By a process which pure reason alone does not suffice to justify, but which the spirit satisfies, or rather insists upon, he was able to penetrate and explore the ways by which the intelligence moves to the point at which he discovered the spiritual appetite within it. In his very philosophy, the philosophical endeavor develops into a mystical flight. The human spirit becomes conscious of its total nature and of its high vocation. He explores all its dimensions and, going beyond the techniques and specializations which obliged him, as it were, to divide himself in two, he seeks to rediscover the simplicity of the mind's essential act.[20] The formal distinctions

---

realm, will be able to bring the soul to an authentic and pure contemplation. In the second case, the very fact that philosophy has undergone a mixing will render the presence of this impulse in it more manifest and more sensible, and it is this all too beautiful testimony to eternal aspirations which, in its very defeat, and whatever may be its price, will always incline a metaphysician towards revering a Plotinus or the thinkers of ancient India. But it is into an empty void — if we suppose the end term of the movement, as well, to be simply natural — that the latter will emerge; or at any rate, if superior influences enter into play . . . , he will emerge again into a mixture, where the part played by deception will be great." Cf. pp. 549-551.

19. This is true even of Descartes, so often accused since the time of Pascal of only being interested in God for the sake of possessing the world. See in particular the well-known *Letter to Chanut*.

20. Hence the definition of first philosophy which appears to contradict the texts referred to in note 9 above. "First philosophy is entirely ordered to the knowledge of God as to its final end, and that is why it is called the divine science" (*Contra Gentiles*, bk. 3, ch. 25). Cf. Etienne Gilson, *L'Être et l'Essence*, pp. 81-83. It is in the same spirit, it seems to me, that J. de Finance writes, in *Être et agir*, p. 351: "If the dynamism of personal life, which expands exquisitely in the religious consciousness, is merely the interiorisation of the dynamism of being, there would not prove to be any conflict or

and oppositions tend to be reabsorbed into unity, although without ever quite reaching it.

The whole of St. Thomas's philosophical research is the search for God.

To reject God because man has corrupted the idea of God, and religion because of the abuse of it, is the effect of a sort of clear-sightedness which is yet blind. For surely the holiest things are inevitably destined to be the victims of the worst abuses. Religion, which is its own source and origin, must continue to purify itself. Moreover, under one form or another man always turns back to adoration. It is not merely his first duty but his deepest need. It is something he cannot extirpate; he can only corrupt it. God is the pole that draws him, and even those who deny him in spite of feeling that attraction, bear witness to him.

God is the Transcendent — but he is also the absolute other. He is the Beyond of the hierarchical universe — but he is equally the unconditioned, the uncoordinated, which no series of conditions brings nearer to us, and which no system of relationships can situate. We can rise up to him — to the threshold of his Mystery — through the "degrees of being," for he is the "being of all beings" — and yet our ascent never really leads us nearer to him, for if we say that "he is," then we cannot really say that other beings are.[21] By comparison with him, all of them are equally nothing:

> I looked upon the earth, and saw that it was empty;
> I looked into the heavens, and found no light.[22]

The universe is a "cosmos" whose beautiful order reflects its Author, the heavens proclaim the Glory of God — and yet that Glory extinguishes the

---

indeed irreducible distinction between what reason demands in order to guarantee the whole order of being and the living God whom a life is in need of in order not to fall away from the plan of the spirit."

21. St. Catherine of Siena, *Vita*, ch. 14: Of all created things, "however beautiful, good, and useful they may be thought to be in this world, it cannot be said that they exist." Cf. St. Clement of Rome, *Letter to the Corinthians*, ch. 27, n. 4: "God has created everything by the word of his majesty, and by this same word he can reduce everything to nothing."

22. Jeremiah 4:23. See the commentary of St. John of the Cross, *Ascent of Mount Carmel*, bk. 1, ch. 4.

light of the stars and reduces everything to dust:²³ silence alone can proclaim it.

Before thy rising Light, everything is a desert!²⁴

Every creature is an image or vestige of the Creator — though nothing resembles God.²⁵ *Similis quidem, sed dispar.*²⁶ (Similar indeed, but different.) *Dissimiles similitudines.*²⁷ (Dissimilar similitudes.) The μὴ ὄν is incurably opposed to the ὄντως ὄν — and yet that radical opposition does not exclude a symbolic relation between that which is not and that which is; the hiatus makes room for participation. "The grace and beauty of creatures are a supreme dis-grace compared with the Grace of God" — the austere thinker to whom we owe that uncompromising maxim is also the great poet who sings of the grace and beauty scattered throughout the creation:

> Scattering a thousand graces,
> He passed though these groves in haste,
> And looking upon them as he went,
> Left them, by his grace alone,
> Clothed in beauty.²⁸

---

23. St. Augustine, *Confessions*, bk. 11, ch. 4, n. 6: "You, therefore, Lord, who are beautiful, have made those things, and they are beautiful; you have made them, you, who are good, and so are they; you have made them, you, who exist, and so do they. And they are not so beautiful, nor so good, nor so existent as are you, their founder, compared to whom they are neither beautiful, nor good, nor existent" (PL 32:811).

24. Paul Claudel, *Vers d'exil.*

25. St. Augustine, *In Psalmum* 85, n. 12: ". . . Whatever else a man may think, what has been made is not like him who made it. . . . Who could properly ponder the great gulf of difference between the maker and what has been made? Therefore he said, 'There is none like thee among the gods, O Lord'; he did not say to what extent God is unlike, because it cannot be said. . . . God is ineffable. . . . Think of the earth: it is not God . . . men and animals . . . ; think of the angels: they are not God. And what is God? This alone have I found myself able to say, namely, what he is not. . . . What is it that you bid rise onto your tongue that does not rise up into your heart? 'There is none like thee among the gods, O Lord, nor are there any works like thine'" (PL 37:1900).

26. St. Bernard of Clairvaux, *In Cantica sermo* 81, n. 4 (PL 183:1172d).

27. Pseudo-Dionysius, *Celestial Hierarchy,* 2, 4, and 5 (PL 3:144a and 145a).

28. St. John of the Cross, *Ascent of Mount Carmel,* bk. 1, ch. 4: "All the being of creatures, compared to the being of God, is mere nothingness. . . . All the goodness of creatures, compared to the goodness of God, is merely supreme badness." *Spiritual Canticle,* strophe 5.

The passage from the world to God is thus effected by a double dialectic.[29] On the one hand there is negation, on the other construction. The one suppresses, the other develops.[30] The one is refusal and rejection, the other is acceptance and enhancement.[31] The two movements are interwoven, and neither is altogether independent of the other. We are not faced by a choice between them, and neither has ever brought its task to completion. No mystical ladder reaches its end unless we renounce it.[32] The soul in search of God explores the whole cycle of creation from matter to pure spirit, from the rhythm of the universe to the march of history, but

---

29. Corresponding with this double dialectic there are two spiritual ways, the way of signs and the way without signs. Like the two dialectics, these two spiritual ways are, moreover, less separate than united; but it is sometimes one and sometimes the other which dominates. These ways have been described by Jules Monchanin, *De l'esthétique à la mystique* (1955), pp. 105-112.

30. St. Augustine, *De vera religione*, ch. 29, n. 52: "Let us see how far reason can advance, ascending from visible things to invisible things, and from temporal things to eternal things. . . . [In an examination of things] a step has to be made towards things that are immortal and everlasting" (PL 34:145).

31. St. Anselm, *Proslogion*, ch. 14: "O my soul, have you found what you were seeking? You were seeking God, you found him to be something that is the highest of all things, than whom nothing better can be thought of" (PL 158:234d). On the "anagogical mediations" used by Richard of St. Victor: G. Dumeige, in *Dictionnaire de Spiritualité*, fasc. 18-19 (1954), col. 326.

32. "Whereas in the course of the initial contemplation, the soul used to attribute to God, to an eminent degree, all the good that she found in creatures, she seeks henceforth to eliminate all of this as notoriously insufficient for the expression of the divine perfections and the consideration of God in the shadow of un-knowing. . . ." St. Axters, O.P., *La spiritualité des Pays-Bas*, p. 72, summarizing Dionysius the Carthusian, *De contemplatione*, pt. 3, ch. 14 (*Opera omnia*, vol. 41).

Cf. St. Hilary, *De Trinitate*, bk. 1, ch. 7, commenting on The Wisdom of Solomon 13:5: "The creator of great things is in the greatest of things, and the author of the most beautiful things is in the most beautiful things . . . , and God, who is most beautiful, must be confessed in such a way that he is not within the sense of comprehension nor outside of the comprehension of sensation" (PL 10:30); and ch. 19: "There can be no comparison of earthly things with God; but the weakness of our intelligence forces us to seek certain images from the realm of inferior things as a touchstone of superior things, so that, admonished by customary and familiar things, we might be drawn from a knowledge derived from our senses to the supposition of sense perceptions to which we are not accustomed" (col. 38).

Compare this with the twin dialectics of progress and rupture that are to be found in Buddhism: Paul Mus, *Barabudur*, vol. 1, pp. 137-140, 217, 222, etc. Gustave Thibon, *Nietzsche ou le déclin de l'esprit*, p. 279: "We should have traversed all the deserts of negation in order to discover the *profound* symbolism of the sensible world."

it never passes from one stage of its ascension to the next except by a series of rejections and denials, for the beings which it questions on the road all reply: "We are not the God you are seeking."[33]

Let us admit that three-quarters, and perhaps more, of all that man says and thinks of God in his worship and his prayer is infected with hypocrisy and superstition, childishness, convention, and routine repetitions.[34] Yet we must be on our guard against contemptuous judgments, because they are the most blinding of all. This enormous wastage must not blind us to the spark of truth that burns in the innermost recesses of the soul. Even when it conceals it from us, it is not always stifled, and from time to time it can be seen glowing and bursting into a pure and upright flame.

Optimi corruptio pessima.
The coating of hypocrisy is never so thick as round the idea of God.

God can never really be thought or recognized apart from a *sursum*, which no proof can ever arouse. It is much less important to prove God to the unbeliever than to open his eyes. Apologetics is to testimony what the sermon is to example.

If, when night comes, I think back to certain privileged moments when the truth of my affirmation was revealed to me in an experience, I am not

---

33. *Confessions,* bk. 10, ch. 6, n. 9 (PL 32:783). Cf. *Sermo,* 53, 12 and 14: "Force your heart to think of divine things; compel it, urge it. Cast away from yourself any thinking that has affinities to the body. Not yet can you say, 'He is this'. Rather say, 'He is not this'. For when will you say, 'This is God'? Not when you see; because what you will be seeing is ineffable. . . . He is not a likeness. The Christian should blush with shame to carry such an idol in his heart" (PL 38:369 and 370). See also the admirable *Enarratio in Psalmum,* 41, nn. 7-10, which is less well known than a similar passage in the *Confessions,* but is nonetheless more complete and more lyrical: "By hearing every day: Where is your God? etc." (PL 36:467-471). I reproduce this passage at the end of the chapter.

34. Cf. Julien Green, *Journal,* vol. 4 (30 June 1943), p. 543: "What happens is that a person thinks so often and so habitually about God in conventional terms that this great reality, which is the sole reality, becomes attenuated behind a screen of phrases that have been learned by rote. . . ."

living on a deceptive memory, on the recollection of a pleasing experience, but recollecting a value perceived; it is not the recollection of the fulfillment of a value which I bore in principle within me, but the recollection of a newly discovered existence which integrates, orders, and judges all human values.

I had been told that the grey canopy of the sky was only a thin curtain of cloud which hid the sun. I had been offered ingenious and even convincing proofs. They explained many things. That fine solution was a correct one. My reason had nothing more to say. And yet its direction was not unalterably fixed. My mind remained perplexed. . . . One day the clouds opened, and I saw the sun appear beyond them. I was unable to fix my eyes upon it, but I was struck by its rays. My countenance was illuminated.[35] From then on the trial was no longer a scandal. The clouds are once again opaque, but they cannot make me doubt the sun.

Perhaps, if I get caught up in a network of argument, it will be enough to meet a man for whom the clouds have in effect opened. Perhaps it will be enough to see a man who has seen, and to believe on his testimony. For that is the miracle which is endlessly repeated, generation after generation, which overcomes our prejudices and all the precautions we oppose to it: it blows a breach in the critical fortress and dynamites negation. Such a testimony is unlike any other we encounter in ordinary life. Through his testimony, through the man who has seen, I really see — or at least glimpse or have an inkling of what he has seen. The sound of his voice awakens an echo in me. The night in which I live is illuminated, without ceasing to be darkness. And what the psalmist says to God I can say to the "man of God": *In lumine tuo videbimus lumen.* (In thy light we shall see light.)

The saints are the efficacious witnesses of God among us.[36]

When we meet a saint we are not discovering at long last an ideal, lived and realized, which had already been formed within us. A saint is not the perfection of humanity — or of the superman — incarnate in a particular

---

35. Cf. St. John of the Cross, *Spiritual Canticle*, ch. 14, n. 24: ". . . like the sleeper who, awakening from a lengthy sleep, opens his eyes to the sight of an unexpected light."

36. See Léonce de Grandmaison, S.J., *La religion personelle*, pp. 177-179, and the beautiful article by Gabriel Le Maître, "Choisir l'espoir," *Etudes* (September, 1950), pp. 216-226.

man. The marvel is of a different order. What we find is a new life, a new sphere of existence, with unsuspected depths — but also with a resonance hitherto unknown to us and now at last revealed. We are shown a new country, a home we had originally ignored, and as soon as we perceive it we recognize it as older and truer than anything we had known and with claims upon our heart.

No feeling of self-satisfaction invades us; we do not see our noblest image reflected in a mirror. This is not the fulfillment of our loveliest dream — or rather there is something further, which is not only more beautiful: we are simultaneously attracted and repelled, and the more we are repelled the more we are attracted. We experience an ambiguous sensation as of something at the same time very near and very far; something disturbing, troubling, and at the same time obscurely desired. The feeling is a mixed one, compounded of a sense of strangeness and of supreme fulfillment beyond all desire. We are both disconcerted and ravished, and the delight we experience is never without a sense of dread. Our worldliness reacts to the threat. Our secret connivance with evil is aroused. We are on our guard. If we had begun to regard ourselves as perfect in some respect, we shall be doubly tempted to reject the provoking vista which is going to oblige us to recognize our misery and, more than that, the wretchedness of what we call perfection.

But in all this we are not left to ourselves, as spectators. It acts upon us as a provocation. It is a summons to choose and to act, unveiling our most hidden tendencies. . . . All of a sudden the universe seems different; it is the stage of a vast drama, and we, at its heart, are compelled to play our part.

If there were more saints in the world, the spiritual struggle would only be more intense. As the Kingdom of God becomes more manifest, it calls forth more fervent adherents — and, correspondingly, more violent opposition. The heightened urgency of the situation provokes tension and becomes the occasion of resounding conflicts.

For if we are more or less at peace in the world, it is simply that we are tepid.

⁂

"Love and do as you will," St. Augustine said — if you love enough to act, in every circumstance, according to the dictates of love.

One might also say "love and believe what you will" — if you know how to extract all the light from love, whose source is not in you.

But do not rush to the conclusion that you know what love is.

If the task of reason is to penetrate sensible appearances, the task of faith is to penetrate all appearances. It must pass through all the nights. That is what sometimes makes it so hard; it is the very opposite of a "lazy solution."

Faith is always a victory.

The solitary mystic sees himself as identical with the Principle of Being, and so infinitely increases his solitude; the believer is brought up short against the Other, is overthrown, and, after the struggle, united with him in love.

When the witness of the saints incites my adherence, I do not confuse the power of their testimony with the force of a rational argument. I know perfectly well that I am not effecting a scientific operation. I can see quite clearly that there are two *genera,* and that their difference cannot be bridged. But although their testimony is not a proof, that does not mean that it is a bad or even a weak proof, any more than it is an apodeictic one. And so I shall not say that it is "reasonable and prudent" to rely on what I am told by men who deserve respect, whose affirmations converge, and whose sincerity is beyond doubt, although the evidence which they claim to bring remains "purely extrinsic" and does not allow me to draw any conclusion with real certainty. I do not need to be told that such an argument is "devoid of scientific value," since I have already admitted that there is no question of arguing. What I contest is that the testimony to which I give my adherence is "purely extrinsic." On the contrary, its whole value — which, to repeat, has nothing "scientific" about it — consists in the echo it evokes in me. It enables me to unravel something essential within myself. That does not mean that it supplies a proof. None is even hinted at. But the two epithets "reasonable" and "prudent" are nonetheless inadequate to describe the adherence which that testimony compels me to give.[37]

---

37. Cf. Jacques Maritain, *Approches de Dieu,* p. 118, who, even while he speaks of the argument founded on evidence, adds: "I do not think that this argument entails a rational or purely natural adherence without belief of a wholly different order being

The witness of the saints does not produce an automatic effect. Nor can it be generalized in the same way as a rational proof. But when it is efficacious, it is an altogether different thing and not a simple and inferior form of proof.[38]

"Once a thing is explained it ceases to interest us" (Nietzsche). So God interests us eternally — and everything else in God through its participation in his infinity.

In the "now" of eternity, everything will be "new, fresh, and present" to us in God.[39]

To some people God is the one who lets them sleep in peace, a reassuring word which dispenses them from the fatigue of inquiry. To others he is the one who tears them from the "false security" in which, according to Pascal, the world lived before the coming of Christ.

The humility of the saints is not the humility we attribute to them. Nor is their love what we imagine it to be. And to say everything — if we must — our God is not their God.

Yet each one of us, at the bottom of his heart, has some inkling of the difference, and can begin to measure the gulf. And that knowledge helps us to reduce it. Each one of us, if he will but attend, can have some premonition of the strange new country in which the saint finds his home.

---

mixed in with it, a belief, indeed, that is founded on an invisible testimony, in the depths of the soul, to the God whom we intend to speak of on the part of his friends." The witness of the saints would thus become a witness to God himself; and this is very much what I think. But without denying, indeed far from doing so, the possible interventions of grace, I believe that there is a place here to make an appeal, first of all — and if Maritain does not say so expressly, he does not at least deny it — to a certain resonance that arises from the connaturality that exists between the soul of a saint and our own soul.

38. Cf. Fernand Van Steenberghen, "Le problème philosophique de l'existence de Dieu," *Revue philosophique de Louvain* 45 (1947), pp. 146, 302.

39. Master Eckhart (*Oeuvres de Maître Eckhart, Sermons-Traités,* trans. Paul Petit, p. 14).

Hell is the work of man, of the man who refuses to give himself and puts himself in bondage: to whom love is unbearable.

As the first Christians understood so well and symbolized so admirably, it is one and the same gesture which both saves and condemns, the serene and majestic gesture with which Christ shows the five wounds. The Redeemer does not transform himself into the Judge, as though tired of his first role; it is the same unique love, the same unchanged love which pronounces the double sentence as it is refracted in our hearts.[40]

It is the same word, the one double-edged sword which comes to some as the word of life and to others as the word of death. *Semel locutus est Deus, duo haec audivi.* (God has spoken, and these two things have I heard.)

It is the same "contemplation" which is obscure or luminous, exquisite or cruel, according to the state of the subject.[41]

In its unchanging essence the same divine Fire is pain for one, Purification for another, and Beatitude for a third.[42]

Noverim me, noverim te. May I know myself, and may I know you, O God, my God! — only that double wish must not be realized at two different times. I cannot get to know myself without seeking to know God — for in my very being I am wholly relative to God. The subtlest investigations

---

40. See, among others, the fresco of the Last Judgement by Cavallini at the farther end of the tribune in the Church of St. Cecilia in Rome.

41. St. John of the Cross, *The Dark Night,* passim, ch. 6: ". . . the unspeakable torment that the soul endures when it is purified by the fire of this contemplation"; cf. also ch. 8.

42. Alexander of Hales, *In Sent.,* d. 37, n. 10: "God is in himself the Alpha and Omega, as it were, he is in the world as creator and guide, in an angel as savior and helper, in the damned as their terror and dread" (Quaracchi [1951], p. 368; text cited as being from St. Augustine, *Confessions*). Adam Scotus (of Dryburgh), *Epistola:* "God is in himself incomprehensible, an object of terror among the damned, and of love among the elect" (PL 198:795a; cf. 778c). Maximilianus Sandaeus, S.J., *Pro theologia mystica clavis* (1640), p. 169; *Theologia mystica, seu Contemplatio divina Religiosorum a calumniis vindicata* (1627), p. 101: "What then is God? — he is no less the punishment of the wicked than the glory of the humble. He is a certain unchangeable and indeclinable uprightness of rational moderation that in very truth touches everything everywhere, and it is for him a necessity to confound every kind of wickedness in this way." Cited by St. Bernard, *De consideratione,* bk. 5, ch. 12, n. 25, who adds: "God is the punishment of those who are evil. For he is light; and what is more hateful to foul and shameful minds? . . ." (PL 182:802).

and the most learned reflections only serve to lead me astray instead of revealing me to myself so long as I try to know myself alone. Man only knows himself — can only desire and love himself — in God or before God. *Noverim te, noverim me.*

The man of prayer discovers in himself and upon himself the light which the man in search of his "self" does not discover.

Man, alas, is above all frightened of God. He is afraid of being burned at his touch, like the Israelites who touched the Ark. That adds subtlety to his denials, cunning to his attempted escapes, and makes the pious inventive in devotional tricks to deaden the shock.... Whether incredulous, indifferent, or believers, we compete with one another in ingeniously guarding ourselves against God.[43]

"Whenever we seem to touch upon God, or when we perceive that he has come to us in our dreams and our wretchedness, we are horrified" (Maurice Blondel).

The mystical impulse is not a luxury. Without it the moral life would run the risk of becoming a form of repression, asceticism a withering dryness, docility a form of sleep, and religious practices a routine, a matter of display if not of fear.

The genuine mystic confides in no one — not because he is prudent or aloof, nor solely from humility or love of mystery. He has no confidences to make.[44] The life of consciousness is beyond the range of psychology, particularly in its highest form, the mystical life.

---

43. Cf. Simone Weil, *La Pesanteur et la Grâce,* p. 77: "We fly from the inner void since God might steal into it."

44. Cf. Marie of the Incarnation, letter to her son, October 1671: "God consumes me in a state of simplicity with him. If I wanted to speak of it further, I would not have much to say, for I would almost always say the same thing." To her son again, 26 October 1653: "... The greatest intimacy has not been in my power. It is this in part which makes me reluctant to write of these matters, although it is my delight to find absolutely nothing in this great abyss and to be obliged to be at a loss for words in losing myself

~

The mystic longs to know God in himself, that is to say, as God knows himself; and — if love has revealed itself to him in some measure — he longs to love God for himself, that is to say, with the love with which God loves himself. And then he will be open on all sides to the inflow of the divine.

~

Cum absens putatur, videtur; — cum praesens est, non videtur.[45] (When he is thought to be absent, he is seen — when he is present he is not seen.)

~

Is mysticism "an intuition of God"? Yes, but always in the dark night. For God is only found by always seeking him. He is always "the one sought."[46]

O Luce qui mortalibus
Lates inaccessa, Deus.[47]

(O God who dwelleth in light which is for mortals inaccessible!)

~

Progress in the knowledge of God there is, but it would not merit the name of progress unless it took us nearer the term, and in another sense left us just as far away. As the infinite allows us to approach it, so it proves the more inaccessible. Moreover, "those who ascend never cease ascending";

---

in it. The older one gets, the more incapable one is of writing about it, because the spiritual life simplifies the soul in a consummate love, the result being that one can no longer find the terms to speak of it."

45. St. Augustine, *De videndo Deo (Epist.* 147, *ad Paulinam),* ch. 6, n. 18 (PL 33:604).

46. St. Gregory of Nyssa, *In Cantica canticorum; In Ecclesiasten,* hom. 7, n. 6: ". . . to find him is always to seek him. For it is not one thing to seek him and another to find him: but the advantage of seeking out is seeking itself" (PG 44:720c). John Scotus Erigena, *De divisione naturae,* bk. 5 (PL 122:1010c-d). Alexander of Hales, *Summa theologica,* pt. 1, bk. 2, ch. 10, n. 2, ad 3m: "Coming to know about God is always within the context of becoming in this life." Correlatively, ἔρχε ται ὁ ἀε ὶ παρώνrchetai ho aei parōn [= "The one who is always present comes"], an insight that comes again from Gregory of Nyssa, *De vita Moysis* (PG 44:472c). Cf. Apocalypse 1:4, 8; 4:8.

47. Gallican liturgy, hymn for vespers.

those who have started on their course move "from beginnings to beginnings, through beginnings without end."

"Once the soul takes flight and begins, insofar as it can, to participate in the divine good, then the Word begins to draw it to itself as though it were still at the beginning of its ascent. . . . 'Arise' it says to the soul which has already arisen, 'Come' it says to the soul which has already come. And indeed those who really rise up must always continue to do so, and those who run towards the Lord will never find their journey to the divine cut short. In saying 'Arise and come,' the Word obliges us to rise up continually, and never to slacken speed, always giving us grace for a new and more perfect ascent."[48]

---

48. St. Gregory of Nyssa, *In Cantica canticorum*, hom. 5 (PG 44:873-876); cf. Hom. 8 (940-944); *De vita Moysis* (PG 44:405). "Thus," comments Louis Beirnaert, "there is indeed an ascent, but this ascent and this progress do not occur between two points which remain fixed. There is never a satisfaction of desire and an achievement of importance, because, for the Christian mystic, desire and its object are both drawn together by a mysterious gravitation, which causes new summits to come into view, even as one scales the heights, and hunger to be rekindled, even as one is sated. What is there to say, except that the greatest and the least, the high and the low, take on their value in this case with reference to an Absolute whose loftiness is of such a kind that one is always starting out on an ascent? But always to be starting out and to recognize the fact unceasingly is, to use the words of Tauler (*Sermons*, French ed. of Hugueny-Théry-Corin, vol. 1, p. 358), to remain 'in the depths of humility, precisely in the spot where one is absolutely like a beginner' (even while one is already being raised up beyond oneself and all things). It is paradoxically to live an ascent which is inscribed in a situation of greater depth, a situation for which the distance between high and low does not have a measurable meaning. . . . This is why in the end the Christian ascent, inasmuch as it is inscribed in time, is a progress towards the depths of humility at the same time as it is a movement towards the lofty heights of divinity, for where God has been humbled 'to the point of death on the cross', the road to the heights wends its way unceasingly through a landscape of humiliation."

Cf. St. Augustine, *De Trinitate*, bk. 9, ch. 1, who cites Sirach 18:6: "For when man brings it to completion, then he begins . . ." (PL 41:961). St. Bernard of Clairvaux, *In Cantica*, sermo 84, n. 1 (PL 183:1184-1185). Maurice Blondel, *L'Action* (1893), pp. 351-352: "As soon as a person thinks that he knows God adequately, he does not know him any more. Without a doubt the moment of his appearance in a person's consciousness has such a resemblance to eternity that a person is fearful, as it were, of entering into it quite entirely, his gaze being fixed on a lightning flash which serves only to deepen the night for him. But the mixture of light and shade remains such that the presumption of the person who thinks he sees and the expectation of the person who supposes he is ignorant are both confounded. Against those who are overly clear-sighted it must be maintained that in the realm of what we know and wish, God remains that which we cannot either know or make. Against those who are wilfully blind it must be maintained

Far from discouraging us, that thought can only strike us with wonder. What it teaches us has nothing to do with Penelope's web or the rock of Sisyphus. Nothing is ever lost, the distance we cover is not wasted, and there is no turning back upon our steps — but everything is greater and more beautiful than we could have imagined or suspected. For God must always be greater than everything "not only in this world but in the next."[49] Everything, therefore, which has to do with God always preserves the freshness of a beginning and the zest of the original departure. No fatigue or satiety "which would dull the spirit"[50] need be feared. The rich autumn harvest will have the savor of the first fruits of spring. And we ourselves shall participate in this eternal youth. We shall understand more and more as we experience it, and as we see better and better that we do not yet understand it, and never shall understand it, what this astounding thing, the discovery of God, means — for it will never cease to astonish us.

Cum consummaverit homo, tunc incipit
Sanctorum sicut aquilae juventus renovabitur.[51]

(When man is consummated, then he really begins.
The youth of the saints shall be renewed like eagles.)

"Not to be able to reach God is our discovery; the failure itself, our success."[52]

---

that, without dialectical complication or long studies, in the twinkling of an eye, for anyone, at any time, God is the immediate certitude without which there is no other, the first brightness, the language that is known without one's having learned it. He is the only one whom a person can never seek in vain without ever being able to find him in his fulness."

"No man can seek you without already having found you. Thus you wish to be found so that you may be sought, to be sought so that you may be found. You can in truth be sought and found, but not, however, anticipated" (St. Bernard of Clairvaux, *De diligendo Deo,* ch. 7, n. 22 [PL 183:987c]).

49. St. Irenaeus, *Adv. Haer.* 2, 28, 3 (PG 7:806a).

50. Leibniz, *Principes de la nature de la grâce,* no. 18. Cf. Gratry, *Connaissance de l'âme,* vol. 1 (1857), 1, 13: "The wine of eternal life, says the Savior in the Gospel, will itself be new."

51. Psalm 102:5. See also St. Augustine, *De Trinitate,* bk. 15, ch. 2, 2; see the lovely commentary on Psalm 104:3-4: "Let the heart of those who seek the Lord rejoice. . . ."

52. Master Eckhart, *Treatise* 14 (F. Pfeiffer, 1857). Cf. St. Gregory the Great, *Moralia*

∽

"God is not a spectacle. The contemplation of him is something more secret, veiled and disconcerting. He is only discovered, and then only in a certain degree, in the fidelity of our movement towards him, in a 'passover' which brings peace out of suffering and gives riches at the cost of stripping ourselves of everything."[53]

∽

... It should not be imagined that the soul always remains or should remain at the highest point of the spirit, and so adheres to God as a most pure spirit, in whose presence all things are as nothing ... in such a way that progress consists solely in inserting, immersing and concealing itself deeper and deeper in the divine spirit. Spiritual profit should be conceived in this way: once the soul has reached the summit in one order or degree, then if it is to be raised by God to another degree, substantially more perfect, it must first of all return to the lower state and begin a new and more searching purgation, an expansion and a fresh disposition, a deeper and more sincere foundation of true self-knowledge than heretofore. Which new beginning, nevertheless, virtually contains in its lowliness all the heights previously attained.

For this must be carefully noted: all that the soul acquired at the summit of its spirit, the sublime fruit and final term, she now possesses in secret by way of principle, by way of being, as basis and substance, hidden and unknown, as something which is joined and identified with her own substantial being in this new beginning at the lower levels: and this, by a singular disposition and artifice of God, in order that the soul should not esteem its interior state too greatly and magnify it; so that being exempt from the danger, she may continue always to grow in God. . . .

Hence it comes that true spirituality does not always consist in enjoying God; nor, similarly, in always being able to persevere continuously at the summit of the spirit; but in being able to follow God according to all the changes and vicissitudes and fruitions and all the

---

in Job, bk. 24, n. 11: "The closer the spirit approaches to divine realities, the further from them it considers itself to be, for, if it perceived none of them, it would be incapable of understanding that it is impossible for it to contemplate him without a veil." Clement of Alexandria, *Stromata*, ch. 6, 40, n. 1: "the contemplation which does not satisfy."

53. Jacques Paliard, *Profondeur de l'âme* (1953), p. 159.

diversity of degrees which he imposes upon the soul. In a word, the ability to follow him wherever he leads.[54]

The real problem is not "the search for God" — for there are ways of searching for him which are no more than provocations[55] — and any search in which man allots himself the principal role is surely a provocation. The real problem is to cultivate the right dispositions so that one may hope to find him without — so to say — having to search for him. The essential thing is to understand that these dispositions themselves can only come from God. For it is he who searches for us and who, in his time, will manifest himself to us.

> Turn towards the East and await God,
> And the dawn of grace will soon rise in you.[56]

Sometimes we think we are looking for God. But it is always God who is looking for us, and he often allows himself to be found by those who are not looking for him.

No critical ingenuity can ever prevail over the clear-sightedness of the pure in heart.

The pure in heart are twice blessed: they shall see God and through them God will make himself seen.

That which man, starting from his own level, calls "God" is a vital impulse, the topmost summit of the world whence the summons leads into the beyond, a jumping-off place for the leap of faith. But if one stops at that point, giving it a definitive value, the result is a "religious" deception, and nature or some ideal or other is turned into God. Such

---

54. Constantin de Barbanson, *Anatomie de l'âme et des operations divines en icelle* (1635), pt. 3, art. 16, pp. 155-158.
55. Cf. Wisdom of Solomon 1:2: "because he is found by those who do not put him to the test."
56. Angelus Silesius, *The Cherubic Pilgrim*, bk. 2, ch. 5.

a divinity, starting with the *numina* of natural religions, and ending with the absolute being of religious philosophy, has no real existence. The God who is, the true and living God, is he who shows himself to us in Revelation. It is with him, whether man likes it or not, that he is concerned in time and in eternity.[57]

Light is the Lord's cloak; rest assured that if you lose the light you have not yet lost God himself.[58]

Beyond all conventions — in the rejection of all untruth — at the cost of security — behind all negations — when everything fails — in the abandonment of everything: The discovery of God.

What is an unhealthy subtlety or at least a superfluous refinement to some is a necessity to others. It is the "flight ahead" to which they are condemned. That narrow defile is their only path to salvation.

They are certain to disconcert or antagonize the easily satisfied mind, more than the clever and the restless, more even than the adventurers in

---

57. Romano Guardini. It should, however, be noted that the "natural" God whom the author excludes is only the one in whose name one would exclude the God of supernatural revelation by attributing to him "a definitive value." By the same author, *Christliches Bewusstsein. Versuche über Pascal,* 2nd ed. (1950), pp. 58ff.: "... The ordinary representations or universal conceptions of God which claimed to be 'pure', and which, to be sure, were in a certain sense such, are immersed in this apparent humanization of God. The two worlds of thought and experience which were capable of being characterized by the formulas: 'God is absolute' and 'God is the one who speaks through Jesus Christ', contend with one another, ... even though they have for their object the same reality, namely the living God. ..." However, "all that a faithful effort at 'the philosophical knowledge of God' was capable of bringing to light keeps its value. And this value is great, in spite of all the despisers of philosophy, either in our own day or times gone by. For the great ensemble of the real, just like the postulates of thought and the power of the spirit from which these concepts are taken, did not take their rise just anywhere; nor is it any more strongly the case that they spring from evil. Rather do they spring from that God who has spoken through Christ. But creation is ordered to grace and is only grasped properly in all its truth in relation to it."

58. Angelus Silesius, *The Cherubic Pilgrim,* bk. 2, 5.

the world of thought with their dubious designs, more than the disguised adversaries of the truth. But how can they help it?

Their choice is between scepticism and the purification of faith. Between despair and the purification of hope. Between hatred of their kind and rebellion, and the purification of love.

And the Peace which comes upon them coexists with an anxious dread.[59]

And the God of their distress is more *God* to them than any other — and is *theirs* more than any other.

And no other God is so contagious — and no distress so effectively appeases the mind without lulling it to sleep.

> No, my Love, you are neither fire, nor water, nor aught that we say. You are what you are in your glorious eternity. You are: that is your essence and your name. You are life, divine life, living life, unifying life. You are all beatitude. You are ineffable, incomprehensible unity, supremely adorable. In a word, you are Love, and my Love. What, then, shall I say of you? You made me for you; for you, I say, who are Love. Why, then, should I not talk of love? But alas, what can I say? On earth I cannot speak of it. The saints who see you in heaven adore you in silence, and their silence is a sacred language in which they taste love. You pour your love into us, O my God, as into them. And you fill us with yourself, as you do them. Why, then, should we not do as they do? Why should we not taste love as they do? For if you are their Love, you are also ours. They see you directly, O my dear life, and that is what they have and what we have not in the lowliness and the misery of the flesh. But when we are delivered from our prison, we shall see you as they do, we shall praise you as they do, we shall embrace you as they do, we shall possess you as they do, we shall be immersed in you as they are, and we shall no longer express your love in humble similitudes, because we shall be nothing but love, because we shall be wholly in love, that is, in you, who are my one Love, my mercy and my All.[60]

---

59. Marie of the Incarnation, *Relation de 1654*, 12: "The soul is carried away passively by a stroke which, in its depths, gives her a very great peace. But beyond this, divine love holds her bound in an anguish which can be vividly felt but not spoken of" (*Écrits*, ed. Jamet, vol. 2, p. 216). There are, however, different forms of anxiety. Cf. Hans Urs von Balthasar, *Der Christ und der Angst*, 6th ed. (1989).

60. Marie of the Incarnation, *Exclamations et Élévations*, 2 (ed. Jamet, vol. 1, pp. 380-381).

Let nothing disturb you,
Let nothing frighten you,
   Though all things pass,
God does not change.

Patience wins all things,
But he lacks nothing,
Who possesses God:
   For God alone suffices.[61]

But if I do not reach my goal? If I fall by the wayside? I shall nevertheless have the joy of having run, strained, and sweated as much as I could, in search of the face of my Lord.[62]

O Lord and my God, my one and only hope, hear my prayer, lest in my wearied state I should find myself unwilling to seek you. But rather let me always seek your face with a burning desire. Give me the energy and power to seek you, Lord, who have made us to find you, and have given us an ever greater hope of finding you. My strength and my infirmity are known to you. Preserve my strength and heal my infirmity. My knowledge and my ignorance are also known to you. When you have opened the door to me, be my stay as I enter through it. When you have closed the door, open it to me when I knock. May I remember you, may I understand you, may I love you. Increase and nurture these aspects in me, until you reshape me completely. . . . Free me, Lord, from the excess of talk and words which I suffer within my soul. . . . Many are my thoughts, which you are well aware of, my thoughts that are all too human, inasmuch as they are a vanity. Grant that I may not consent to them . . . , nor dwell upon them like one in a daydream. . . . When, therefore, I finally reach you, many of the things we speak of now shall cease, . . . and you alone will remain all in all, and we shall speak of

---

61. St. Teresa, *Poems*.
62. Richard of St. Victor, *De Trinitate*, bk. 3, ch. 1 (PL 196:915-916).

you alone as being without end, even as we praise you together, having been made one in you. . . .[63]

O ergo, quem nemo quaerit vere et non invenit, quippe cum ipsa veritas te quaerendi in conscientia quaerentis non suspectum jam habeat responsum aliquatenus inventae veritatis! [64]

(So no one truly seeks you without finding you because the very truth that you are being sought in the consciousness of the seeker contains in itself the unsuspected answer of a truth which, in a measure, has been discovered already.)

To await God is to possess him.[65]

---

63. St. Augustine, *De Trinitate*, bk. 15, ch. 28, n. 51. Translation provided here is by M. Sebanc.
64. William of St.-Thierry, *Speculum fidei* (PL 180:397a).
65. Fénelon, *Oeuvres* (Paris), vol. 8, p. 557. Cf. St. Augustine, *Enarratio in Psalmum*, 41, 7-10 (PL 36:467-471). A translation by M. Sebanc appears on the pages following.

Where Is Your God?

Hearing every day the words, "Where is your God?" feeding every day on my diet of tears, I have pondered day and night on what I have heard.... Also I have sought my God, so that, if it were possible, I might not merely believe in him, but even see him to some extent. For I see what my God has done, but I do not see my God, the very one who has done these things.

But because I long like a hart for flowing streams, and the font of life is to be found in him, and the Psalm is written to be understood by the sons of Korah, and the invisible things of God come within our ken through the things which are made: what am I to do, so that I might find my God?

I shall examine the earth: the earth has been made. Great is the beauty of the earth. But it has an artificer. Great are the marvels of seeds and plants. But all these things have a creator. I declare the greatness of the encompassing sea. I am awestruck, I marvel. I seek an artificer. I look up at the sky and the beauty of the stars. I marvel at the splendor of the sun which suffices for the putting forth of day, the night-time moon that mitigates the darkness. These things are marvellous. They are praiseworthy, even stupendous. For these things are not earthly in character, but are already heavenly. — Nor, indeed, does my thirst linger with a view to being sated by them. I marvel at them, I praise them, but I thirst for him who made them.

I return to myself, and I search out who it is that I myself am, I, who ask such questions. I find that I have a body and a soul, etc. But is God actually any such part of myself as is spirit? Indeed, God cannot be seen except by the spirit, but he cannot, however, be seen in such a way as the spirit can be seen. For this spirit seeks in some way to find out what God is, and those who say, 'Where is your God?' do not insult him. This spirit seeks a certain unchangeable truth, a substance that has no defects. The spirit itself is not such. ... Its kind of mutability does not fall to the lot of God. ...

Therefore it is in seeking my God in visible and corporeal things and not finding him, in seeking his substance in myself, as if he were something like what I am, but not finding it, that I feel that my God is something above my soul. Thus, so that I might touch him, 'These things I have pondered, and I have poured out my soul above myself.' ...

... Let them still say: 'Where is your God?' Thus I seek my God in every body, be it earthly or heavenly, and I do not find him. I seek his substance in my soul, and I do not find him. I have pondered, however, the search for my God, and through the things which have been made, desiring to catch sight of and understand the invisible things of God, 'I have poured out my soul above myself'. And now there remains no one whom I might touch, except for my God. For the home of my God is there, above my soul. There he lives, from there he views me, from there he created me, from there he guides me, from there he takes an interest in me, from there he inspires me, from there he calls me, from there he directs me, from there he leads me, from there he shows me the end of my way.

For he who has the loftiest of homes in solitude also has a tabernacle on earth. His tabernacle on earth, his Church, is still a wayfaring pilgrim. But the seeking must occur here, because the way homewards is found in the tabernacle. . . . Beyond the place wherein the tabernacle is situated I shall roam as I seek my God; 'Because I shall enter the place of his wonderful tabernacle, even to the house of God.' . . .

. . . Behold how many things I marvel at in his tabernacle! For the tabernacle of God on earth is the faithful . . . and I regard the soul herself in her obedience to God, . . . I regard justice and charity which are near . . . and I marvel at those virtues in the soul. But I am still walking in the place wherein the tabernacle is situated. And now I pass beyond a discussion of these matters. For I am awestruck at how wonderful the tabernacle is when I reach the home of God. . . . In the home of God there is everlasting festivity, the face of God is present, there is unblemished joy. . . . The sound of this festivity wafts caressingly to the ear of the person who walks in this tabernacle and who considers God's miracles in redeeming his faithful. It carries off the hart to flowing streams.

But because, brothers, for as long as we are home in this body, we are a stranger to the Lord, and the body, which is corrupt, weighs down the soul, and living on this earth weighs down the mind that muses on many things. Even though in some ways the foggy mist is dispelled by our journey through the realm of yearning, and even though now and again we come within reach of those festive sounds, so that by our efforts we acquire something from this house that is God's, still, on account of a certain burden of infirmity, we fall back on our accustomed ways and we come to grief on those old habits. And just as we had found in the former situation the source of our joy, so there will not be lacking in the latter something for us to bewail.

For that hart . . . is seized by desire for flowing streams, that is to say, the interior sweetness of God, and pours out his soul above himself so that he might touch what is beyond his soul, journeying to the place of the marvellous tabernacle, even to the house of God, led by the delight of interior, rational sound, so that he despises all exterior things and is enthralled by interior things. Still, however, he is a man, still he sighs and groans here, still he bears his fragile flesh, still he is exposed to danger among the stumbling blocks of this world. Therefore he has cast his gaze back at himself, saying: "Why are you sad, my soul, and why do you throw me into confusion? Behold, already we rejoice in a kind of interior sweetness; behold, we catch sight of something unchangeable with our keenness of mind, even though we have been able to examine matters only cursorily and superficially. Why then do you still throw me into confusion, why are you still sad? For you are no longer in doubt about your God. For this is what you say to yourself, against those who say: 'Where is your God?' 'Already I have felt something unchangeable. Why, then, do you throw me into confusion? Hope in God.'"

And his soul answers him in silence, as it were: "Why do I throw you into confusion, except for the reason that I am not yet in that place of sweetness, by which I am so caught up as by a rite of passage? . . ."

But "Hope in God," he answers his own soul as it throws him into confusion. . . . Meanwhile live in hope. For hope which is seen is not hope. If, moreover, we hope for what we do not see, we wait patiently. . . . (Cf. Romans 8:24-25.)

7

God in Our Time

Whenever it abandons a system of thought, humanity imagines it has lost God.

The God of "classical ontology" is dead, you say? It may be so; but it does not worry me overmuch. I have no inclination to defend the petrified constructions of Wolf. And if "classical ontology" disappeared, it was surely because it did not correspond adequately with being. Nor was its idea of God adequate for God. The mind is alive, and so is the God who makes himself known to it.

"God is dead!" or so at least it seems to us . . . until, round the next bend in the road, "we find him again, alive." Once again he makes himself known, in spite of all that we have left behind on the road, all that was only a viaticum for one stage of our journey, all that was only a temporary shelter till we had to make a fresh start. . . . And if we have really progressed along the road, we shall find God himself greater still. But it will be the same God. *Deus semper major.* And once again we shall move on in his light.

God is never left behind among the dross. . . . In whatever direction we go, he is there before us, calling to us and coming to meet us. . . .

It is only too true, often enough "a deist is a man who has not had time to become an atheist."[1]

---

1. De Bonald. Cf. Peter Wust, *La crise occidentale,* in *Le Roseau d'or,* Chroniques (1929), p. 330: "The God of the Deists is no more than an absolutely dead shadow of the paternal God of the Christians." Jacques Maritain, *Les degrés du savoir,* pp. 446ff.; Paul Hazard, *La pensée européenne au XVIIIe siècle,* vol. 1, p. 153; *La crise de la conscience . . . ,* vol. 2, p. 31. Proudhon put it quite crudely in his *Philosophie de la misère:* "I know a man who would be ready to draw his sword in God's cause, and,

The deist's God, the God of several modern "theodicies" which weigh and measure him rather than defend him, the God who can hardly say "I am" any longer, the God who tends to be no more than "the universal harmony of things," who rules over a beyond where "everything is the same as here,"[2] the God imprisoned "within the limits of reason," who no longer intervenes in the world, who is really nothing but the projection of natural man, who is distant yet without mystery, a God made to our measure and defined according to our rules, a God merged in the "moral order of the universe" as man understands it, a God who is not adored and whom one can only serve by the cult of morality, a God who is "only accessible in pure knowledge" and who is "nothing but that knowledge itself," a God in fact whose thoughts are our thoughts and whose ways are our ways: such a God has proved very useless in practice and has become the object of a justified *ressentiment*.[3] And when at last man decided to get rid of him altogether in order to enter into his own inheritance, he was only a shade, "reduced to the narrow limits of human thought."[4]

---

like Robespierre, to set the guillotine going till the last atheist had been destroyed, little suspecting that he would be the last." Let us say, at the very least, that rationalist deism provides the denial of God, on behalf of man, with its most redoubtable argument.

2. Cf. Jules Lachelier, criticizing Leibniz's conception, *Lettre à Jean Baruzi*, 10th December 1906.

3. Cf. already F. Pillon, "Une dénonciation épiscopale," *La Critique philosophique* (1876), vol. 2, pp. 122ff.: "Was it desired only that he should be decorously respectful to the God of Cousin and the *Revue des Deux Mondes?* Is he wrong to disdain, indeed, to scorn this colorless, bourgeois religiosity of dilettantes and those of a doctrinaire disposition, a religiosity which is of no consequence, which exerts no influence on life, which is not in any way incompatible with a profound, subconscious skepticism, which puts an obstacle, by virtue of the place it occupies in terms of habits and customs, to every spontaneous and original manifestation of true religious thought?" For Hegel, cf. Jean Hyppolite, *Logique et existence* (1953); the thought of Hegel himself is ambiguous yet, but this was the case, moreover, in his first works already; cf. Marcel Méry, *G. W. F. Hegel, Premières publications* (1952), p. 299; and *La critique du christianisme chez Renouvier*, vol. 2 (1952), conclusion (pp. 500ff.).

4. It should, however, be remembered that each case is unique, that something active very often survives, that there are ambivalences, that the "quarrels over atheism" are often muddled, and that what looks like a degradation in one light may sometimes be in fact the beginning of a rediscovery. . . . Gabriel Marcel notes, for example, that "among the greatest representatives of idealism" — he is thinking in particular of Fichte — "there existed an extraordinarily vigorous recognition of values": *Le mystère de l'être*, vol. 2 (1951), p. 89.

∾

"To convict Voltaire of atheism is not really a great victory over Christian thought"[5] — nor is it, for that matter, to show that the God of Fichte or Hegel easily turns into the Man of Feuerbach. "Let them reach what conclusions they please against deism," Pascal prophetically remarked.[6]

∾

We have witnessed, during the last few centuries, "the rationalistic evaporation of God."[7] But it was the rationalist God. A single puff will disperse the vapor. We shall not be disturbed. We shall even breathe more comfortably. The true God, the God we continue to adore, is elsewhere. He is everywhere you think to find him. He is everywhere, even when you do not find him.

∾

When "God's cause" is lost, then God is victorious once again. Then "he is his own defender."[8]

∾

It is generally conceded that Christianity "inaugurated the struggle against false gods." But some people would like to take over from it, as though it could not complete the task itself. They would like to make philosophy the heir to Christianity. Yet the philosopher, it is said, is "the man who understands" and not "the man who chooses."[9] In that case the false gods still have a promising future!

∾

One must "reject the gods," a certain writer says, "all the gods." That is precisely what the disciples of Jesus taught us to do from the beginning. If they were taken for atheists, it was not because they were making the banal claim to have discovered *another god*, who would simply have been one among many, but because they proclaimed him who is *totally different from*

---

5. Etienne Gilson, replying to Leon Brunschvicg in *Querelle de l'athéisme*.
6. Cf. G. Fessard, *La main tendue* (1937), pp. 124ff., with regard to the Hegelian formula proclaiming "the death of the abstraction that is Divine Essence."
7. Georges Gusdorf, *Mythe et Métaphysique* (1953), p. 221.
8. Cf. Leibniz, *Causa Dei* . . . .
9. Merleau-Ponty, *Eloge de la Philosophie* (1953), p. 65.

the gods, and who frees us from their tyranny. They denied everything that the men around them took for the divine — everything that man, at every epoch, tends to deify in order to adore himself and tyrannize over himself, in and through his gods.

The Gospel is the only "twilight of the gods."

It is possible to maintain that religion — faith in God in the first instance — is a system invented by nature with the object of *reassuring* man who would otherwise be paralyzed by fear in face of a hostile mystery.

But there is another way in which man can reassure himself: the rationalist way, the way of the short-sighted optimist who does not even rise to the level at which the mystery can be felt and proudly announces that there is none to know.

Which of the two is nearer the truth?

Faith in God certainly gives us confidence.[10] That is undeniable, and there is no reason to be ashamed of it, as though it were more intelligent not to have been touched by dread or anguish, or nobler not to wish to be delivered from it. Faith, indeed, reassures us — but not on our level, or so as to produce a paralyzing illusion, or a complacent satisfaction, but so as to enable us to act. It gives man the confidence to become worthy of himself, and helps him not to succumb in the great crisis in his growth to maturity, when consciousness awakens from animality. Faith gives him confidence, but it does so by establishing him in the truth and by communicating a disquiet of a higher order.

What could be more horrifying than a world without God, without stability, and without mystery, convinced of its own transparency, falling headlong into an abyss of meaningless and endless change, *dum nil perenne cogitat,* while the soul thinks of nothing eternal? or a society entirely given over to temporal idols, in which the *mens avida aeternitatis* is suffocated to death — a world of inexpressible horror and despair?

---

10. Cf. Clement of Alexandria, *Texts Chosen from the Prophets,* nn. 21 and 26: God is at once "inaccessible light" and "devouring fire"; as fire he engenders fear, as light he gives back security.

To compare Nietzsche to Jesus: Jesus was killed because he proclaimed the Father who is in heaven; Nietzsche killed himself, his mind foundered in perpetual night, because he proclaimed, accepted, and willed "the death of God."

Since that decision was taken, in spite of deliberately persuading himself that he possesses a "carefree knowledge," man is obliged to admit, with Nietzsche, that his knowledge leaves him "frozen stiff with fear" — he is a prey to "a sacred terror."[11]

The divine right of kings, the divine right of peoples: both of them human inventions and instruments of oppression. The divine right of God is the only source of freedom.

The anti-theist — the militant atheist — claims to know God, otherwise he could not oppose him. But by that very fact, and whatever he may say, he is not really opposing God. For God cannot be known in that way.

Even from the point of view of sociological analysis, the Marxian theory of religion is hardly exact — or at least it is incomplete. Religion, let us admit for argument's sake, might really be the opium of the people if the people had that particular craving. In certain favored circumstances, perhaps, they have. But observation suggests that as a people becomes a proletariat, it loses that taste. Far from stimulating the religious impulse by a sort of mystical compensation, the increasing "alienation" and isolation which goes with the proletarian condition tends, on the contrary, to smother any interest in religion. It turns those whom it dehumanizes away from God.

For in fact a certain degree of social "alienation" very often involves the alienation of the consciousness. And the alienated consciousness is the exact opposite of the religious consciousness.

"The proletarian has no country." In an analogous sense and for similar reasons, the proletarian has no religion. In a society such as ours, religion tends to become a luxury article, which is denied to a whole section of the

---

11. Cf. the present author's *Affrontements mystiques* (1950), ch. 3, "Nietzsche mystique." Also similarly in *Drame de l'humanisme athée*, 7th ed. (1983), pp. 493-532.

population. Though the suppression of the proletariat will not automatically give God back to man: but it is, up to a point, a condition of God's being given back to him.

~

The famous Marxian dialectic is another perfectly authentic, though very heterodox and shameful, example of a "Christian philosophy."

Hegel was a theologian; his main categories were supplied to him by a rationalization of the Christian mysteries. Marx had been a Hegelian. It took a double inversion, a double "apostasy," to produce the final result: the divine was made immanent by Hegel; then the human was materialized by Marx (what Marx called standing the dialectic on its feet again). But in spite of its double metamorphosis, the texture remains unchanged: it was furnished neither by experience, nor by science, nor even by pure reflection (does pure reflection yield anything?), but by faith. It is the Mystery of Christ, God incarnate, dead and risen. A keen eye can still detect the "theft of sacred things" at the source of categories which are in appearance the most profane. Even now, after so many changes, so many denials, negations, and corruptions, the Marxist ideology is still really a parasite that draws life from the Christian substance.[12]

Long after people have stopped talking about "the absolute history of the divine idea" or its "supreme alienation," faith in the God who is incar-

---

12. Cf. Franz Gregoire, *Aux sources de la pensée de Marx* (1947), p. 77: "Hegel's attachment to the Christian dogma of redemption, even though it dates from a time after the philosopher had lost his faith and was purely symbolic, certainly contributed to his idea of the dialectical process as the fundamental law of things." And G. Van der Leeuw, *L'homme primitif et la religion*, pp. 194ff.: "The stronger atheism grows, the more we are able distinctly to notice in its features the traces of past religious experiences, as in communist atheism we notice the vestiges of eschatology and the religion of human community. The man who does not wish to be religious is so nonetheless, precisely through this wishing. He is quite well able to take flight before God, but it is not possible for him to avoid God."

In *Le Génie des Religions* (1841), Edgar Quinet had already noted this kind of absorption of Christianity that had been effected by the teachings of the German metaphysicians who were most opposed to the Christian faith. But his liberal point of view caused him to regard this fact in an optimistic light: "Christianity, which had entered into the theories of these metaphysicians almost wholly and entirely, was never abolished in their minds, even for one single day. The result is that (Germany) has made the transition from religion to philosophy without violence.... Never for a moment did Germany find itself confronting nothingness...."

nate in history, and who was "destroyed" for our sake, will still be alive. When the "Good Friday of Speculation" and the "Calvary of History" are long forgotten expressions, the Cross of Jesus will still bear the Fruit of Life.

If I meet a saint, I know what I have seen — or at least glimpsed. But some people say they can do without God from now on, and can find something better. I wait for them to show me a new type of saint.

To think that people can convince themselves that "metaphysical anxiety" is a thing of the past! "We are cured of our obsession," they tell us, "cured of our folly: of our obsession with God, with being and with nothingness, of the searing burn of the unknown in the heart of the known, and of *the other* whom we pursued in our dreams." We are no longer "haunted by the absolute," they tell us, for we have shaken off the burden of "eternal truths." . . . Poor mutilated wretches who think they have achieved freedom, and celebrate the most lamentable abdication as a "tremendous victory." They had better sing their hymn of victory while there is time. For even in them the mutilation is not final and they do not realize that man cannot abdicate. A sudden awakening can put everything in doubt, and a single spark can relight the fire that seemed to have died out. The soul comes to life again though we think we have killed it. Then he realizes with terror that he bears it within him:

> Not like a satisfied cow ruminating on its feet,
> But like the virgin mare, its mouth still burning from the salt
>   it has taken from its master's hand,
> How can he keep back and restrain that huge and terrible thing
>   that rears and cries out in the narrow stall of its personal will,
> When the smell of the grass comes in through the cracks in the door
>   with the wind at dawn?[13]

Man is wounded — a sign of his greatness, often hidden and always indelible. When the wound breaks the surface of consciousness, it assumes the most varied forms. It becomes the source of a continual unrest, of a

---

13. Paul Claudel, *La Ville,* Act 3.

deep dissatisfaction which not only prevents the sufferer from being content with any one position, but from being satisfied with progress in any single direction. It is the motive-spring of thought which drives him to break through the successive circles in which the life of the human animal tends to unfold, and disposes in turn of the critical systems and of the positivist wisdoms which seemed able to dispose of it. It may take the form of dread without any precise object:

Aliis oppressa malis in pectore cura. (With heart weighed down by other evils.)

This anguish cannot be described in all its forms and psychological expressions — not even "depth"-psychology can reach it except in its manifestations. Sometimes it is a presentiment, the presentiment of another existence, and those who experience it vividly can sometimes communicate its flavor, or at least the suspicion of it, to those around them, thanks to the connivance of the spirit which is found everywhere, though it is almost always dormant and subject to the mysterious laws of germination. It has been called "the appeal of transcendence". . . .

One might try to give comforting explanations of this universal phenomenon. Equally it is possible to criticize many of its cruder manifestations. One may condemn its many distortions and point out many counterfeits of it — which are all the more serious when they hinder the normal growth of the spiritual life. One could go on almost indefinitely unraveling the confusions which the undeveloped mind entertains on this subject.[14] It may be further observed that many people who are on the whole satisfied with themselves have not the faintest idea of it; whereas it is often remarkably clear in certain states of illness or when the social organism is not in sound health. But it would be a very poor observer who thought that it was just an anomaly, a passing disease, a sort of excrescence which could be removed altogether one day, a phantom of the mind which could be dissipated, a strange voice which could be reduced to silence. It would be most unrealistic to imagine that physical or social health or the progress of science were the cure. That would be to misconceive all that is most human in the human being and which "makes him more than man."

---

14. Gabriel Marcel is right to observe that although "the need for transcendence presents itself above all as a kind of dissatisfaction," "the converse," however, "does not seem to be true, it does not seem that one would be right in saying that every kind of dissatisfaction implies an aspiration towards transcendence." *Le mystère de l'être,* vol. 1, *Réflexion et mystère* (1951), p. 50. This should put us on our guard against a romantic illusion, and equally against the opposite, anti-romantic illusion.

Let us suppose, however, that the cure has taken place. We should have no hesitation in preferring worse health if such good health were to condemn us to a complacent humanism, if the balance reached left man glutted, and he no longer regarded himself as a problem. What a depressing ideal it would be — a terrestrial existence undisturbed by struggle or contradiction, without suffering but also without aspiration and untouched by the search for the Absolute! A perfectly ordered world with no room for either saints or heroes! An ideal world, perfect in its circumscribed reality, completely adapted to its surroundings, where there is an exact balance between the objective and the subjective, where man's idea of himself and his concrete existence are identical,[15] so that there would not be the smallest fault or crack through which to communicate the mystery of being, no further adjustment in the wonderfully balanced machine of the human universe, no room for man's struggles with himself or for a genuinely personal decision! One might go on using the words "humanism," "culture," and "spiritual life," but in what a degenerate sense! And from the Christian point of view, what a monstrosity! Even from the merely human point of view, what misery it would be! Does the vast effort which carries us forward today lead to that prison-cell?[16]

But in fact we are not faced with such a dilemma. On the contrary, the truth is that certain social conditions, where the injustice or the misery is too great — although they favor, perhaps, certain crude aberrations — shut man off from the life of the spirit. So we should work with all our hearts and with no misgivings, and certainly without the slightest danger of going too far, to improve the lot of man and to promote progress on every front: success, however great, can never heal the wound. Even if "the leap into the reign of liberty," which Engels foretold, were to be realized on earth, the

---

15. Cf. Henri Niel, "Athéisme et Marxisme," *Lumière et Vie* (1955), p. 78: In Marx's view, "religion is born of the dualism between the idea and reality, between the idea which man forms of himself and his concrete existence. As long as that hiatus exists there will be religion. Marx's aim was to put an end to that sense of insufficiency and lack of adaptation by realising a world where man would feel really at home." Cf. Emmanuel Mounier, *Carnets de route*, 2, p. 415: "What is a happy man? — A man who is well adapted, one would think, gliding along like a perfect mechanism in his meshwork of biological, affective, and social cog-wheels. . . ."

16. It almost seems as though the Marxists themselves were somewhat uncomfortable, and this perhaps accounts for the fact that they much prefer to draw an ideal portrait of the Marxist man in society as it is at present than to depict man in Marxist society.

wound would still remain. Our consciousness of it would only be keener and purer. What social disorder has not created, social order is powerless to cure.

The belief that man's hour had sounded became general for the first time in our age; it came in like a racing tide: man was sufficient unto himself in his immanence and in his finitude, usurping the prerogatives of God. This was the madness of Kirilov, of Zarathustra and of Feuerbach, of the "humanist" and the "superman". . . . It has rightly been called a "tragic mistake." Man excels, it is true, in transmuting the actual conditions of his misery, whether physiological or social, into all manner of dreams. There is certainly much truth in the opposed psychologies of Marx and Freud, to mention two great parallel examples. There is truth, too, in Comte's idea of a first "theological" age and in analogous ideas in the worlds of our philosophers and historians. One of the signs of a mature spirit is without doubt to renounce false forms of transcendence, and all the luxuriant vegetation which draws off the sap and produces no fruit. But let us not forget the wisdom of the first great "reductionist." When old Xenophanes of Colophon uttered his seemingly skeptical words: "If oxen and horses had hands and could paint and draw . . . ," he was bent upon purifying, not destroying, the idea of divinity. Let us not forget either that the reality of nature and the reality of man, once recaptured, if they needed to be, still have to be explained, and also to be explored and penetrated, preserved and saved. We must be careful to see that when, like Xenophanes, we begin by "reducing," we do not end by mutilating, and that the conquests of science, wrongly interpreted, do not confuse and cloud the mind, and that in ridding ourselves of one illusion we do not fall into another, its antithesis. For there is indeed an illusion of the absolute, but there is also an illusion of the relative; there is the illusion of the eternal, but there is also the illusion of the historical; there is the illusion of transcendence, and also the illusion of immanence; a mystical illusion and a positivist illusion. That is to say, if one misconceives the relative and the historical, one can, of course, only obtain a pseudo-absolute, a pseudo-eternal, and one's liberation is a dream. But, on the other hand, it is no less true that if we misconceive the eternal and the absolute, we are left with only a pseudo-historical, a pseudo-temporal, a path that does not lead to liberation. In short, "mystification" takes place in more than one direction.

There is a mystical or celestial illusion — and there is a positivist or terrestrial illusion. Let us call the one spiritualist and the other materialist. Now, they are not only individual illusions or illnesses. Either can stamp long periods of history. Normally the celestial illusion comes before the terrestrial, which is why the second is a double illusion, taking itself for critical sagacity. Yet it serves no purpose to dissipate one illusion if we fall into the other.

The man whose guide is the Gospel will be on his guard against both. The idea of transcendence implies immanence. The dogma of the resurrection and the biblical behest to work the soil are reliable guides; so is the precept of brotherly charity. The intellectual maturity and the technical progress of the last few centuries help us to deepen our understanding of it. We believe with St. Paul that *"the figure of this world passes,"* and we refuse to sacrifice either side of this truth, recognizing their solidarity. We do not want a spiritual life in a dream-world, nor an eternity which is not prepared for us by time. But neither do we want a closed humanism, an "inhuman humanism." "Nothing but the earth" is the cruelest of all illusions.

The heaven of the mystical illusion does not exist. But the earth of the positivist illusion, the temporalist illusion, does exist — and takes its revenge.

We do not protest enough against the way in which the idea of God is distorted among Christians. We are always anxious to spare the weak; we avoid startling the weak-minded and keeping the impure away, in the hope that contact with the Church holds out a possibility of enlightening and converting them; and we forget that there are others, no less weak, the unbelievers, who are scandalized by our accommodations.

To allow the truth to be obscured is invariably a cause of scandal somewhere, even if one has been tempted to prevaricate in order to avoid scandalizing this or that individual.[17]

---

17. Jacques Leclercq, *Dialogue de l'homme et de Dieu* (1948), pp. 23ff. Cf. Louis Bouyer, *Le sens de la vie monastique* (1950), p. 105, on the blasphemies that "we utter on our knees."

No proof gave me my God, and no critique can take him from me.[18] However acute it may be, that critique will provoke another. But perhaps it must first fulfill its salutary role. Without forcing me to make any concessions, it stimulates me to make progress. Without depriving my proof of value, it compels me to unearth its secret spring, to deepen and purify my faith.

Moreover, unbeknown to and in spite of himself, the atheist is often the greatest help the believer can have. Like the biblical Ecclesiastes, his criticism marks one of the stages of the dialectical process. He cooperates, unintentionally, in the "purification of faith," which consists in "freeing it more and more from the senses and human reasonings." He provides the salt that will prevent my idea of God from petrifying and so becoming false.

The idea of God cannot be uprooted because it is, in essence, the Presence of God in man. One cannot rid oneself of that Presence. Nor is the atheist a man who has succeeded in doing so. He is only an idolater who, as Origen said, "refers his indestructible notion of God to anything rather than to God himself."[19]

Industrial civilizations are naturally atheistic, and agricultural civilizations are naturally pagan.[20] Faith in the true God is always a victory.

---

18. History is instructive in this regard. "Critical idealism" thought that it had definitively discarded, or at least radically transformed, many of the proofs. What part of this idealism, taken as a whole in all that it purports, holds good today?

19. Origen, *Contra Celsum*, bk. 2, ch. 40 (PG 12:861b): . . . τοὺσ, δὲ πλανωμένουσ πε ρὶ θε οῦ καὶ παντὶ μᾶλλον ἢ θε ῷ ἐφαρμὸζοντασ τὴν πε ρὶ αὐτοῦ ἀδιάστροφον ἔννοιαν, ὑπολαμβάνοντασ ε ἶναι ε ὐσε βε στάτουσ [= ". . . but those who stray as regards God, and who refer their indestructible notion about him to anything rather than to God, and who suppose that they are very religious . . ."]. J. Leclercq, *Dialogue de l'homme et de Dieu* (1948), p. 19: "We ascribe God to things, because we do not know God. However, we do know him, since it is He whom we seek in things. We do not seek these things for themselves, as they are, but rather for the Ineffable One with whom we vest them."

20. Cf. Joseph Folliet, *L'avènement de Prométhée* (1951), pp. 21ff.: "As a prelude to the soaring flight of the natural sciences and technology, Descartes and Bacon prepared the way for the coming of the great proponents of denial, the enemies of God. The

As they gradually become more profane, modern civilizations expose us to the risk of losing God.[21] Perhaps they will enable us to rediscover him at a deeper level, and the rediscovery may well prepare the way for new syntheses, without involving a return to earlier and indistinct ideas.[22]

Promethean man lives in a world which is his own creation, far from a nature whose cruelty and beauty filled primitive man and the peasant as well with rapture and terror. The lights of the city hide the stars from him. . . . Amid the universe that he spins out, he no longer experiences a need for the Creator. The fear of the unknown which remains in him is the fear of a human and social unknown, more so than of a natural or supernatural unknown."

21. Cf. Henri Niel, "Athéisme et Marxisme," p. 80: Through the technological revolution "man in some fashion experiments with his creative power and compares it with the creative power of nature. In revealing to man a new aspect of his greatness, this revolution obliges us as a consequence to undertake the task of cleansing and purifying the idea that we have of God."

22. Cf. G. van der Leeuw, *L'homme primitif et la religion,* p. 207: "What we call secularization is not merely a decay of religion, but a phenomenon going hand in hand with the dawning awareness of *homo religiosus*. What religion loses in breadth, it is able to gain in depth. Primitive man never eats without bringing religion into it, whereas for modern man the fact of eating, even if he is religious, is the most ordinary thing in the world. But primitive man cannot 'convert', and it is precisely this that modern man is in a position to do. What primitive man possesses to a much lesser extent is the possibility of secularization. The man who has discovered the world can find his perdition in it. It is in this way that the loss of the notion of the sacred character of life can become the pre-condition of the notion of the sacred character of God. But it can also lead to the loss of any notion whatever of the sacred."

Also to be pondered are these other reflections by the same author (pp. 167ff. and 187): "The sovereignty of abstraction, which in its idealist and materialist forms, dominates to a great extent the nineteenth century, has come to grief, in our era, at the hands of the implacable forces of reality. Man has recovered himself as a being of flesh and blood, he has recovered his instincts. He has discovered anew the powers which dominate the world. Similarly he is in the process of rediscovering the reality of his gods, even sometimes the reality of his God. All kinds of influences that are apparently extremely contradictory converge to shatter abstraction. It is here that we can find lined up side by side the names of Nietzsche and Kierkegaard, of Barth and the Third Reich, of Klages and Berdyaev, of Guardini and Rosenberg, of Buber and Chesterton. The modern 'mentality' as an abstraction of reality, dominating this reality, is a transitory phenomenon, a phantom that still lurks in our midst, but condemned soon to disappear." Only this liquidation of rationalism constitutes at the same time the irruption of a no less dangerous irrationalism. We must be warned of this: "However great and stable, in the ensemble of human life, may be the importance of the structures of primitive and mythic life, they should never set us at odds with reason. Otherwise we would

No man without values — and no values which establish the value of man absolutely unless there is an Absolute which establishes them.

Man is of absolute value, because he is illuminated by a ray of light from the face of God; because, although he develops as he acts in history, he breathes the air of eternity. Unless that is true, any philosophy of man must be a mere vulgarity, a cynicism, or an empty dream.

People imagined that by reducing everything to immanence, everything, beginning with himself, would be given back to man; on the contrary, it meant robbing him of everything he possessed and "alienating" him absolutely. For it implied reducing everything to *duration* — to a duration without an eternal foundation, so that despite all one's efforts the moments of which it is formed disintegrate into fragments or add up into a mass but never form an interlocking structure. It was even thought that "the treasures wasted in the skies" had been saved; that the Absolute belonging to a dream-world had been brought back to earth; but it was not brought back from God into Man; it collapsed into the relative, carrying the whole of man with it.

The world is the real work of a beneficent God and has a real value. It is not just the stage on which man has to act and choose, nor is it simply an instrument for him to use; it is, so to speak, the stuff of the world to come, the matter of our eternity. Man's task, therefore, is not so much to liberate himself from time as to liberate himself through time. His task is not to escape from the world, but to raise it up. Only, in order to understand time and the world, it is necessary to look beyond it: for it is its relation to eternity which gives the world its consistency and makes time a real be-

---

commit the fault that is exactly opposite to that of those . . . who present the rational structure as the only beneficial structure. We would in a way be returning to the glorification of Rousseau's 'noble savage.' . . . The considerations that are prized by the mortal enemies of the spirit, particularly those put forth by Klages, cause us to think about this issue . . . , even though these considerations aspire to a very different end. . . ."

That is why, if we do not wish to escape from Charybdis only to fall into Scylla, it is so very important nowadays further to recover and emphasize in its completeness the idea of the spirit that comes to us from the Christian tradition. . . .

coming. And it is the hope of radical and final transformation which saves our terrestrial effort from futility.

Humanism, it has been said, "is a fully articulated anthropocentrism which starts from the knowledge of man and purposes to give him value, thus excluding everything which alienates him from himself, whether it does so by subjecting him to supra-human truths or powers, or by disfiguring him by putting him to some sub-human use."[23] But if the refusal, as it is called, to subject man "to supra-human truths and powers" is a refusal of God and of divine truth, it would very soon lead to the disfigurement of man "by putting him to some infra-human use." The guarantee of man's value is to be found above his own sphere. The way in which humanism, which regards man as the supreme value, "gives value to man" ends by resembling the exploitation of land or livestock.

Man has a twofold character; there is the historical aspect and the inward aspect, and the one cannot be dissociated from the other. He possesses the one by virtue of the other; but for the fact that his historical character is real, fruitful and clearly orientated, his inwardness would only be phantasmagoria, a psychological epiphenomenon; were it not for his substantial inwardness, his historicity would disintegrate in time, itself reduced to dust.... Man makes himself in and through history — that can be affirmed without presupposing any particular theory of "progress" — and that is why each generation only fully understands itself as a link in the chain of humanity on the march. But the march of man would have no meaning, or rather humanity would not be on the march, and the very name by which we designate it would be a mere *flatus vocis*, if there were not, at the very heart of the world, an Eternal, drawing us to an End, impressing upon each one of us the seal of his image, and conferring upon each of us his unalterable inwardness.

If man wants to find himself, he must aim above and beyond himself. It is not enough for each individual to take on a task that transcends him;

---

23. C. Brunold and J. Jacob, *De Montaigne à Louis de Broglie, introduction a l'étude de la pensée française contemporaine* (Paris, 1952), p. 4, Entretiens de Pontigny.

the same must be true of each generation and for each community, and in fact for humanity as a whole. Otherwise our successes will only be external and precarious, threatened each time by a more radical crisis of nihilism, and turning, in the end, against man himself. No human fortune is worthy of absorbing man's attention. Humanity can only find equilibrium and peace — an active peace, an equilibrium in movement — by keeping its gaze fixed above the earthly horizon, by being faithful to its divine vocation.

Man needs a beyond which can never be grasped, a beyond that always remains beyond. He cannot find himself without losing himself.

At each stage, the final solution of the human problem lies in adoration. It can only be found in ecstasy.[24]

"Man surpasses man." Many of those who regard themselves as "humanists" in the most exclusive and strict sense of the word, are prepared to recognize the fact. No man, according to them, is worthy of the name without a *sursum*. The doctrines that incarcerate him in a nature already fully realized seem to them untrue and contemptible. They require a movement towards transcendence at the very heart of immanence.

. . . But in what sense can that movement be efficacious? Dreams of a collective future are vain unless there is an eschatological Beyond, already present and active in the womb of becoming. Equally our dreams of spiritual development are vain if there is no Beyond which is both transcendent and immanent at the same time.

Those who do not recognize the attraction of a Transcendent Being in themselves have nothing to offer but a transcendent movement towards nothing.

---

24. To anyone who catches a glimpse, at least, of the need for adoration which is in the heart of man, all positivist solutions to the problem of religion will appear derisory. This is one of the faults of the Kantian solution. Cf. my *Drame de l'humanisme athée*, pt. 2 (Eng. trans. *The Drama of Atheist Humanism* [London, 1949]). The same applies to the sketch by Julian Huxley: "Religion as an Objective Problem," *The Uniqueness of Man* (1940): "The disappearance of God means a recasting of religion, and a recasting of a fundamental sort. It means the shouldering by man of ultimate responsibilities which he had previously pushed off on God" (p. 282). For example, the responsibility for becoming an object of adoration, the proper object of his own proper adoration? The utopia of integral laicism is at least more logical. . . .

At one moment we are told that we make our heaven in the image of this — all too real — world; and at another that our desire creates, by contrast, a mystical region where all the signs are inverted, in order to escape the bondage of society here below and fly to the freedom of our dream world.

But we know quite well that our God is different. We know quite well that he is the Living God. Our faith in him does not depend upon those processes, and the hope that he pours into our hearts does not deceive us.

Indeed, we see the processes which are pointed out to us quite as well as others. The mind cannot do without analogies in its attempt to represent God — so the door is wide open to risks. The oppressed naturally tend to find in the sky a refuge from their hardships and the malign influence of man — and that involves risks of another kind. It is only too easy, too "natural," to mobilize the divine in the service of social realism, or to call it to the rescue of a utopian subjectivism. The one can call God the principle of his revolt, the other the principle of his tyranny. But the believer is on his guard against both abuses. He does not allow himself to be the dupe of analogies or of contrasts. He does not deify the earth, or hypostatize a heaven without reference to it. And yet he knows full well that, in the end, only his hope in heaven gives relish to the earthly work that prepares him for it.

Man, they say, is alienated by his God. But alas, the truth nowadays is rather that he is alienated *from* his God, deprived of his ultimate wealth, the most precious of all, where he could rediscover the principle not only of his *having* but of his *being*.

How sharply the traditional formula has been thrown into relief in modern times: he who is in me is *more than I myself!* — a formula adopted confidently by many of those who live its truth without reflecting upon it, and which a terrible experience of emptiness has demonstrated anew!

Man without God is dehumanized.

There have been tyrannical gods — and there is the God who makes us free.

Tyrant gods, nowadays, do not, as a rule, assume the names of gods. They prefer pseudonyms. But their tyranny remains the same.

You reject faith in God as an intolerable "theocracy"? Yet with every day that goes by it is surely increasingly obvious that this could only favor a "mythocracy" more terrible still. Empty the heavens and they are at once occupied by an army of myths more compelling than hunger, more despotic than the worst despot....

Non habebis deos alienos coram me. (Thou shalt not have strange gods before me.) Such is the everlasting "precept of liberty."[25] Those strange gods, those false and mythical gods, are the ones who alienate us — monsters that devour us like the human passions of which they are the hypostasis.

You made the true God resemble them and believed that in rejecting him you rejected them all with a single gesture. But that proud gesture was the result of a misunderstanding, and you failed to perceive that one must choose between him and them. The dark gods who vanish as the Sun of Justice dawns, and whom he keeps at a distance, return at once under other names.

Whether the names be new or old, the names of gods or pseudonyms, they invariably possess some characteristic of the man who adores himself in them, and makes himself his own slave.

How far are we destined to go in that slavery before humanity, with one voice, begins to cry out, "I hold out my arms towards my liberator!"

God is rejected as limiting man — and people forget that it is man's relation to God that confers upon him "a sort of infinity." God is rejected as enslaving man — and people forget that it is man's relation to God that frees him from all servitudes, in particular the historical and social. God is rejected because he obliges man to ratify everything — and it is forgotten that it is this same relation to God that confers upon him "an infinite capacity for rejection."[26] Men reject God on the ground that he alienates man by his transcendence — forgetting that "it is in the affirmation of transcendence that man finds his most authentic truth."[27]

A purely humanistic consciousness, which will not recognise anything outside man, can never be quite certain whether the impulse which

---

25. Origen.
26. The expression is André Breton's in *Position politique du surréalisme*, p. 11.
27. F. Alquié, *Philosophie du surréalisme* (1955), p. 211. Cf. Albert Cartier, "Le probleme de Dieu dans la philosophie de Blondel," *Giornale di Metafisica* (1955), pp. 833ff.

drives it towards life is hope or despair. To say that man is everything is surely to say that he finds himself faced by nothing. . . . Can man be saved if we can have recourse to nothing beyond man?[28]

∼

Unless God is at the source a revolt and its ally, it invariably ends in servitude.

Whenever we say No, we imply that on a deeper level there is a Yes which provokes and originates it; rebellion always implies an acquiescence which is both deeper and more free.

∼

One can never, even for one generation, bracket off, as in a parenthesis, the immediate problems of existence or the whole problem of destiny.

Humanity is always a present question, with its elementary needs and its passion for the absolute.

∼

The believer can hardly help being saddened at the sight of humanity caught in the quicksands — and who knows for how many centuries it may be? — at the very moment when it seems to aspire more fervently than ever to be free. He sees it shun its God as "a strange being."[29] He sees it alienate itself in the very act in which it believes it has finally freed itself. How can one avoid being saddened at the thought that it is lowering itself in a movement that seemed as though it were struggling to greater dignity?

In time, perhaps, those in whom the original aspiration lives on will see the danger. And then, perhaps, they will recognize that the believers they first took for adversaries are really their indispensable allies.

∼

Homo sapiens has again become *homo faber* — but this time he is the builder of a whole world, and so more than ever the builder of himself. He is no longer the hard-pressed animal, but a creator. All that is true enough, but does it not mean that once again he must go farther and rediscover a

---

28. F. Alquié, pp. 210ff.
29. Cf. Karl Marx, *Das Kapital:* "It has become practically impossible to ask if a foreign being exists, a being placed above nature and man, since the question implies the non-essentiality of nature and of man."

new wisdom? And how can that be achieved except by a higher and richer contemplation?

In order to avoid acknowledging that I have received from the Creator the traits which make me a man, shall I consent to alienate them in favor of some future, or rather mythical, Entity, which means nothing to me and cares nothing for me?[30] On the one hand, if I acknowledge the gift the inalienable nobility of human nature is ensured, and if I sacrifice myself for my brethren my sacrifice has meaning. On the other hand, my consciousness itself is sacrificed,[31] and as a result of a complete and final alienation, I am simply a cog in the vast machine for producing, in the distant future, which I cannot know, what is called, I know not why, Humanity.[32]

    30. Cf. Henri Niel, "Athéisme et Marxisme," p. 83: "Indeed the concrete individual finds merely his own present reality of social being in the idea of a perfect society. This reality is one that is determined by the representation of a society which does not yet exist. Represented as producing the reality of the present as a function of an ideal yet to come, the actual individual is alone in incurring all the expenses of this representation of the perfect society. If therefore he considers as already real for him a term that is purely representational and that contains nothing other than his strictly actual efforts and if he believes that he recognizes in this representation a real presence of the perfect society, it is in this case that he becomes estranged, for he provides nourishment from his own proper substance for a future which has no other reality than that of his present under the guise of a mythical projection. The representation, in fact, of the perfect society has for its necessary condition of existence the living endowment of the individual who produces it. We are very much in a full state of alienation, and the remedy against death, in reality, is merely an ideological usage it undertakes, for the life and death of an individual are of benefit to a representation of society. We do not proceed beyond ideology and its particular alienations."

    31. Cf. Friedrich Wilhelm Foerster, *Europa und die deutsche Frage* (1937), p. 27: "There is nothing more grandiose than the way in which Revelation describes the growth of this collective beast, which puts its mark on each person's forehead and each person's hand. That is to say, it standardizes the thought and the action of each person, and opens its mouth wide to blaspheme and vomit forth lies. Quite such as this is contemporary society, where the individual conscience, attached to the invisible world of morality, no longer counts. This is a society which is a mass lump deprived of any moral center, careless of all eternal values, returning to that gelatinous semblance of jelly-fish, from which humanity had escaped by the slow progress made by individual consciences."

    32. Cf. Gaston Fessard, *France, prends garde de perdre ta liberté* (1946), p. 146: "Because it sets aside the individual conscience and its relationship with others and with

~

The idea of God within us is perpetually menaced with extinction, but is always reborn. Everything threatens it with ruin, for everything is a scandal to us, when lo and behold! the very threat that menaced it with death gives it fresh life. Each day brings a new witness of it. For man will never finish wrestling with God. The mysterious struggle between Jacob and the Angel, so foolhardy and yet so necessary, so necessary yet so unequal, lasts through the night — throughout the night of our somber history.

"It is originally God himself," Bossuet says, "who is brought low and rises again for the human race."

~

Sub nocte Jacob caerula
Luctator audax angeli,
Eo usque dum lux surgeret,
Sudavit impar praelium.[33]

(Jacob in the dark night,
The bold wrestler with the angel,
Sweated in the unequal struggle
Until the breaking of dawn.)

~

Exaudi me, Domine, Deus meus, Illumina oculos meos, ne unquam obdormiam in nocte.[34]

---

the universe, it (human nature as understood by Marxism) is, moreover, merely the generic concept of Man or Humanity: abstract individuality or a universality purged of all human reality."

33. Prudentius, *Book of Hours,* Hymnus 2.
34. Psalm 13:4.

Hymn to God

O Thou who art beyond all — is this not the sum total of all that we can sing of Thee?
What hymn will human language raise to thee? No word can give expression to Thee.[1]
What would our minds cling to? Thou dost surpass all intelligence.
Thou alone art unutterable, for all that is spoken has arisen from Thee.
Thou alone art unknowable, for all that has been thought has arisen from Thee.
All beings, both those which speak and those which are mute, acclaim Thee.
All beings, both those which are given to thought and those which are devoid of thought, render Thee homage.
The desire of the universe, the groaning travail of the universe, tends towards Thee.
Everything that exists entreats Thee, and towards Thee every being that considers thy universe lifts a silent hymn.
All that remains remains by Thee. By Thee subsists the movement of the universe.
Of all beings Thou art the end term. Thou art every being, and Thou art not any of them.[2]
Thou art not a single being. Thou art not a great collection of beings; Thou dost possess all names,[3] and how is it that I shall name Thee, Thou, who alone cannot be named?

---

1. Cf. St. Ephrem: "Who is totally foreign to all tongues" (Edmund Beck, "Die Theologie des hl. Ephraem in seinen Hymnen über den Glauben," *Studia Anselmiana* 21, p. 247).

2. Cf. M. Sandaeus, S.J., *Pro theologia mystica clavis* (1640), p. 167: "If these things are understood as they should be, nobody or perhaps a Scholastic censures them. For as God is spoken of as *All*, because all things are contained in him through one very simple reckoning of Deity, whereby it turns out that he is All either formally or equivalently or eminently: so he can be said to be *Nothing*, because he is beyond all things."

3. "God's having many names is a frequent phenomenon from the end of the Hellenistic period on." Festugière, O.P., *La Révélation d'Hermes Trismégiste*, vol. 4 (1954), p. 65.

What celestial spirit could penetrate the clouds that cover the heavens themselves?
Do Thou take pity,
O Thou, who art beyond all, — is this not all that we can sing of Thee?[4]

4. This hymn, which figures among the works of St. Gregory of Nazianzus, may be by Proclus. (A. Jahn, L. J. Rosan; against this hypothesis are: J. Draseke, A. Ludwig, Schmid-Stahlin; cf. Festugière, *La Révélation d'Hermes,* p. 67.) It is certain, in any case, that, for the expression of their "negative theology," the Fathers of the Church — and after them the Christian philosophers of all the following centuries — owe much to Neoplatonism. This certainly does not mean that their idea of God, taken in its totality, is Neoplatonic, nor indeed that it is not very profoundly different. — Bossuet has translated a part of the hymn in his *Instruction* on the states of prayer, second treatise, ch. 22, *Théologie et contemplation de saint Gregoire de Nazianze* (ed. E. Levesque [1897], pp. 58-61).

Not only in the writings of the Fathers, but in the liturgy itself, one finds a type of thanksgiving, or rather praise, "in which the Christian theme of the knowledge of God assumes the style of Hellenistic philosophy. The inaccessible greatness of God is conveyed here by the accumulation of negative attributes; generally formed with a privative alpha prefix: 'uncreated, inscrutable, ineffable God, incomprehensible to all created substance'. Thus in the Anaphora of Serapion . . .": Joseph Andreas Jungmann, S.J., *Missarum Sollemnia. Eine genetische Erklärung der römischen Messe,* vol. 1 (1952), p. 41. Cf. in an early manifestation already the beautiful passage from Sirach 43:27-31 (RSV):

> Though we speak much we cannot reach the end,
>   and the sum of our words is: 'He is all.'
> Where shall we find strength to praise him?
>   For he is greater than all his works.
> Terrible is the Lord and very great,
>   and marvelous is his power.
> When you praise the Lord, exalt him as much as you can;
>   for he will surpass even that.
> When you exalt him, put forth all your strength,
>   and do not grow weary, for you cannot praise him enough.
> Who has seen him and can describe him?
>   Or who can extol him as he is?

Cf. Angelus Silesius, *The Cherubic Pilgrim,* bk. 5, 196-197:

> The Most High can on the one hand be named with all his names,
> While on the other hand not one name can be attributed to him.
> God is nothing and he is all, and this without frivolous subtlety:
> For say what he is or name something that he is not!

... Abraham, desiring to know what should come to him through the blessing of his first father, inquired about the God for whom he was to wait. And as, following the inclination and tastes of his soul, he journeyed about the world, asking where God might be, and as he grew faint, and ceased his inquiries, God took pity upon him who sought him only in secret: he revealed himself to Abraham by means of the Word, as though by a ray of light, and made himself known. . . .

St. Irenaeus, *Demonstration*, 24

In giving us his Son, God gave us everything. By delivering up to us his unique Word, he revealed everything to us. There is nothing further to wait for after Jesus Christ.

St. John of the Cross, *The Ascent of Mount Carmel*

No man hath seen God at any time: the only begotten Son who is in the bosom of the Father, he hath declared him.

John 1:18

No man hath seen God at any time. If we love one another, God abideth in us. God is charity: and he that abideth in charity abideth in God, and God in him.

1 John 4:12, 16

God is greater than our heart.

1 John 3:20

Now this is life eternal: that they may know thee, the only true God, and Jesus Christ whom thou hast sent.

John 17:3

That which was from the beginning, which we have heard, which we have seen with our eyes, which we have looked upon, and our hands have handled, of the word of life: — for the life was manifested: and we have seen, and do bear witness, and declare unto you the life eternal, which was with the Father, and hath appeared to us — that which we have seen and have heard, we declare unto you, that you also may have fellowship with us, and our fellowship may be with the Father and with his Son Jesus Christ. And these things we write to you, that you may rejoice, and your joy may be full.

And this is the declaration which we have heard from him, and declare unto you: That God is light, and in him there is no darkness.

If we say that we have fellowship with him, and walk in darkness, we lie, and do not the truth. But if we walk in the light, as he also is in the light, we have fellowship one with another; and the blood of Jesus Christ his Son cleanseth us from all sin.

1 John 1:1-7

Sed in hac quaestione Deum videndi, plus mihi videtur valere vivendi modus, quam loquendi.

(But in this matter of seeing God, our manner of life seems to me more important than our manner of speech.)

William of St.-Thierry, *Aenigma fidei* (PL 153:398c)

Vere dignum et justum est, aequum et salutare, nos tibi semper et ubique gratias agere, domine, sancte pater, omnipotens aeterne deus: quia per incarnati verbi mysterium nova mentis nostrae oculis lux tuae claritatis infulsit ut dum visibiliter deum cognoscimus per hunc in invisibilium amorem rapiamur. . . .

Postscript

The attentive reader will have seen at once that there is nothing in this little book which has not been borrowed from the double treasure of the *philosophia perennis* and Christian experience. The author imagined that the same was true of the first two editions, which appeared under the title *De la connaissance de Dieu*. He was astonished, at first, to hear that this had been questioned by some readers. For such a doubt to be possible there must, however, have been some risk of misunderstanding. Though one might say of questions touching the knowledge of God what St. Augustine said of that knowledge itself: *Nomen quippe non sonaret aenigmatis, si esset facilitas visionis*[1] (the word would not sound enigmatic if we had the power of vision), or again what St. Leo said of supernatural mystery: *Inde oritur difficultas fandi, unde adest ratio non tacendi*[2] (the difficulty of expressing oneself arises from the same source as the need for not keeping silence). To speak of God is as dangerous as it is necessary.

The danger, however, is no excuse for silence. "God's truth is at once so exalted, and of so delicate a nature, so to say, that human language cannot touch upon it without in some way wounding it. . . . Yet after all, if you wait to find words worthy of God you would never speak at all."[3] Bossuet's wise words seemed to us to clinch the matter.

Nevertheless, the need to speak of God is not in itself an excuse for

---

1. St. Augustine, *De Trinitate*, bk. 15, ch. 9, n. 16 (PL 42:1069); cf. chs. 23 and 24 (cols. 1090-1091). See also St. Thomas Aquinas, *In Cor.*, ch. 13, lectio 4.
2. St. Leo the Great, *Sermo 9 in Nativitate Domini*, ch. 1 (PL 54:226b).
3. *Sixième Avertissement aux Protestants*, no. 38.

lack of skill. Whatever the "intentions" of an author may be, not only in the ordinary sense of the word but in the purely intellectual sense of *intentio*, the *intentio* of his thought, the general meaning which his aim gives to his work, the direction in which it is engaged,[4] it is always possible that some abbreviation of thought, some elliptical expression, or some word with more than one meaning may put some reader on the wrong scent; the stress or the tone may be too weak at one point or too strong at another, and so may endanger the delicate balance of truth in some minds. It might be added that a discontinuous form makes greater demands upon reflection and makes a full understanding of the various formulas more difficult. That is why I have closely revised the text in response to well-intentioned and authoritative requests. Many precisions have been added, aiming at greater clarity. It was, however, impossible to ignore the fact that each time one touched on essentials, the supplementary explanation gave rise to new problems, so that the more one explained oneself the more explanation became necessary. The inevitable weaknesses of human nature will not be made a ground of complaint against us. Moreover, like the earlier editions, this edition, in its recast form, does not deal with all the problems treated in the classical works on "natural theology." Nor does it claim, any more than former editions, to be a substitute for them. At some points at least, it has been expanded so as to complete, or to illuminate, certain passages which seemed to us important in themselves, or which seemed likely to embarrass certain minds; and at the risk of weighing down the book, some notes have been added with the aim of incorporating further explanations or necessary justifications.

The character of the original work has, as a result, been somewhat modified. My first intention had simply been to lend a helping hand to a few people in their search for God (and my reward has been that it was more than once accepted). Readers of this kind have little use, as a rule, for the citation of "authorities." Quotations, in fact, were reduced to a minimum, to a few specially chosen texts whose beauty or force seemed particularly telling. Now they are printed out, or referred to, in footnotes.

---

4. Cf. St. Thomas, *Quodl.* 3, a.17, ad 1m7; *De substantiis separatis,* 12. See also *In 8 Physic.,* 21, 13; *In 1 de Caelo,* 6, 5; *Contra Gentiles,* bk. 1, ch. 20 etc. St. Anselm, *Monologion,* preface: "For I think that a person will derive great advantage towards arriving at an understanding of what he reads therein, if he first ascertains the intention or the manner in which matters are discussed" (PL 158:144a-b).

It will henceforward be still more clear to all, I hope, that I attribute the same importance as the Catholic church itself to "the power of human reason, starting from created things, and without the help of supernatural revelation or grace, to demonstrate the existence of a personal God." I do not confuse that power — presupposed by this whole endeavor — with particular concrete conditions in which it is put to use, and, for example, to recall the words already used, if the taste for God is one thing, we know that the proofs are another. There is not a page in this book which does not bear witness to my attachment — as profound, I dare say, as that of anyone — to "the sane philosophy which we received as a legacy and as a heritage of long standing, from the Christian centuries"; and, while recognizing that it is right and suitable in a work which is not a manual of instructions, "to disengage it from certain of its scholastic forms, less suited to the present time," I am very far from regarding it as "an imposing monument, certainly, but belonging to another age." It is the philosophy which nourished me, and my thought continues to live in that climate. I should like to be able to show that it is still richer and more nourishing, that it has more sap and is more fertile, than even its adepts imagine. Everyone will see, moreover, that here, as everywhere, I profess no indulgence for the sort of "philosophical neurasthenia"[5] which seems to eat away the minds of a certain number of our contemporaries, and that we have no excessive leaning towards the "novelties of the day" which preach an exclusive preoccupation with "individual beings and the flux of life" or the simultaneous adoption of "diverse doctrines." In any case, I can safely leave to specialists the task of taking up the necessary discussions; our ambition has always been, and still is at this moment, simply to recall some eternal truths in a language that is not too antiquated. And finally, if I consider, with all believers, that "the teachings of the faith in a personal God and his precepts, are in perfect accord with the necessities of life," I do not regard this as in any way detrimental to their truth-value but, on the contrary, by virtue of it.[6]

I must now beg the reader's indulgence to draw attention to one or two special points.

---

5. The expression is Michele F. Sciacca's, with regard to "a certain existentialism": "L'esistenza di Dio," *Filosofia e Metafisica* (1950), p. 110.

6. All the passages in this paragraph between inverted commas are taken from the encyclical *Humani Generis,* pt. 3, "The position of traditional philosophy in the Church."

One critic suggested that it was my design to "return to the Fathers" in a sense which implied renouncing all the subsequent acquisitions of Christian thought. That was an error on his part; the present work should make this sufficiently clear. I attach great value to many of those acquisitions. The mania for novelties and for all forms of archaeological thought repels me equally, and I know full well how far they are from the spirit of catholicism. If what is called "a return to the sources" has sometimes given rise, in our time, to rash statements, it must be granted, in justice, that this is not our fault. On the other hand, it would surely be a novelty to regard the patristic contribution as simply obsolete, either in thought or in expression. Can it really be imagined that the patristic tradition, which is still the source of "spiritual life" in a narrow sense of the expression, is no longer of any use in our intellectual inquiries? Is it no longer fertile? Has everything it contained been completely assimilated, digested, systematized, and "surpassed" by subsequent speculation, and is it now a waste of time to turn to it? Not one of the great Christian thinkers down the ages would concur with that view. Their example is in the opposite sense. Thought does not progress like a technique. That sort of break, that sort of practical contempt, would surely be full of dangers. Were it necessary, the warnings so clearly set out in the encyclical *Humani generis* should suffice to preserve us from them.[7]

Another critic, in a much more moderate form, informed the author that "even when he gives the impression of following St. Thomas faithfully, his thought develops outside the synthesis and the spirit of St. Thomas." Perhaps that impression resulted from the fact that in the earlier text there were fewer references to St. Thomas than to subsequent systematizations.

---

7. ". . . Both sources of divinely revealed doctrine contain rich stores of truth, stores so great they will never be exhausted. That is why the sacred sciences are continually rejuvenated by the study of sources, whereas speculation which fails to promote the study of the revealed deposit becomes, as experience has taught us, sterile." What is said here of theology in the strict sense of the word is no less true of the whole of Christian thought, and it would clearly be contrary to the spirit of the encyclical to exclude everything which concerns philosophy. It is well known that Zigliara played a leading role in the restoration of traditional philosophy in the last century: "I do not believe," he wrote in *Della luca intellettuale e dell'ontologismo secondo la dottrina de' Santi Agostino, Bonaventura e Tommaso di Aquino* (Rome, 1874), vol. 1, p. xiv, "that the priest can really be what he should be, a man of piety and knowledge, a father to his people and a defender of the Church, if he is not formed in the school of the Fathers and Doctors of the Church. . . ." What a host of similar testimonies a person could adduce!

Let us translate the observation into more exact terms by saying that in fact my constant concern in this matter, as in others, was not to present St. Thomas as standing against the whole Tradition, but rather to throw into relief the traits in which that Tradition finds in him its most eminent witness. I do not regard the "common Doctor" as an "exclusive Doctor" who dispenses us from the task of familiarizing ourselves with the others; and I deem it regrettable that a certain partiality, inspired by a misguided strictness and artificial controversies, should sometimes have obscured the sense of profound unity which exists among the great masters — a unity which M. Gilson, himself a subtle analyst of their individual characteristics, recently recalled to mind.[8]

To regard this as eclecticism would be entirely false. In a work which is not in the technical sense a philosophical work but a series of free reflections on the most fundamental themes, such an attitude is not only legitimate: I regard it as necessary. It safeguards the unity of the *philosophia perennis*. Among other advantages, it allows the assimilation, as far as possible, of many thoughts whose significance or power of suggestion overflows the meaning given to them by their immediate context. Other studies, more scholarly or more historical, belong to a different category. But in addition to these, there are what we have called marginal notes, and these humbler efforts should at least be tolerated alongside others, since they may sometimes have more chance of answering the needs of a certain number of minds. It is well to attend to the serious objections which are so often brought against us: not in order to give in to them, but in order to answer them; not that we should be intimidated by them, but because we must face them honestly. Those who are groping their way should be treated with respect and with sympathy. It is a mistake to conclude hastily that the truth could lose by so doing; it can sometimes even gain. And one should make a real effort to remember that God does not belong to a few professionals.

In fact, it should be added that the traditional philosophy is not exactly what certain oversimplified *exposés* might lead one to expect. St. Thomas

---

8. Etienne Gilson, *L'esprit de la philosophie médiévale*, 2nd ed. (1944), p. 356, note. Between St. Augustine and St. Thomas especially, the difference is at once more irreducible and less contradictory than is sometimes supposed, because it is not exactly the same problem that is being tackled by these two parties. Cf. Gerson, *Secunda lectio contra vanam curiositatem,* 5a consideratio: "It is a sign of curiosity and singularity . . . to rejoice more in an attack on the Doctors or in the pertinacious defence of one of them than to take pains to harmonize their teachings" (*Opera,* vol. 1, col. 99b).

himself, "the most intellectualist of Christian philosophers,"[9] offers "a constant resistance to the threats of rationalism."[10] He requires "that one should institute a severe criticism of our knowledge concerning the things of God."[11] His negative theology is not the anemic and timid theology of so many modern "spiritualists." His doctrine of analogy, often wrongly understood, has more than one aspect: it is not the milk-and-water theory one finds here and there whose sole aim seems to be to reduce the chances of vertigo. His criticism of the concept, insofar as it concerns our knowledge of God, is far-reaching. The best interpreters have shown this very clearly: for example, M. Gilson in his fine book on Thomism, or, among others, Father Sertillanges who praises its "audacity, which is as tranquil as it is liberating,"[12] and who, commenting on one of the texts of the *Summa*, once allowed himself an exclamation of amazement: "What," he asks, "is this unbreakable unity, so rich and so full that our concepts approach it from all sides and are swallowed up in it."[13] ... It is easy to take comfort in the thought of the classical distinction between the meaning of a concept and the mode of its meaning, and in principle nothing is more just;[14] but it is

---

9. Gilson, *ibid.*, p. 36. With regard to Augustinian illumination and Thomistic abstraction cf. the same author's *Introduction à l'étude de saint Augustin*, 2nd ed. (1943), pp. 112-125.

10. M. D. Chenu, O.P., *Introduction à l'étude de saint Thomas d'Aquin* (1950), p. 139.

11. L. B. Geiger, O.P., *La participation dans la philosophie de saint Thomas d'Aquin*, 2nd ed. (1953), p. 262.

12. A. D. Sertillanges, O.P., *Les grandes thèses de la philosophie thomiste* (1928), p. 52.

13. A. D. Sertillanges, commenting on *Prima*, q.14, a.4 of the *Summa theologica*, in *Revue des Jeunes*, Dieu, vol. 2, p. 346. Cf. Louis Bouyer, *Le sens de la vie monastique* (1950), p. 172: "In reaching him we leave far behind all that the mind can conceive. Not only all our imaginations, but all our concepts vanish at his approach."

14. This is the very formula of analogy. As was recalled again quite recently by Taymans d'Eypernon, S.J., this formula posits "the realism of a knowledge in which the concept drawn from human experience remains, in the application that is made of this concept to the transcendent, the latter being objective and true according to what it positively denotes, but not according to the restrictions and limitations of finite reality from which it draws its origin." "L'encyclique 'Humani generis' et la théologie," *Nouvelle revue théologique* (1951), p. 7. Only the use that is sometimes made of this distinction shows that it has not been understood. On the *modus significandi*, cf. St. Thomas, *Prima*, q.13, a.1, a.2, and especially a.3; q.45, a.2, ad 2m; *Contra gentiles*, bk. 1, ch. 30: "As for the mode of signifying, every name has a defect." Jac. Alvarez de Paz, S.J., *De inquisitione pacis*, bk. 5, pt. 1, apparatus 3, ch. 7, "De cognitione Dei per negationem": ". . . We take away all the perfections of creatures from God, because they do not exist in the way in which we conceive of them, but in another way, infinitely

sometimes applied too materially, as though one flattered oneself it was possible to lay the former aside and retain the latter intact, as though one could, at least at the high point of one's thought, conceive that *modus altior*, starting from our human qualities, the *modus altior* in all its purity, which is found in God and in God only. That is simply to reestablish, in a roundabout way, an element of univocity in our analogical knowledge which is in fact denied by it. It is to forget that, in reality, the analogy is not in the concept but in the judgment, that it expresses similarity and dissimilarity at the same time, indicating a "relation" *(ordo, proportio)* which allows us to affirm the former while taking account of the latter.[15] Or else, fearing quite rightly to have to admit that our concepts are only approximate, people refuse, quite wrongly, to admit their inadequacy, which, without robbing them of their truth, inevitably affects them.[16] Such excessive timidity comes, perhaps, from a lack of sufficient regard for the compensating elements which ensure the equilibrium of the traditional doctrine. To tell the truth, the reluctance which such attempts reveal derives from a pragmatic rather than an intellectual concern, and it is by no means certain that they give full due to the spirit of faith. Would everything be lost if one were not able to present God in tabloid form?

---

more perfect, which we have no knowledge of" (*Opera,* vol. 6, p. 486). On analogical knowledge see the relevant chapter of J. Defever, S.J., *La preuve réelle de Dieu, étude critique* (1953), pp. 70-90.

15. St. Thomas, *Prima,* q.13, a.5: "Names of this kind are used of God and creatures analogically, that is to say, proportionally"; "A name which is thus used in a multiple sense signifies different proportions with reference to some single thing."

16. That is because the epithets "inadequate" and "approximate" or even "inexact" are taken to be equivalents — a regrettable confusion (when it is not merely a matter of words). The encyclical *Humani generis* uses more precise language. It rejects the claim that the mysteries "cannot be expressed in true terms, but only in approximate and changeable terms which indicate the truth to a certain degree, but which also necessarily deform it"; a claim which is not so much a daring idea as a vague and inconsistent one; not so much a desire for accuracy as a confusion. God himself, in his answer to Moses (Exodus 3:14), "reminds us that all our statements about him are inadequate" (A. M. Dubarle, O.P., "La signification du nom de Yahweh," *Revue des sciences philosophiques et théologiques* [1951], p. 18). Maréchal explains, as many others have done, that the "signification" of the divine attributes, that is to say, the objective value which the affirmation in judgment confers upon them, rests upon a "very inadequate representation, inadequate because it is borrowed from our experience of creatures" (Notebook 5, p. 234). Cf. A. D. Sertillanges, *St. Thomas Aquinas* (4th ed., vol. 1, p. 404): "The doctrine of analogy makes it possible to attribute to the divine names a value which is positive, although inadequate."

A firmer conviction is justified in being less tentative in its approach. It is not tempted to stop halfway to the truth, and so sacrifice its respect for mystery to a cowardly instinct for security. That is because, however far it extends the scope of "negative theology," it knows full well that the solidity of the first affirmations which support that theology remains undisturbed. It is in no danger of confusing the *démarches* of negative theology with the withdrawals or hesitations of agnosticism. It knows, as we shall see, that the "no" which follows on the "yes" is not (to use the Sartrian jargon for once) "annihilation": the "yes" lives on secretly within the "no" as its necessary correlative; it orientates, determines, and qualifies it. Even if everything suddenly seems to have been engulfed, it knows that nothing is lost. It knows, with St. Thomas, that the *remotio* is the fruit of the *excessus*. And it can say with St. Augustine: *Non parvae notitiae pars est, cum de profundo isto in illam summitatem respiramus, si antequam scire possimus quid sit Deus, possumus jam scire quid non sit.*[17] (It is a part of no small knowledge, when we have emerged from this depth to breathe on that summit, if before we can know what God is we can already know what he is not.)

Criticism, moreover, is not rejection. It would certainly be wrong to reduce intellectualism to "a logicism which identified the ground of being with concepts. It would be a strange misunderstanding to confuse the idea, in its pure and luminous realization, with the concept, that pale spark that the human intelligence extracts from the most obscure participations in the Idea."[18] But it is not less true that the concept remains indispensable, and the truth it involves is not in any doubt; it only needs to be defined. The critique of the concept which I instituted, or rather which I recalled in certain pages, is also its justification — "for there is always more in the concept than the concept itself" — and I should be the last to wish to give in to the mirage of some other form of knowing as part of the normal life of the mind. It has been excellently said that the concept and the discursive method, by themselves, would undoubtedly build nothing but an unreal world; but there is "a basis of intuition" in our knowledge which is implicit

---

17. St. Augustine, *De Trinitate*, bk. 8, ch. 2, n. 3 (PL 42:948). Cf. St. Thomas, *Prima*, q.84, a.7, ad 3m. "If one must always end with a negation," Xavier le Bachelet asks (*Dictionnaire de théologie catholique*, vol. 4, col. 1024), "what would become of our knowledge?" But this agonized question is answered a little further in the same article (col. 1111): "Not an absolute but a relative silence, and one which has its place not at the beginning, but at the end of our knowledge." See above, Chapter 5.

18. Charles Boyer, *L'idée de vérité dans la philosophie de saint Augustin* (1921), pp. 226-227. Cf. Pierre Rousselot, *L'intellectualisme de saint Thomas*.

in them, and confers a real value upon them, while at the same time requiring them in order to express itself and perfect itself.[19] The "natural knowledge" or the "necessary affirmation" which I have discussed, awkwardly perhaps but certainly in the spirit of an ancient and unbroken tradition,[20] cannot be objectified otherwise than in concepts — although it always remains a living force at the mind's center, and prevents it from settling down in the conceptual order.[21] Interpreting it in this way, that is, by refusing to admit that, in this world, natural man can have a direct "intellectual vision" of Being, or intuition sufficient unto itself, and again rejecting "innate ideas" in the proper sense of the word, even in regard to the first principles of the reason or the *prima intelligibilia*, I was in opposition to all the doctrines which tend to "ontologism."[22] Furthermore, I believe myself to have followed the essential scheme of Thomistic thought on this essential point, in preference to any other philosophy approved by the Church. And very certainly I was more faithful to St. Thomas than those who thought themselves in a position to criticize me on this matter. As Josef Pieper has recently reminded us, neo-scholasticism was no doubt not wrong in wishing to "wash its master St. Thomas of the least trace of agnosticism"; but (provided one recognizes at the same time the profoundly positive element of his inspiration) that should not involve ignoring the "negative element" in his philosophy, most specially in regard to the prob-

---

19. J. Defever, *La preuve réelle de Dieu*, pp. 107, 123; cf. pp. 16, 20-21, 130-135.

20. It is contained in the well-known passage of St. John Damascene, *De fide orthodoxa*, bk. 1, ch. 1: "Therefore God cannot be explained in any words nor can he be comprehended in any way. . . . However God did not suffer for us to stay in total, blanketing ignorance. There is, indeed, no mortal for whom the knowledge of God's existence is not naturally implanted by God" (PG 94:790). Cf. St. Hilary: "Indeed, there is no one who does not have the seeds of the understanding of God," etc. See Thomassin, *Dogmata theologica*, *De Deo*, Bk. 1, c. 3, n. 1: "The holy Fathers of the Church agree unanimously that the anticipated notion of God is implicit in the minds of all, even before our first attempts at being taught, before the experiences of the senses . . ."; n. 4: "Thus, after sin, there remains in every person's spirit a notion that somehow remembers God, but it is a notion that is rather hidden . . ." (Ed. Vives, vol. 1, pp. 8 and 10). Only the interpretation that we propose for it is inverse to the interpretation that had prevailed in the doctrines with an innative or, more or less, ontologistic tendency. See Chapter 2, note 7.

21. "An intuitive movement," writes Defever (*La preuve*, p. 125), which takes up and transcends the representation.

22. To whatever variety they belong, they are always characterized by the idea of a certain objective apperception of the Being of God.

lem of the knowledge of God. God known as the "unknown": for St. Thomas that is the highest degree of our human knowledge.[23]

St. Thomas has "described the imperfection of the instrument" which we must use in our search "better than anyone else." That imperfection, however, "does not arrest its intrepid flight."[24] That is because he, too, knows that there is something more fundamental in the human mind: not outside, but at the very heart of the intelligence. To banish from intellectuality the element which is neither form nor representation, that dynamic element, the movement of thought which is not the concept, since it explains the formation of the concept, but which gives it its soul — that would be to destroy "intellectuality" itself, and to imprison the intelligence within the sphere of the relative. One may hesitate about its nature, or rather focus attention on one or other of its aspects, according to the problem involved, but — once one has perceived what an enigma knowledge is to itself, and the sort of questions which it sets — it is quite impossible to get rid of it. Everyone is free to desire a more "clear-sighted intellectualism" as the rather misleading catch-phrase goes. But it is perhaps opportune to recall that it is not a matter of taste, and that the most clear-sighted intellectualism is not always the most authentic. Genuine intellectualism is not a narcissism of the concept. It is not the love of the intelligence for its own sake, or a complacent delight in its products: it is the free and confident use of the intelligence in search of the truth. It would be as well to guard against reintroducing, by some subtle deformation, a new subjectivism. Nor should presumptuous declarations be accepted too easily: it costs nothing to announce, with the aid of peremptory proofs, some definitive distinction or to present a thing as perfectly clear and without shadow of doubt; but, as has been very truly said, a philosophy is not judged by its promises but by its achievements.

An analogous preoccupation was at the root of yet another misunderstanding. Several readers failed to understand the prime object of the chapter in which the origin of the idea of God is considered. Enclosed within the sheltered circle of their scholastic disputes, they imagined in all good

---

23. *In Boethium de Trinitate*, 1, a.2, ad 1m. J. Pieper, "De l'élément négatif dans la philosophie de saint Thomas," *Dieu Vivant* 20 (1951), p. 45. Cf. the later German edition of this book: *Philosophia negativa. Zwei Versuche über Thomas von Aquin* (1953), p. 43; 2nd rev. ed.: *Unaustrinkbares Licht. Über das negative Element in der Weltansicht des Thomas.*

24. J. Webert, *Saint Thomas d'Aquin* (1934), p. 48.

faith that these pages were written for them — against them, as they thought. Miraculously protected against the very sound of the assaults delivered upon our faith in God, they do not appear to have suspected for a moment the principal adversary which those pages had in mind. And yet that adversary is legion. It has proliferated for a whole century. Turn by turn it assumes the masks of ethnology, of sociology, of psychology, and of the history of religion. It has invented a hundred different systems, from the animism of Tylor to the lucubrations of a certain school of psychoanalysis which denounces the grand illusion from which humanity needs to be liberated. It explains the whole idea of God in human consciousness by a series of transformations starting from dreams, belief in spirits, the mystification of language, cosmic fear, social alienation, etc., and confident that it has in this way established the "genesis" of the idea — one might even say its empirical genealogy — concludes to its nonentity.[25] To contest that pretended genesis is not to profess belief in innate ideas, nor to undermine the value of ratiocination, of the rational operation by which we affirm God: on the contrary, it means giving that operation a free field. To extricate the affirmation of God from the meshes of an immanent "dialectic," in which so many contemporary thinkers, Marxists and others, would like to enclose it and make it relative, does not mean, either, cutting it off from its logical foundations; quite the contrary, by removing it from the interplay of "otherness and negation," the affirmation of God is given back its foundations and established once again upon the absolute. Was it not Engels who said: "This dialectical philosophy dissolves any idea of absolute truth"? And is it necessary to remind philosophers that in present-day language the two words "dialectic" and "logic," far from being equivalents, are often opposed to one another? Only recently an intelligent critic and analyst of doctrines defined Thomism as "a repudiation of dialectic."[26] In any case, unless some attempt is made to resist the invasion of the dialectic when it goes beyond certain points, it becomes impossible to preserve the decisive purity of the *logos*. In the same way, when we showed how, in the course of history and of the evolution of religion, certain "analogies" hard-

---

25. Thus Gustave Belot, after recalling certain "modes of thinking" God and distinguishing various types, according to him irreducible in principle, of the idea of God, writes: "The initial term of these complicated processes is posited by man's mythical imagination." "Note sur la triple origine de l'idée de Dieu," *Revue de métaphysique et de morale* 16 (1908), p. 721.

26. Etienne Borne, in *Philosophies chrétiennes* (1955), p. 163.

ened and became fixed, we were very far indeed from bringing metaphysical analogy to book. We were simply reproducing one of the observations of the Book of Wisdom. We merely observed that, in certain minds or among certain peoples, sensible things such as the vault of heaven or the sun or lightning, through which divinity could be perceived as in a symbol, become at one point opaque, and instead of sustaining religion, imprison the religious impulse. Hence the diverse forms of "naturism," which are only too easy to discover in history, and which some would have us believe to be the origin and final explanation of all religion.

The words "analogy," "dialectic," and "genesis," in the context in which they occur, seemed to me to be clear enough in themselves for anyone who was to some extent in touch with the sort of problem which is met with everywhere nowadays. No doubt those who are misunderstood are always in the wrong. It would have shown greater wisdom to have been more emphatic in forestalling misunderstanding. And yet, if the misunderstanding was limited to a small number of people, and if it is, furthermore, quite easy to recognize what engendered it, perhaps the author of it may not be held entirely responsible. Perhaps those who fell into the misunderstanding might even be invited to examine their own attitude, to see whether it does not in fact make it quite impossible to fulfill a task which is unfortunately indispensable and thus prevent the pressing recommendations of the Holy See from being obeyed in any way.[27]

Reviewing this work with his usual sympathy, Father Joseph Huby, since then entered into the Light of God, expressed one regret. The knowledge of God through Jesus Christ, only just mentioned at the end of the volume, is nowhere examined. The lacuna is undeniable, and is, I freely recognize, not without its disadvantages. By delaying too long among the problems

---

27. Cf. the allocution of Pius XII, *ad Patres Societatis Jesu in XXIX. Congregatione Generali electores*, Castel Gandolfo, 17 September 1946: ". . . [The members of the Society of Jesus] should speak to men of their time either orally or through the written word in such a way that they may be intelligently and willingly heard. Wherefore it must be inferred that in proposing and advancing questions, in conducting arguments, and in choosing their mode of speech the Society's members ought wisely to adjust their discourse to the genius and inclinations of their time" (*Acta Apostolicae Sedis* [1946], p. 383). Similar texts were brought together by Bishop Blanchet in his address given at the beginning of the academic year at the Institut catholique de Paris, 3 November 1950 (*Documentation catholique* [1950]). To be of a positive, not negative, nature, this task is no less imperative than the complementary task. Which of us could testify in the forum of his heart that he has seriously and adequately performed it?

of natural theology, one does indeed run the risk of forgetting how abstract the method is, and allowing oneself to be caught in a sort of "religious philosophy" which usurps the place of religion itself. One runs the risk of turning into an object of speculation, even if contemplative speculation, the Being to whom one should give one's faith — and give oneself in faith. This speculation, it is true, cannot fail to develop sooner or later into negative theology, for it is certainly true both that natural reason cannot enter into God whom it affirms and that the knowledge of God *per negationem* is on any hypothesis the most perfect.[28] But in a climate of unbelief, negative theology has a fatal tendency to drift towards agnosticism, if not towards an altogether negative mysticism, or towards atheism pure and simple, concealed only for a time. "The definition of the Absolute," Hegel said, "can only be negative," and everyone knows the end of the story in its living posterity. . . . Even supposing the risk were less, it may seem at least that reflection obliges us to discard any personal qualification from the Absolute as being imaginative or anthropomorphic, and then the mystery of the Divine tends to be substituted for the mystery of the living God, all the more hidden for being personal.[29] As all sense of the values which Christianity engendered in our consciousness is lost, people cease to understand that respect for the mystery of God becomes an avowal, all the stronger, of his Personality.

These dangers must not, however, be allowed to mislead us into overlooking the legitimacy, the necessity even, of a "natural theology." The history of ideas reminds us that, in fact, it needs the climate of faith in order to attain its proper balance. It was formed and developed by the great thinkers of the Christian tradition within the faith, though they may have treated it as relatively autonomous and stressed its rationality. That is

---

28. Cf., among others, Maximilien Van Sandt (Sandaeus), S.J., *Theologia mystica, seu Contemplatio divina Religiosorum a calumniis vindicata* (1627), pp. 89-125, particularly pp. 118-119.

29. For "the first effort at reflection is represented spontaneously (an ineffable reality) under an impersonal form: the natural light of reason leads to a result 'that is at once valuable and deceptive.'" Revelation permits a more confident audacity. In revealed knowledge, "God is no longer aimed at by the efforts of a universalizing and abstractive upward movement. He is given and transmitted as someone concrete who condescends." And a knowledge thus "communicated by condescension can arouse, in the spirit that receives it, potentialities that it would have been incapable of developing all on its own." Charles de Moré-Pontgibaud, "Sur l'analogie des noms divins. Au centre de l'analogie révélée," *Recherches de science religieuse* 42 (1954), pp. 322, 324, and 328.

manifestly true, as the latest histories of Christian philosophy have once again brought to light, and as the Council of the Vatican has fully explained.[30] That is the basis on which I, in my turn, have proceeded. No attempt has therefore been made, at least not directly, to fill the lacuna which Father Huby pointed out. That would have demanded a whole book and a direct appeal to faith. But the historical perspective which preponderates in the first chapter, and the concrete point of view which appears on almost every page, do something, I believe, to remedy the defects which we have admitted. Moreover, how could the Glory which the disciples of Christ contemplated, fail to throw some ray of light here and there, if secretly, upon our path? How could I, or anyone, have abstracted entirely from all that the Christian revelation has definitely given us? When Jesus invited the philosopher, in a sense, to the same metamorphosis.[31] In principle the realm of reason and the realm of faith are quite distinct, and various affirmations can of course be classified accordingly without the smallest difficulty — as belonging to the one or the other. The mysteries of the faith remain inaccessible to rational investigation, while the authority and the laws of reason remain essentially unchanged in the believing intelligence.[32] Nevertheless, it is a fact that it is often a nice point to determine into which category great works matured by Christian thought should really be placed; it is open to question whether they are really philosophical or really theological. The discussion goes beyond not only the meticulous analysis of the text but also the general historical context of the work; for example, we have only to look at the literature on St. Anselm's *Proslogion* and on St. Thomas's *Contra Gentiles*. There is not, in fact, a single Christian whose philosophy would be in every respect what it is without his faith. And whatever some may say, that is eminently true of St. Thomas. The "sublime truth," the keystone of his rational structure, is in the Bible, though one could not say that the Bible imposed it upon him, nor that his reason imposed it upon

---

30. Constitutio *De fide catholica (Dei Filius)*.
31. A. D. Sertillanges, O.P., *Le christianisme et les philosophies*, vol. 1, p. 7.
32. Cf. First Vatican Council, 3rd session, Constitutio *Dei Filius:* "The perpetual consensus of the Catholic Church has held and holds that there is a twofold order of knowledge, an order that is distinct not only in its principle, but also in its object. It is, indeed, distinct in principle because in the case of one we come to learn by natural reason, in the case of the other by divine faith. It is, moreover, distinct in its object, because, beyond what natural reason can attain, mysteries hidden in God are proposed as needing to be believed by us. And if these mysteries were not revealed by God, they could not be known."

the Bible. His most rational thought derives part of its vitality from the soil of Revelation. It springs from the religious life and flowers in a religious act. "Dialectic and contemplation are happily married in an exalted experience."³³

I have certainly not sought in any way to imitate the manner or the tone of the great Doctor, nor of anybody else, any more than I have erased all trace of the "conflict of thoughts"³⁴ which inevitably agitates the mind when it allows itself to be filled by the Mystery of God; nor have I attempted to exclude the personal coefficient from my reflections. Provided the substantial unity of doctrine is safeguarded and the adhesion of all to the teaching Magisterium is assured, there are still many mansions within the great Catholic family. There are diverse forms of exposition, answering to a wide diversity of temperament, itself willed by God. There are, furthermore, various historical situations with the needs which they imply. Fundamentally always the same, like the mind of man itself, the problem of the existence of God appears, in the course of ages, under new aspects which, even if it were not a necessity, would remain an obligation to take into account to the best of one's abilities if one wished to enlighten one's brethren. Whether, as some would have it, this is due to a deepening of the mind, or at least to an improvement of its technique, or whether, on the contrary, as others would say, it is due to a sickness of the mind, or whether,

---

33. Cf. Etienne Gilson, *Le Thomisme*, 4th ed. (1943), pp. 120-136. M. D. Chenu, *Introduction à l'étude de saint Thomas d'Aquin*, pp. 161, 275. See also A. M. Dubarle, "La signification du nom de Yahweh," p. 20: "One may ask whether this single name of Being would have contained the riches which Christian thinkers discovered in it if it had not been placed in the framework of biblical revelation, etc." Cf. Chapter 5.

34. "Cogitationum conflictus": St, Anselm, *Proslogion,* prooemium. St. Thomas, *In Joannem,* ch. 1, lectio 1, n. 1: ". . . the understanding is tossed this way and that way . . ." — And who is the person, if he is not "puffed up with vain knowledge," who has not said to himself more or less the same thing as St. Augustine, in *De catechizandis rudibus,* ch. 2, n. 3: "My talk almost always displeases me. For I am desirous of something better, which I often enjoy inwardly, before I begin to explain it with actual, spoken words. But when I discover that my ability to express myself falls short of my knowledge about the subject, I am despondent, inasmuch as my tongue cannot equal the workings of my heart . . ." (PL 40:311). Cf. *De doctrina christiana,* bk. 1, ch. 6: ". . . And there occurs some mysterious battle of words . . ."; "this battle of words must be guarded against by silence rather than pacified by the spoken word." But how could we not add, using Augustine's words again: "Although, indeed, we can say nothing that is worthy of God, God has allowed for the pliant obedience of the human voice, and has desired us to rejoice in his praise by means of our words" (PL 34:21)?

more simply, it is just a change in perspective, it is in any case a fact that the question marks — the objections and the negations — do not occur at exactly the same point, nor with the same emphasis. Now it is they that dictate the starting point.[35] Moreover, the believer's faith is not satisfied with a literal repetition in all cases. Without comparing this very modest and limited essay with the giant efforts of our predecessors, I can safely say that it follows wholeheartedly in their train in the service of the same Truth.[36]

The Christian knows that the only way to a real encounter with God is the Living Way which is called Jesus Christ. It was that thought which suggested the French title of this work: *Sur les Chemins de Dieu*[37] — without implying directly, even about the first steps of natural knowledge, whether they are the ways by which we go to God or those by which God draws us to him.

---

35. St. Thomas, *In lib. I de Caelo*, 22, 2. *De perfectione vitae spiritualis*, ch. 26.

36. Of the many authors to whom I am in debt, I particularly wish to recall Joseph Maréchal, S.J. (d. 1944), whose work has inspired many passages (though his thought has "too often been simplified and perverted"): L. B. Geiger, O.P., in *Revue des sciences philosophiques et théologiques* (1954), p. 273; cf. J. Defever, S.J., *La preuve réelle de Dieu* (1953), and, where the historical interpretation of Thomism is concerned, Etienne Gilson.

37. St. Augustine, *De civitate Dei*, bk. 11, ch. 2: ". . . So that (man) might walk more confidently towards the truth, Truth itself, God, the Son of God, who assumed manhood without destroying his Godhead, established and founded this same faith, so that there might be for man a way to the God of man through a God-man. For this is the Mediator between God and men, the man Christ Jesus."

Cf. *Sermo* 117, *De verbis evangelii Joannis*, ch. 10, n. 16: "If we cannot yet see the Word-God, let us listen to the fleshly Word: because we are made as beings of flesh, let us listen to the Word made flesh. For thus he came, thus he took on our weakness, so that you might be enabled to grab hold of the strong words of the God who bears your weakness."

www.ingramcontent.com/pod-product-compliance
Lightning Source LLC
Chambersburg PA
CBHW022006160426
43197CB00007B/296